BUSINESS CONSULTING

OTHER ECONOMIST BOOKS

Guide to Analysing Companies
Guide to Business Modelling
Guide to Business Planning
Guide to Economic Indicators
Guide to the European Union
Guide to Financial Markets
Guide to Management Ideas
Numbers Guide
Style Guide

Dictionary of Business
Dictionary of Economics
International Dictionary of Finance

Brands and Branding
Business Ethics
Business Strategy
China's Stockmarket
Dealing with Financial Risk
Globalisation
Headhunters and How to Use Them
Successful Mergers
The City
Wall Street

Essential Director
Essential Economics
Essential Finance
Essential Internet
Essential Investment

Pocket World in Figures

BUSINESS CONSULTING

A Guide to How it Works and How to Make it Work

Gilbert Toppin
and
Fiona Czerniawska

THE ECONOMIST IN ASSOCIATION WITH
PROFILE BOOKS LTD

Published by Profile Books Ltd
3A Exmouth House, Pine Street, London EC1R OJH
www.profilebooks.com

Typeset in EcoType by MacGuru Ltd
info@macguru.org.uk

Printed and bound in Great Britain by
Creative Print and Design (Wales), Ebbw Vale

A CIP catalogue record for this book is available
from the British Library

ISBN 1 86197 702 6

Contents

Acknowledgements

MANY PEOPLE HAVE HELPED in the writing of this book, and the authors are indebted and grateful to all of them. Some deserve a special mention: Sarah Taylor at the Management Consultancies Association for allowing us to make use of the detailed research the MCA has carried out into the consulting industry; Brad Smith at Kennedy Information who was kind enough to answer our queries and provide us with global data, which is so difficult to find; Mike Sedgley for his enormous help in gathering additional research, and Deborah Vallez for the considerable time she gave to reading our draft with the detachment it required. We would also like to thank the publisher, Stephen Brough, for his support throughout the project, and Penny Williams for her invaluable editorial role.

How to use this guide

This book has six parts:

1 Business consulting today
2 The client world
3 The consulting world
4 The worlds connect
5 Routes to success
6 A blueprint for the future

Part 1 introduces business consulting and describes a new way of looking at how it works: the business consulting ecosystem.

Parts 2 and 3 focus on what happens within the ecosystem, looking internally at the client market, the consulting industry and other components. Part 2 describes the client world. It looks at the client market for consulting: What drives the demand for consulting? Why do clients hire consultants? What kinds of consulting projects are there? Part 3 describes the consulting world. It examines the equivalent issues on the supply side: How is the consulting industry's structure changing? What are the main challenges facing consulting firms? What skills and behaviours are required of today's consultants?

Part 4 focuses on seven interactions outlined earlier. It explores the nature of these interactions and how they have changed, highlighting the implications for the future. It focuses on the intricate maze of connections between client and consultant worlds, brought alive through the themes of reputation, isolation, metamorphosis, relationship, portfolio, career and life cycle.

Part 5 translates those implications into practical realities. What are the routes to success? What can clients do to maximise the value they get from consultants? What are the factors that will determine success for consulting firms in this more complex, interdependent environment? How can organisations which work closely with this market develop more effective relationships? What are the characteristics of the best consultants?

Part 6 lays out a blueprint for the future, drawing some conclusions on the likely evolution of the business consulting ecosystem, highlighting where improvements are likely to occur and where progress may be more disappointing.

The quotations on the part title pages are from people interviewed for the book.

1
BUSINESS CONSULTING TODAY

"Everything has changed, and most things are more difficult."

1 Business consulting at the crossroads

CHANTILLY IS ONE OF THE LOVELIEST CHATEAUX in France. In the glow of a warm day, it is easy to see why it became a favourite playground of the French nobility – and to forget that it was razed to the ground during the French Revolution, its owners fleeing abroad to escape the guillotine.

Drive past Chantilly, down the immaculate tree-lined avenues of the kind you find only in France, and you reach Les Fontaines, a house built by the Rothschild family and now a training centre for Capgemini, one of the world's largest consulting firms. It is hard to find a better metaphor for the turbulent fortunes of the consulting industry than Les Fontaines. Bought by Capgemini in 1998 at the height of the dotcom boom, when the consulting industry was growing by 10–20% a year, it is now home to state-of-the-art teaching facilities and campus-style accommodation for visitors. With modern art, marble flooring and wireless networks, it epitomises the way business consultants like to think of themselves: cool, polished, pricey. Beneath the smooth surface, Les Fontaines went through a difficult time after the dotcom bubble burst and a sweet boom the consulting industry had been enjoying turned sour. Capgemini's attentions shifted to laying off staff, not training them. It outsourced the management of the centre to a conference company in the hope of recouping its investment by hiring it out to other companies. Ironically, the company is now in a position where, as it begins to recruit again, it has to fight for space at its own training centre.

"I have been in consulting for almost 20 years," said Bjorn-Erik Willoch, Capgemini's global head of consulting, in 2004, "but I have never seen restructuring as brutal as that of the past two years. Everything has changed, and most things are more difficult. Clients are more demanding – and with good reason. During the 1990s, you could win good consulting engagements without much effort; there was a lot of learning on the job by consultants; you could be credible just by reading the right magazines. Clients could not attract the people they needed, so consulting represented a mutually useful way of getting good work done. Now you need to be a world-class expert with a very good idea upfront."

A tale of two projects

Everyone is a consultant these days, from sales people to beauticians, so what do we mean by "business consulting"? The more traditional "management consulting" is usually associated with one particular high-end style where the consultant's role is to advise senior managers. But this ignores the large proportion of consulting that is now involved in implementation: systems integration, outsourcing, and so on. These days, most consultants are expected to provide not just advice, but also solutions. If that is the case, what is it that distinguishes business consultants from all the other consultants out there? Why consultants, not contractors? The point is that business consultants are supposed to improve businesses: they are not hired to maintain the status quo but to change it. This might be changing a company's strategy or revoking, even taking over, a process in order to transform it, but it does not include managing an existing process or taking over a function in order to deliver the same levels of service at a lower cost. Consultants should be defined less by what they do (offering advice, implementing systems, outsourcing processes) and more in terms of the changes they achieve.

For the technical support staff at Sun Microsystems, spread across 46 countries, everything hangs on being able to resolve straightforward problems as quickly as possible and on having a watertight process for dealing with more difficult ones. A good support organisation, like Sun's, will solve almost all problems quickly. The remaining small proportion of problems will, however, absorb 50% of its resources. Things go wrong; no one knows why; finding the cause is a matter of discipline, not luck.

The term "rational troubleshooting" comes from psychological research conducted by Charles Kepner and Ben Tregoe in the mid-1950s and refers to a structured thinking process aimed at helping people solve problems and make decisions more effectively. For many years, the problem-solving concepts of rational troubleshooting were aimed at helping technicians on assembly lines pinpoint problems quickly and accurately. Sun dabbled with the idea in the early 1990s, sending some of its support engineers on training courses, but did not take it particularly seriously and by the mid-1990s had pretty much given up on it. But in 1995, the company recruited a considerable number of people from DEC, another technology company, all of whom had been trained in this way of thinking. The improved ability to solve difficult problems was impressive. Sun approached Kepner-Tregoe, which specialises in consulting and training in rational troubleshooting, and asked for help in training its technical support staff. Steve White, Sun's global manager for a programme that has trained and supported more than 2,300 technical engineers, explains that "the fundamental problem we had was how to improve the handover of a problem from one engineer to another as it went from expert to expert. We were not thinking about how we think. We were wasting too much time double-checking information and going through the same thinking process again and again. Case files were being passed over in a mess; data you would expect to be there was not. There was no protocol for saying what information would be needed."

Kepner-Tregoe trained groups of engineers and managers in troubleshooting and how to work coherently on outstanding problems. These people then had three responsibilities: to train their colleagues; to specify explicitly where and when these troubleshooting skills should be used at Sun; and to help solve the most serious problems. "The training aims to make thinking visible," says Mike Bird, a partner at Kepner-Tregoe who has worked with Sun since 1995. "We took a team of Sun's top engineers and gave them new skills in diagnosing difficult issues. Classically, people make meaningless statements about what has gone wrong – a server is broken, performance is poor – and support engineers end up working on problems without having done enough to identify the cause. We teach people to be like doctors working on a diagnosis, to ask the right questions and to rule out possible causes before drawing conclusions."

The secret of the project's success, however, is that both Sun and Kepner-Tregoe share a common vision of success. As a result, the training programme has been only one of three project pillars. The second was aimed at changing Sun's work processes to make use of these new skills, and the third set out to identify how to adapt the work environment to help engineers work differently and support this through rigorous coaching of Sun engineers by their peers. Following the pilot work there has been a sustained improvement in customer support, and Sun has demonstrated that it can solve the most difficult customer problems on average in half the time it used to take.

The longevity of Kepner-Tregoe's relationship with Sun is a testimony to the contribution consultants can make to their clients. According to White, Kepner-Tregoe's approach is that the consultants follow and are honest about what works and what does not work. Sun employs 35,000 people. "If someone from Sun approaches Kepner-Tregoe directly, Mike Bird will let me know so we can discuss it." "We will not train and run," Bird agrees. "If a client wants us to do that, then we will turn the work down. And we will not sell work for the sake of it: delivering value is more important than quick cash."

That does not mean it has been smooth sailing throughout; indeed, the relationship is stronger precisely because Sun thought the original training programmes were too geared towards a manufacturing environment and collaborated with Kepner-Tregoe to come up with something specifically for a support environment. White is just as pleased as Bird that that the programme they have developed together has become one of Kepner-Tregoe's standard interventions: "If we can sell the concept to Sun's customers, we will be able to collaborate with them more effectively. Mike and I are on the same side – working for Sun."

A cramped room overlooking Whitehall in London is Richard Granger's office. As a partner at Deloitte Touche Tomatsu, Granger managed the implementation of London's congestion-charging scheme for motorists; he is now employed by the UK's National Health Service (NHS) to oversee its £6 billion National Programme for IT. It is a Herculean task, aimed at bringing together myriad pieces of information on patients into a single, electronic record. "The existing NHS IT team is fully occupied running the current systems," says Granger, "600 organisations, 5,000 clerical systems, 30,000 people across 28,000 locations – all serving a health service that is the world's second largest employer after the Chinese army. You couldn't have engineered a bigger challenge if you'd tried. And now we have to overlay a national infrastructure in which information will be available anywhere at the push of a button."

Delivering the systems over a five-year period has already meant a fast procurement cycle, unprecedentedly so in the context of the European Union's Byzantine regulations. "Most large-scale IT systems need replacing every ten years. In the public sector, it is typical to spend three years mapping out the project and looking at potential suppliers, between one and two years choosing suppliers and negotiating with them, and between two and three years deploying the technology. You are lucky if you've got the first wave of benefits out before your supplier wants to change the platform on which you are operating. The overall business case is pretty poor; your asset is heavily degraded before you have implemented it. We wanted to break out of that approach. We wanted to spend more time on specification (as this is always what gets squeezed most) and less time on procurement. We sent out the request for proposals for the electronic booking system in January 2003, appointed a supplier in October 2003 and had the first live transaction in July 2004."

Success also depends on finding more effective ways of making the multitude of companies involved genuinely accountable. "I use a husky dog-sled racing analogy when I am talking to suppliers," says Granger. "If one of a pack of huskies is lame, you kill it and feed it to the others. This speeds up the pack in three ways: it is not held back by the lame dog; the other dogs go faster because they are better fed; and the remaining dogs also know what will happen to them if they do not keep up. If a supplier falls behind, we can remove work from them and give it to the supplier who is doing best. It gives the suppliers who fall behind the chance and incentive to catch up, and they can focus more effectively on a diminishing portfolio. We want them to realise how much they stand to lose, much as some of the suppliers involved in congestion charging ended up hiring specialist subcontractors at their own expense because it still cost them less than the delay-deduction would have done. You need to have a contestable framework and a degree of contestability to make this work. We had to design our procurement process with this in mind."

It is, in his own words, a toxic environment in which British cynicism about ambitious projects, hostile media and rivalry between suppliers create difficulties. "I was only 37 when I started this project; a couple of years later I was feeling more like 50. We have a once-in-a-lifetime opportunity to lay the foundations for something which the majority of people in this country see as a cornerstone of what differentiates us as a society: a high-quality public health service. But on a day-to-day basis, it's like chopping bits off my body – it's just incredibly painful. I'd like my life back sometime."

Granger contrasts his desire to make a difference with those of consultants more generally. "The consulting industry is lost," he says. "It needs a new blueprint. It lacks a sense of its role at a societal level and has become very self-serving as a result. Accounting firms professionalised themselves as a result of trade-sale and capital-market frauds in the 19th century; the consulting industry is immature by comparison, it still needs a roadmap. There are consulting firms out there which pay their consultants 50% more than their basic salary if they sell goods and services. That means there is absolutely no incentive for their consultants to turn round to a client and say, 'I'm not making a difference, I wish to leave' or 'this is my advice, I appreciate you may ask me to leave because it is contentious'. They will do everything in their power to keep the meter running – and they're doing the industry an enormous disservice. It is exactly the type of behaviour clients do not want to see."

"Some of the messages put out by consulting firms – come and join us, together we can change the world – have been inward-looking, unsustainable," claims Dave Higgins, consulting marketing director for Deloitte in Europe, the Middle East and Africa. "Senior executives in business have grown tired of the over-promising and under-delivering, the do-everything approach, like the famous German *Eierlegenvollmilchsau* – 'egg-laying woolly pig' – vainly trying to do everything for everyone." Mark Leiter, who runs Leiter & Company, a consulting firm specialising in the professional services sector, agrees. "Four years ago, people were sitting on the beach. The consulting industry faced a crisis of confidence in terms of whether the consulting proposition made sense. The erosion of many traditional consulting markets, such as corporate strategy, is being masked by a series of management ideas, years of cost cutting and now outsourcing. If you look under the cover today, you'll see western consulting firms selling more services in the developing world where ideas that have peaked here are still new. That lack of innovation and clear thinking eventually catches up with you. Answering the big question – who are we? – is the biggest challenge facing the consulting industry today."

If not this way, how?
You can tell a lot about the reputation of an industry by the jokes made about it. People have always made jokes about lawyers and now they make them about consultants. It is not hard to see why: there is no shortage of clients who still harbour bitter memories of the amount of money they spent on a succession of management initiatives – from business process re-engineering and enterprise resource planning, through e-business to customer relationship management – which yielded little in the way of quantifiable benefits. They are choosier about when and where to use consultants, preferring to hire a small number of experts rather than a cadre of bright, freshly minted graduates.

"We are seeing more clients focused on becoming intelligent clients," says Paul Hayes, who leads BT's technology transformation team, part of the company's rapidly growing consulting practice. "The 1990s were typified by organisations taking a 'me too' approach to implementation in order to keep pace with the latest trend and the increasing pace of change. Consequently, there was a tendency to lurch from one bandwagon to another, rather than concentrating on their real business needs. This created a credibility gap as consultancy and systems integration firms failed to deliver real value. The consulting industry's challenge now is to be more pragmatic and to focus more on delivering tangible and sustainable benefits." "Clients have become more reluctant to use consultants," agrees Michael Traem, head of consulting at A.T. Kearney in Europe. "They have built up their own internal consulting teams, often hiring consultants who have lost jobs with major consulting firms. They have the capacity to do much of the work themselves that they used to hire consultants to do." Part of this is cyclical: clients have established internal consulting units in the past only to sell them off when the market changes. But it also points to a longer-running trend: "Clients want less in the way of strategic booklets and presentations, and more in the way of concrete results," says Traem. "They want to get things done."

Evidence of a change in attitude to the use of outside consultants is provided by the numerous examples of high-profile projects that have run into difficulties or been cancelled part-way through. For example, in the summer of 2004, J.P. Morgan Chase, a financial services company, cancelled an IT outsourcing deal with IBM estimated to be worth $5 billion over seven years and plans to bring back the 4,000 employees and contractors who transferred to IBM. Eighteen months earlier, the company terminated an existing £1.25 billion outsourcing contract with CSC, Accenture, AT&T Solutions and Bell Atlantic in favour of IBM. Both deals were initially lauded as groundbreaking.

The story is the same everywhere
"The biggest change we've seen has been in client behaviour," says Ken Favaro, the New York-based chief executive of Marakon Associates, a strategy consultancy. "Projects are smaller and more focused on tangible outcomes – a reaction to the experience of the late 1990s when many consulting firms were guilty of making big promises that they failed to meet. As an industry, we've gone from enjoying the benefit of the doubt to suffering from the 'tyranny of doubt', where we have to all but guarantee results. Moreover, that so many people have left the consulting industry to join clients' organisations means we're seeing a lot of insourcing going on in the market for high-end advisory work. That will dissipate as managers realise that fresh thinking is always valuable. People who join clients from consulting firms can be very helpful in the short term, but their intellectual capital is effectively frozen and over time they become compromised by the inherent momentum, habits and politics in any organisation, particularly the largest ones. And when does it ever make sense to in-source when there's a highly competitive and innovative market, like the consulting industry, to meet one's needs?"

Even high-end advisory work, Favaro believes, has been tarnished by the actions of a few firms during the late 1990s which promised far more than they could deliver. "Unlike doctors and lawyers, anyone can call themselves a consultant. We have seen – and will continue to see – periodic calls for this to change, for the consulting industry to have some type of qualification or regulatory body. But management science is still too young a discipline to make that possible, let alone effective. The one good thing to have happened since the bubble burst is that it flushed out those people who went into consulting purely for the money. As with medicine and law, the consulting industry now has a higher proportion of people who feel passionate about the work they do, and are not solely interested in the financial return."

"There has been less money and clients are less willing to spend what they have on consultants," says Anders Grufman, who runs a specialist consulting company, Grufman Reje, in Sweden. "The market has shrunk and competition is fiercer. Clients are overwhelmed with consultants selling them things and are bothered by all the propositions out there. My company is a small one and we see clients increasingly choosing the consultants they work with on the basis of their specialist knowledge. But I suspect that larger consulting firms are finding things just as difficult. Demand for general strategy consulting seems almost dead, while consulting firms that actually implement concrete results have an advantage."

In eastern Europe, where capitalism has had less than two decades to find its feet, organisations have become more sophisticated and demanding in their use of consultants. "Clients want tangible results in shorter timescales," says Mihai Svasta, who runs a consulting company in Romania. "When we established our business in 1991, consulting was regarded as a minority sport; now it is definitely a fashion. Despite that, we still find clients looking for alternative pricing strategies (particularly where they can make consulting fees contingent on success). Performance measurement and quality assurance are important, particularly as the supply of consulting services is now growing more quickly than demand for them. Previously, clients tolerated mediocre, even poor performance from consultants."

The consulting industry is at a crucial stage in its evolution. The principles by which it grew in the 1990s – the focus on big management or technology ideas, the emphasis on raising revenues at the expense of just about everything – have not served the industry well. The downturn in demand for consulting in the early 2000s has provided the industry with a salutary reminder that consulting firms, like other companies, exist at the whim of their customers. "When the phones stopped ringing in 2001," recalled one consultant, "I had a nightmare that they might never start again, that clients might just stop using consultants." As the market picks up and the phones start ringing again, consultants will be tempted to think that things have returned to how they where. That would be a mistake. The number of jobs shed by the consulting industry in recent years may well be equivalent to the number gained during the fattest years of the e-business bubble, but the downturn should not be dismissed as just a normal cyclical adjustment. There are long-term, more deep-rooted sources of dissatisfaction with the way consultants operate that need to be addressed if the reputation of the industry as a whole is to recover.

"Clients continue to be very demanding," says David Owen, head of Deloitte's consulting practice in London, "and our responsibility is to respond to this. Clients make substantial investments in the work that we do and have increasingly high expectations in terms of the relevance of the work consultants undertake and the quality of the service delivered. Consulting is a serious business which is addressing serious things."

The aims of this book

The ultramodern, Richard Rogers-designed Lloyd's building in London may seem a strange place to start thinking about how the reputation of the consulting industry might be best restored. But for Geoff Dodds, formerly PWC Consulting's global brand director and now responsible for Lloyd's own brand, there are illuminating parallels between his past and present employers. "The insurance sector has an atrocious reputation," he says, "not far above tobacco and real-estate agents. What we have had to do is go back to the fundamental reasons why insurance exists – and why Lloyd's in particular exists. Lloyd's oils the world economy: we often insure the things that no one else can or will. Without Lloyd's lots of things would not happen – we would not launch satellites, we would not fly airplanes. The same may be true for the consulting industry – lots of the things corporations do they could not do without consultants. The trouble is consultants do not make the point very well."

There are several reasons for using consultants, providing they are good at their job and are used thoughtfully:

■ In the same way that effective non-executive directors can make a profound difference to a company, every organisation benefits

11

from being scrutinised and challenged by an objective (and therefore usually external) person. Everyone, whatever their position, can lose sight of the overall wood because they are too busy thinking about individual trees; having someone come in and ask fundamental questions about what they are doing, and why they are doing it, can be enormously valuable.

◪ Consultants offer their clients "economies of knowledge". Even though they may seem expensive, used intelligently, their clients spend much less time and money either recruiting people with the right skills or training existing staff to carry out a specialist task which may only take a few weeks. Consulting firms, by spreading those costs among their clients, are able to recruit, develop and deploy experts on a short-term basis.

◪ Consultants can provide energy and momentum in projects where clients, often taking a few minutes out of an already busy schedule to sit on a committee, are unable to do so. Consultants can provide the essentials, the roadmap and the resources to help organisations do what they could not do for themselves.

But there can be no doubt that a lot goes wrong. Between the ideal of consulting and the practical reality falls a shadow. Consultants can ride roughshod over the wishes and constraints of the clients they are supposed to serve. They can take longer and cost more money than clients expect. That they sometimes deliver less than they promised does not mean they will not try to sell their clients even more.

As Dodds says: "Consulting firms do not do themselves any favours because they are often arrogant. They are reluctant to acknowledge that clients and consultants go up – and down – the greasy pole of learning together. Some days, the clients will be learning from the consultants; some days, it will be the other way round. Together, they can do more than they could independently. What counts is what really happens."

The past ten years have demonstrated that consulting is no longer simply about a relationship between clients and consultants, but about more complex issues. Clients and consulting firms are far more interdependent than they once were. The pressures each side faces are interlinked, and success comes only from both sides working together and understanding what can be called the "ecosystem" in which they are working.

This book aims to guide you through the new business consulting ecosystem and to help you understand how to operate within it to your advantage. It provides a blueprint for today's and tomorrow's complex consulting interrelationships. As a client, it will help you extract most value from using consultants; as a consultant, it will help you deliver consistently great consulting.

2 The new business consulting ecosystem

W HEN YOU ASK CLIENTS why a particular consulting project has gone well, the following are typical of the responses you get:

◼ "It is amazing what can be accomplished by a small number of people, when focused on a challenging goal and working together effectively."

◼ "There was absolutely no demarcation along the lines of 'I am the client, so you must do it this way'."

◼ "This was an integrated team, with close relationships developing between the senior consultants and our executive directors. We trusted each other and could discuss issues frankly."

◼ "We often asked: 'How would it be if'? Or: 'How could we get more into this'? This gave both parties an opportunity to go beyond what had been initially planned."

◼ "We would be hard pressed now to say which elements were generated by the client and which by the consultant. Both trust the other to deliver what they say they will."

◼ "As true partners with a common goal, trust grew as we both sought the best solutions for mutual success. Issues were raised and resolved in this spirit, and the consultants' commitment was evidenced by the energy and single-mindedness with which they undertook all challenges."

Although people habitually talk about the consulting industry in terms of discrete components – the consulting firm, the client, the consultant, and so on – the most effective and valuable consulting takes place when clients and consultants work together in teams, sharing skills and expertise and focusing on common goals.

Clients need to look at how their actions, in procurement, project management and governance, change the way consultants behave. Consultants, on the other hand, must understand the way in which they do (or do not) transfer knowledge to their clients, deliver advice and implementation, and initiate cultural change. In other words, the collaboration that happens in the most successful consulting projects should not just be the standard for all projects, but should become the benchmark for the consulting industry as a whole, dictating the behaviour of firms as well as people.

Two trends are becoming increasingly clear:

◪ Individual clients (especially in the public sector, but increasingly elsewhere) are adopting a more rational approach to consulting and exchanging information with each other.
◪ Consulting firms are beginning to take on the characteristics of a maturing and responsible industry after a period of intense structural change.

Clients, consultants and their respective industries are part of the same internally dependent system. At the simplest level, consultants exist because there is a demand for their services, driven by pressure in the external marketplace, regulation, the emergence of new technology and management ideas. But the relationship is a symbiotic one: consultants help to create demand by promoting new technology and by helping to disseminate new ideas.

As needs increase in scale and complexity, the classic model of the client–consultant relationship begins to break down: results come from interdependency and diversity; more players become involved; third parties, such as technology vendors and outsourcers, become important.

Six key components interact in a systematic way. On the demand side, there are client markets, individual client organisations and client projects; on the supply side, there is the consulting industry, consulting firms and individual consultants. These components and their interplay form a new system, the business consulting ecosystem (see Figure 2.1 on the next page).

This book explores this system and its components. It focuses on seven important relationships, or interactions, between these components. This is a system in early formation and turmoil, with great imbalances and shifts of power in very short periods. Widespread mergers, radical rethinking of client procurement methods, the increased role of third parties and huge changes in the human resources market for consultants demonstrate that much more is at stake than changes to the traditional client–consultant relationship.

These seven "interaction" themes map out the way the business consulting ecosystem works:

◪ **Reputation.** Whether consulting firms like it or not, their industry

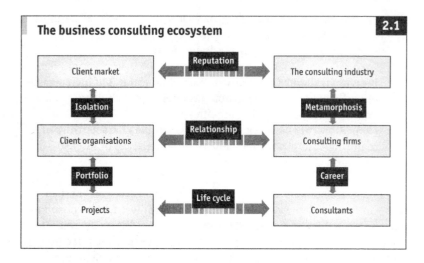

The business consulting ecosystem 2.1

Client market ← Reputation → The consulting industry

Isolation | Metamorphosis

Client organisations ← Relationship → Consulting firms

Portfolio | Career

Projects ← Life cycle → Consultants

has a reputation. Many firms choose to believe they are insulated from any problems that may ensue from this. Well-known firms believe their brands will differentiate them; smaller ones think their client relationships and the quality of their work will protect them. In reality, no organisation can entirely escape the way clients view the collective industry.

◙ **Isolation.** Clients buy consulting in an imperfect market. Although clients believe they are responsible for their choice and use of consultants, they also think their responsibility is compromised where they do not have access to sufficiently reliable information. It is a case of buyer beware, but only if you know what to be wary of. Yet clients rarely share views on consulting performance with each other. This seems ironic in an environment in which consulting firms are falling over each other to publish books, articles and papers on every conceivable client issue. Yet quantity of information is of course no guarantee of quality. Little of the "thought leadership" or "industry practice" material offered helps clients make informed choices.

◙ **Metamorphosis.** Consulting is not a profession: there is no governing body which sets standards and certifies qualified consultants. Qualifications exist, as do trade associations, but participation is entirely voluntary. Would you go to an unqualified doctor? Would you ask an untrained lawyer for his or her opinion? At the moment, clients rely on the brand of a consulting firm to provide them with the confidence that they are buying a high-quality product, but this focus on individual firms, at the expense of the industry as a whole, is unsustainable.

◨ **Relationship.** Clients are accustomed to treating consulting projects as discrete and self-contained. But there are three reasons why this is changing: the remit of central procurement departments has, for the first time, been extended to cover professional services; clients are increasingly using several suppliers for projects where before they might have used only one; and new governance rules are being established that seek to make consulting firms keep the promises they make of working "in partnership".

◨ **Portfolio.** A corollary to complexity is that clients need to manage their consulting projects not in isolation, but as part of a portfolio. They need to balance costly projects against cheaper ones, and difficult ones focused on long-term benefits against simpler ones designed to produce immediate results. A big component of success in using outsiders is getting things lined up internally too.

◨ **Career.** Consulting used to be a career. However, as a result of the downturn in the early 2000s, many consultants left their firms, some to join clients, others to become freelance or to find non-consulting jobs. In common with many other industries, consulting never really offered a job for life. Nevertheless, good consulting relies on good experienced consultants, so how is this to be reconciled?

◨ **Life cycle.** When it comes to actual consulting projects, clients invest too much time in the preparatory stages and too little in adapting to changes during the course of a project. Time, budgets and quality standards are typically set from the outset and ignore the way in which projects change during the course of their life: governance, management style and mindset need to be adaptable over time, not set in stone.

The idea of a client–consultant, mutually dependent ecosystem makes it possible to focus on how the elements of the two worlds of demand and supply interact with each other. It also highlights the inter-actions as the things that are easiest to change so as to achieve better results. Psychologists will tell you that it is much simpler to change people's behaviour than their underlying personalities, and this applies just as much to an industry like consulting. Institutions – consulting firms, client procurement departments, and so on – have processes, people, systems and cultures which make them inflexible. But an interaction is a fulcrum: the point where small changes have disproportional effects, where a little effort can make a big difference.

The premise of this book is that if you understand how your organisation interacts with clients or consultants, or how your clients or consultants interact with other clients or consultants, you can change how you manage that interaction for the better. You cannot beat the system, but you can work it to your advantage.

2
THE CLIENT WORLD

"Companies engage consultants for three broad reasons – brand, bodies and brains – but often they don't take the time to understand which of these they need and end up paying for one when they wanted the other."

3 The client market

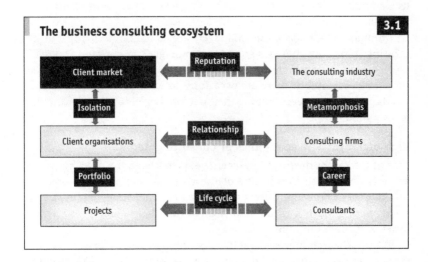

The business consulting ecosystem `3.1`

Reputation

| Client market | The consulting industry |

Isolation — Metamorphosis

| Client organisations | Relationship | Consulting firms |

Portfolio — Career

| Projects | Life cycle | Consultants |

THERE IS HARDLY A BIG OR MEDIUM-SIZED corporation in the developed world that does not make use of consultants in some way. Most consulting firms will also say that between two-thirds and four-fifths of their business is repeat business: that is, additional work undertaken for existing clients.

One reason is certainly to do with money. Consulting firms offer economies of scale: because they work on similar projects for several different clients, they can spread the cost of investing in specialist people and skills in a way their clients cannot. A company seeking to reduce costs might therefore hire an outside consulting firm because their wider experience and specialist know-how should help them spot waste the client might miss. That they can be up-and-running as soon as the contract has been signed should mean that the savings are realised more quickly. Similarly, a client considering launching a new product might hire a consulting firm that can reduce its time to market. Either way, the business case for using consultants – at least on paper – will be compelling.

The second reason may well be related to simple wishful thinking. Clients hire consultants to try to achieve a competitive advantage – to do something either so much better or so much more quickly than their rivals that the economic advantage gained is both substantial and sustainable.

Alexander Pope, an 18th-century poet, rightly advised that: "Hope springs eternal in the human breast/Man never is, but to be blest." But is it realistic to expect that consultants will be better at finding a route to competitive advantage than a firm would be as a result of its own efforts and insights?

Ambition, too, plays a role. Managers are as human as the rest of us: if hiring some consultants is good for a manager's organisation, all well and good; if hiring them is also good for the manager's career, even better. But, inevitably, there are occasions when clients hire consultants to advance their careers, putting their personal agenda ahead of the collective good.

Rich pickings? The economics of consulting demand

One of the myths destroyed in recent years has been the one about consultants doing well irrespective of the woes of their clients. Thus, the thinking went, consulting firms were able to supply creative ideas when times were good but could switch to cutting their clients' costs when times were bad, winning either way.

In fact, research suggests that there is a broad correlation between the state of the economy and demand for consulting. It makes intuitive sense, too. Companies are more likely to consider new initiatives when the economy is buoyant and confidence levels are high; rising stockmarkets make it easier to invest. Conversely, when the climate overall is harsh, clients are more likely to defer purchase decisions and the average size of consulting projects (in terms of both duration and fees charged) will shrink.

Regional variety

Consulting is a global business, but its fortunes depend not only on the local economic climate, but also on the structure of the economy in terms of the number of large, medium-sized and small enterprises, levels of inward investment and the level of investment in technology. Over half of all consulting fees are earned in North America and almost one-third in Europe (see Figure 3.2).

It may not come as a surprise that large companies are more likely to use consultants than smaller ones. They are usually able to spend more and have more complex issues to resolve, so the average size of projects in large companies will be significantly bigger than in smaller ones. The greater the number of large-scale businesses a country has, the larger the market for consulting there. Inward investment is a good measure of how

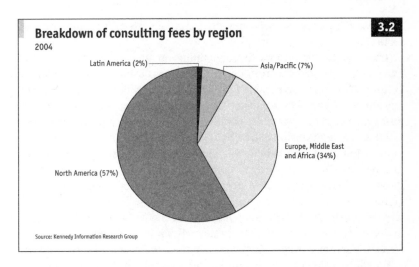

Breakdown of consulting fees by region
2004

Latin America (2%)

Asia/Pacific (7%)

Europe, Middle East and Africa (34%)

North America (57%)

Source: Kennedy Information Research Group

3.2

international the business environment of a country is: the higher the level of investment, the greater is the flow of management ideas (which boosts demand for consultants) and the number of foreign-owned companies that are likely to bring their own consultants with them. Lastly, there is a direct and positive correlation between IT investment across an economy as a whole and the amount of money spent on IT-related consulting. IT-related consulting has fuelled much of the growth in consulting in the past decade and it follows that countries which spend the most on IT are likely to be the largest markets for consulting.

Some sectors are more equal than others ...
The demand for consulting varies among different industry sectors. One reason for this is that levels of IT-related investment vary widely from sector to sector, as does merger and acquisition activity, another important source of consulting projects in the past.

Financial services has historically been by far the largest market for consulting firms, accounting for one-third of the total in some countries, because of its heavy reliance on and investment in technology, the need to accommodate regulatory changes and the sheer difficulty of finding an edge in a ferociously competitive market. But it is also a market which is peculiarly reliant on the health of the financial markets: falling stock prices between 2001 and 2003 triggered a dramatic fall in both the number and value of consulting projects. Consulting firms specialising in this sector saw their revenues slashed: many went out of business.

Business is now recovering: the stock markets are more buoyant and regulation is boosting demand.

One of the survivors in consulting in the financial sector is m.a.partners, which was founded in 1996 and is based in New York and London. The year 2002 was a tough one for Jon Moore, the firm's chief executive: "Clients rationalised their supplier lists; they were much more focused on effective supplier management and reduced the number of relationships that had proliferated during the late-1990s boom." But 2004 was better: "We have been very busy. Financial institutions have been starved of investment. In order to cut costs they downsized significantly, and now they will need to invest if they are going to respond to opportunities for business growth on a more sustainable basis." Although financial-services clients have started to bring in consulting teams again, rather than rely on independent contractors, Moore, like many others, questions whether there will ever be a return to the large-scale systems integration projects which were the source of most consulting income in the past. "Most systems integration work has gone to India. There is still a lot of tactical work, responding to a short-term need," he says. "Moreover, the 'we will do it ourselves attitude' is still there. Some clients are reluctant to use external people if there is a chance the work can be done in-house."

Both the telecoms and the energy sectors have become a source of frustration for consultants. The market for consulting in telecoms companies has also suffered in recent years, as most mobile companies remain saddled with Third Generation (3G) debt. Although energy companies have money to spend – as a result of the high price of oil – they are not spending it on consulting.

Overconsulted during the enterprise resource planning (ERP) boom of the mid-1990s, manufacturing has become a consulting backwater. Although some consumer products firms are spending more on consultants, there seems little prospect of a broader upturn. Even pharmaceuticals companies, historically big spenders on consulting, have cut back and are looking hard at how they buy consulting, buying more selectively and trying to reduce dependency on consultants.

The exception to the doom and gloom since the millennium has been government spending on consultants. BearingPoint's experience is typical: its public sector practice now generates $1.2 billion in fees (one-third of the total). In terms of growth, it is the most successful line of business for BearingPoint, having increased at a rate of 20% a year for the past couple of years.

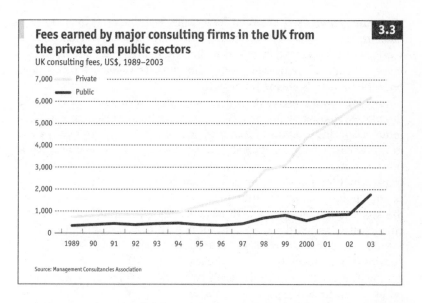

Fees earned by major consulting firms in the UK from the private and public sectors

UK consulting fees, US$, 1989–2003

Source: Management Consultancies Association

When the Management Consultancies Association (MCA) published its annual report on the UK consulting industry in 2003–04, it was the size of the public-sector consulting market that raised the most eyebrows. MCA members earned £1.3 billion ($2 billion) from public-sector clients, twice as much as in 2002. This surge in public-sector consulting is mirrored in the United States as well as in the world's other large consulting markets.

Figure 3.3 shows that between 1989 and 1997 public-sector consulting in the UK remained relatively stable, at around £200m. Interestingly, between 1997 and 2003, when consulting fees from the private sector rose by a factor of three, those from the public sector rose by a factor of four. But even in 2003, when consulting-fee rates were at their lowest ebb, public-sector clients generated only one-fifth of all fees – and that in a year when the private sector was very depressed – still well below historic levels. The evidence is therefore that it is not so much that public-sector spending on consultants is spiralling out of control, but that the entire UK economy is using consultants more than ever before. The public sector is not out of line; if anything, it is getting into line.

... as are some services

But what of the different services that make up the consulting market? What do clients actually buy? The picture emerges of an industry increasingly polarised between large-scale "solutions", which contain outsourcing as well as consulting, and smaller-scale, higher-margin work, which represents a return to the value of traditional "management consulting". Squeezed from both sides is IT-related consulting, once the industry's engine for growth.

Looking more widely, at implementation as well as advisory work, the biggest market of the past few years has been outsourcing and its more recent incarnations: offshoring (outsourcing to a supplier based in a low-cost economy, typically India), business process outsourcing (BPO – outsourcing of business functions other than IT) and even transformational outsourcing (see Chapter 11). It is always a sure sign of an up-and-coming consulting market when no one can agree on the right terminology – the three-letter acronym that will lead the charge into the board room – and these manifestations of outsourcing are no exception. Terms like "right-shoring" and "near-shoring" and "business transformation" are already rolling off people's tongues. Although it is easy to dismiss such terms as management-speak, they point to an underlying, more significant trend: the shift of consulting away from its traditional model as knowledge arbitrage (taking new management ideas and best practice from client to client) to labour arbitrage (trading client staff for consulting staff and, further, trading consulting staff for offshore outsourcing staff) – in effect, outsourcing and offshoring.

But underneath the marketing hype, it is clear that a significant shift has taken place among clients and consulting firms. For clients, outsourcing offers a way of restructuring their business, allowing them to concentrate on their core activities rather than a host of peripheral tasks which do not contribute to their competitive edge. Starting with facilities management and the most mundane IT tasks, outsourcing is now an acceptable approach for activities such as financial and human resources administration and customer query handling. For consultants, this is unquestionably a massive opportunity. Market maturity has not yet reached the stage where organisations feel comfortable making their sourcing decisions in isolation. Consultants can help in developing their overall approach and can advise on supplier selection and contract negotiation.

Advisory work ("management consulting") accounts for only 16% of the global business consulting market (see Figure 3.4), compared with IT outsourcing (36%), business process outsourcing (28%) and systems integration (20%). BPO is expected to grow at roughly 10% per year in the

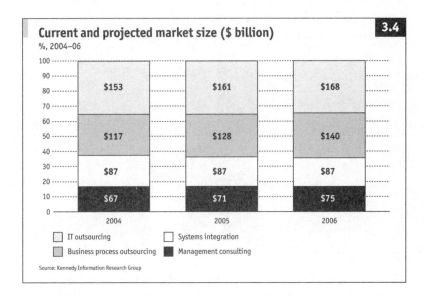

Current and projected market size ($ billion)   **3.4**
%, 2004–06

	2004	2005	2006
IT outsourcing	$153	$161	$168
Business process outsourcing	$117	$128	$140
Systems integration	$87	$87	$87
Management consulting	$67	$71	$75

☐ IT outsourcing   ☐ Systems integration
☐ Business process outsourcing   ■ Management consulting

Source: Kennedy Information Research Group

next few years, twice the rate of management consulting and pure IT outsourcing. Systems integration is not expected to grow at all.

If you strip out government consulting and outsourcing, the picture for other types of consulting is mixed. Operations management (improving the performance of businesses) remains the bedrock of the more advisory end of consulting. As Figure 3.5 on the next page shows, it accounts for nearly half of all fees earned, with strategy accounting for one-third, human resources (HR) consulting for one-fifth, and IT strategy and planning just over one-twentieth of this market.

- Between 2001 and 2003 clients turned away from implementing new, large-scale IT systems in favour of making better use of their existing technology. As the market recovers that trend may reverse, but many people believe that firms still have plenty of work to do in improving processes around the use of technology before they think about buying new technology. Where organisations are making small-scale changes, they are staffing the project internally rather than calling in consultants; for larger-scale changes, they are more likely to outsource or offshore the work.
- Customer relationship management (CRM), the fuel of much growth in marketing consulting during 2001–02, has had its day.

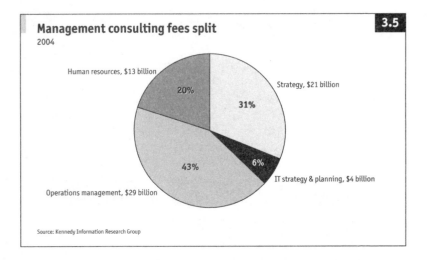

Management consulting fees split
2004

3.5

Human resources, $13 billion

20%

31%

Strategy, $21 billion

43%

6%

IT strategy & planning, $4 billion

Operations management, $29 billion

Source: Kennedy Information Research Group

Many CRM implementations were predicated on the idea of cross-selling products or services. This did not happen, and clients rightly blame consulting firms for overstating the potential returns.

◪ HR consulting continues to battle against perceptions that it is focused on repetitive, formulaic compensation and benefits consulting. While organisations are increasingly looking to consulting firms to help in "talent management", leadership issues and organisational redesign, these remain comparatively small parts of the overall market.

◪ It is tempting to predict the death of strategy consulting every time there is an economic downturn, but it never dies. The need among the most senior management of global corporations to have an external, advisory input – a sounding board backed with hefty analysis – never goes away. Fashions and focus may change, but for this type of consulting demand is constant.

◪ Much consulting stems from firms' need to improve the operational performance of their business, but surprisingly little translates into the archetypal consulting where someone comes into a factory and works out where the bottlenecks are. Most businesses now have such skills in-house. The days when there was a huge divide between clients' and consultants' know-how have passed: clients are just as well-equipped when it comes to streamlining processes or improving productivity. But there are two exceptions. First, clients will still seek out consultants who have in-depth knowledge of a highly specialised area, perhaps a record of solving a particular problem that is new to the client. Second, much operational improvement consulting has been subsumed into IT consulting and outsourcing. Rather than try to re-engineer a process, a company may be tempted to change the technology it uses or hand it over to someone who can fix the problem on its behalf.

Financial engineering?
Of course, it is not just the amount of money that managers have available to spend on consultants that drives demand, but also how they account for it.

Consultants like to tell themselves that it is uncertainty and regulation or the quality of the services they provide that drive demand for consulting. But they may be underestimating another factor: the pressure that organisations have been under to keep their headcount low. For the past 20 years this has been the way in which big corporations have kept a lid on their costs – managers controlled people rather than budgets. Companies employed half as many people doing just as much, and paid them only one-third more in compensation for their additional workload. Asked to do more with less, managers discovered a way round the problem: employing consultants who did not show up on the headcount.

Since the early 1990s, this has been matched by the realisation that outsourcing is a means of instant cost reduction. Increasingly, this approach is being applied to consulting services too: for the largest projects, suppliers may now be expected to finance the work for the first one or two years, until an interim milestone is achieved. Losses made in the early years of a contract are recouped later.

"Why don't people see how dangerous these kinds of deals are?" asks John Kopeck at Compass Management Consulting, which specialises in benchmarking IT costs. "I was sitting in a restaurant in New York late one evening. At the other end of the emptying restaurant was a client talking to an outsourcing vendor, speaking loudly so I couldn't help listening. 'I don't mind what it costs,' said the client, 'I just want to get it off my books.' You should have seen the smile on the vendor's face. Clients like an immediate kick in their return on capital employed when they outsource something, but they don't consider the longer-term impact their decisions have." He believes the 2002 Sarbanes-Oxley Act, affecting corporate governance, financial disclosure and the practice of public accounting, will make clients more cautious. "The primary aim of this legislation is to alert investors to creative financial engineering by management and to hold management responsible when it affects the firm's value. Some outsourced service contracts can look an awful lot like off-balance-sheet financing."

Sarbanes-Oxley may reduce the demand for project financing, but, with the pressure to deliver to ever-shrinking budgets, it is likely that consulting firms will want to find other ways of helping their clients which do not break the bank. Perhaps the change will be semantic: re-labelling consultants as "contractors". "People do not see contractors in the same light as consultants, even though they might be doing the same job," commented one executive. "No one would question the presence of a contractor in the way they would scrutinise a consulting team." Contractor does not sound as good, especially to the ears of consultants themselves, but needs must when the devil drives.

Very stupid? Fads and bandwagons

Between 2001 and 2004 there was a wide disparity in the fortunes of consulting firms – some grew and others shrank by as much as 50%. To understand these variances, it is helpful to look at the role management ideas play in determining the size and shape of the consulting market.

New management ideas unquestionably boost demand. The major waves of growth in consulting have coincided with surges of interest: in total quality management in the 1980s, in business process re-engineering and then enterprise resource planning in the early 1990s, in e-business and the internet in the late 1990s. Consulting firms have been the medium by which many of these ideas have been spread and have earned substantial fees on the back of them.

When a consulting firm says that it has outperformed the industry because of the brilliance of its management or its unique corporate culture, it is telling only a small part of the story. Consulting firms succeed because they have a service which is disproportionately popular in the markets where they operate: they are in the right place at the right time. The turnover of Index, a consulting firm (later acquired by CSC Computer Sciences), grew from $30m in 1989 to $200m in 1997 on the back of business process re-engineering. IBM's consulting practice was worth only around $350m in 1994, but the e-business boom took it to over $10 billion by 2001.

Management fads and fashions have become a growth area for academic research, but it is still difficult to pin down what triggers the take-up of a particular idea. After all, many ideas never make it off the *Harvard Business Review* starting blocks. Equally, how do you measure the extent to which an idea adds value? Clearly, ideas make money for consulting firms, but do they do so for clients? A 1992 study of the Boston Consulting Group Matrix, which became one of the most widely used management tools of the 1980s, by two professors, J. Scott Armstrong at the Wharton School and Roderick Brodie at the University of Auckland in New Zealand, concluded that the BCG matrix, rather than aiding profit maximisation, actually interfered with it. "We suspect", they say, "that decision-makers use the BCG matrix because it legitimises an intuition that many people have about business decisions ... that you should 'stick to your winners'."

Reliable data and objective analysis are thin on the ground, so why do companies continue to adopt unproven ideas? Why do managers believe what consultants tell them? This is what John Micklethwait and Adrian Wooldridge, authors of *The Witch Doctors: What the Management Gurus are Saying, Why it Matters and How to Make Sense of It*, have to say: "Anxious managers grasp at management literature as a panacea for all their worries. Many firms turn to management theory only when they are desperate. Their minds clouded by panic, they start out with exaggerated expectations, put the theory into practice for a few months, start to despair when it fails to produce results, and then turn to a new theory. Two years and 20 theories later, the business may well be bankrupt." It is an argument "reformed" consultants have been happy to confirm.

Even where it is possible to correlate performance with the adoption of a particular fad, it is nigh on impossible to prove there is a causal link. That one company performs better than another will be because of a host of factors – its products and services, patterns of demand, location, management, even luck – and a new management tool can only be a part of this.

But interesting research has been carried out. Eric Abrahamson, a professor at New York University, has spent 15 years researching "fads and bandwagons" and is one of the few academics to draw some conclusions about the impact of management ideas. There is, he argues, a wide disparity in the value obtained: early adopters do best, laggards do worst. Two factors appear to account for the difference:

- Early adopters invest more time in assessing whether a particular idea makes sense for them. In the early stage of the idea's evolution, it will not be clear how it will work in practice. Pioneering companies have to think harder about the appropriateness of the idea, but laggards may be more tempted to jump on the bandwagon without giving due consideration to the return on investment.

■ Early adopters have to customise the idea to suit their own needs. There is no pre-existing manual or methodology for implementing it, so they inevitably write one which suits their own needs. By contrast, laggards are more likely to think there is a standard methodology they should apply; they become focused on the means and lose sight of the end.

Abrahamson's research is borne out by consultants themselves. At Bain & Company, Darrell Rigby has been researching management theories for more than a decade. He believes the secret to making good use of such tools and techniques does not lie in discovering the one unifying theory but in applying the right techniques at the right time in the right way. "Management tools have an important role," he says. "Things go wrong when a guru describes something as a cure-all. Managers should think in terms of a tool chest full of techniques they can apply in different situations. They should not be attracted by big ideas but build up a portfolio of different ones, each appropriate to a different situation." Managers also underestimate how hard it is to apply management tools. Reading an article in the *Harvard Business Review* is the easy part; the problem is how to make the theory stick. "You can't transplant tools any more easily than you can transplant an organ from one body to another. The system (the body) that surrounds the tool determines whether the tool (the organ) will work or not. In some cases, managers trigger corporate antibodies which attack the new idea. They shouldn't just be looking at the ideas other companies are using but questioning whether the conditions that make an idea valuable in one organisation apply to their own."

But managers cannot, he thinks, throw management theory out altogether, however tempted they may be to do so from time to time. "The tools people find helpful vary in line with the changing economic climate. In 2001–02 there was a significant rise in the level of interest in cost-reduction techniques, but now that organisations think they have explored all the avenues that lead to greater efficiency, tools that focus on top-line growth – such as innovation – are picking up speed again. They cannot afford to throw them out and do things by hand."

David Collins, author of *Management Fads and Buzzwords* and a lecturer at the University of Essex in the UK, argues that managers could not give up looking for panaceas even if they wanted to. Work, he believes, is fundamentally about co-operation, but management is about control: "There is a tension at the heart of management. Managers are not the passive victims of fads. They actively seek them out because they are always hunting for new means of establishing control. The irony is that the harder they try to impose control, the more difficult it becomes, and so they never get to a point where they can stop."

Very ambitious? Consulting and the wannabe CEO

Of course, there is a personal dimension to all this. Managers use consultants because their organisation is facing a particular challenge, because they want to try out something new, or because they want to copy something a competitor is doing. But they will not do any of these things if they think bringing in consultants will damage their career. Indeed, they expect consultants to have a positive effect on their career as well as their business. Hiring consultants may also make them feel important. There is nothing quite like having a team of bright young MBA graduates hanging off your every word, or expanding your empire by using an army of consultants to implement your new IT system. Some clients are reluctantly intrigued by consultants. If they have never been one, they want to find out why some consultants are apparently worth more than the people who hire them. They may even be contemplating consulting as a career and think it is useful to establish contact with a potential supplier.

Consultants know this and behave accordingly. They know that, in order to win work, they have to help their clients at a personal level. At its most innocuous, it might mean they simply do the best possible job in the hope that this reflects well on the person who hired them. Equally benignly, it may lead a consultant to take on a coaching role, advising a manager on his or her personal style, helping them prepare for meetings, and so on. Rarely – but it certainly happens – the relationship becomes more manipulative. A manager might be quite clear about how he or she is using the input of consultants to score political points; the consulting team might become more focused on helping a particular manager than on the broader interests of the business as a whole.

It sounds insidious, but it is reality. People will always choose things that make them look good – whether it is a new car, their children's school, the restaurants they eat in – provided they have enough money to pay for them. Consultants will rarely want to make the managers who hire them look bad in front of those they report to, whether it is a more senior manager or the board. Only those with ultimate responsibility can make sure that the client–consultant relationship is one that has probity.

Much more of a problem are those people who use consultants from habit. Maybe they have been a consultant and it is easy to tap into their alumni network when they need help. Maybe the use of consultants is so endemic in their organisation that no one really questions the decision. There are some places that use consultants like junkies use heroin: they are the consulting addicts.

The litmus test

Economic gain, competitive advantage or pure ambition: when is it right to make use of consultants? The answer is far more fundamental. Bringing in people to administer an existing process or to fill a short-term skills gap is perfectly justifiable, but it is not consulting. Consulting involves improving business performance – short-term or long-term, directly or indirectly, but improving it nonetheless.

4 Client organisations

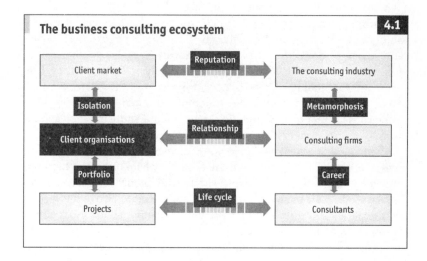

The business consulting ecosystem   4.1

Client market — Reputation — The consulting industry

Isolation — Metamorphosis

Client organisations — Relationship — Consulting firms

Portfolio — Career

Projects — Life cycle — Consultants

So what do clients say about consultants?

The operations manager

Brian Ablett is maintenance manager at an ExxonMobil refinery. "We come across a lot of consultants offering their services," he says, "but we employ few of them and only where we lack some specific expertise. Wherever possible, we will use our own people. What consulting firms can do is provide additional resources – for example, when we implemented SAP software worldwide, we had some internal expertise but we needed to be able to bolster that. We will also use tried-and-trusted consultants on specialist tasks. We use one particular company which carries out industry benchmarking because they are experts at that. But we try to avoid having people hawking their services around."

ExxonMobil now uses fewer consultants than in the past. Building up internal centres of excellence and encouraging people to network more effectively mean that the company is better able to draw on its own skills, rather than seek those of outsiders. An organisation the size of ExxonMobil will have a huge number of experts to call on. Moreover, internal consultants are already familiar with the business – scale means they can be just as objective as external consultants and they have a track record of doing things. "Most consultants have just seen things happen, not made them happen," says Ablett. "We try very hard to avoid becoming dependent on consultants and it is probably this more than any other factor that puts us off using them."

A more accessible pool of internal expertise also means that Exxon-Mobil can be clearer about exactly why it is bringing in external consultants when it does. "We'll pick and choose. We also tend to go to specialists: when firms bundle too many services together, they lose focus and the quality of service goes down across the board. No firm can do everything, even though many imply they can. I cannot see why, just because someone has expertise in the refining industry, they should also have process consulting skills."

Ablett and his colleagues are looking for specific skills and experience so they are more likely to search the market systematically rather than rely on using the same consultants. However, ExxonMobil managers do not start with a clean sheet of paper for each project. "If we have good prior experience with a firm then we will certainly include them alongside the new firms," says Ablett. In any case, the fluidity of the consulting industry means that good contractors join together to form consulting firms, and small consulting firms are taken over by larger ones; it is impossible to have an exclusive list.

So what, apart from specialist knowledge, helps consultants win work at ExxonMobil? Not so much the brand as the ability to work together, according to Ablett: "A firm can have a great reputation, but success comes down to the individual consultants you get." Nor is global coverage always important, even in an organisation as far-flung as ExxonMobil. So much depends on the skill of the individual consultant that buying locally is often preferable. Where a firm has a niche product, ExxonMobil will go to it rather than expect it to be based around the corner. "Clearly," says Ablett, "much depends on the project. We are not going to hire two men in a shed to implement SAP worldwide, but we're more likely to hire an independent consultant to coach senior managers."

One way that consultants can add value is when they help one organisation share developments in best practice with others. But organisations themselves are making increasing efforts to do this. "We are a big enough company that we have some very good practices," says Ablett, "even if no one refinery is best at everything. If we can transfer that learning from one part of the business to another, then we can cut out the middlemen – the consultants – and all the costs and inefficiencies that typically come with intermediaries. But if a consulting firm has expertise that we do not, perhaps because it is not a core part of our business, then manifestly it can add value."

The strategy director

"Vodafone UK's use of consultants varies widely, although overall we bring them in less than we did, partly because of expense and partly because we're aware that we do not always make best use of them," says Craig Tillotson, the company's UK strategy director, who spent ten years at McKinsey and then Mercer before moving into industry. "At the UK company level, we employ strategy consultants, especially where an issue is particularly challenging, perhaps because the answer is unclear, perhaps because we need access to some very specific expertise. Elsewhere, we make widespread use of highly specialised consulting companies. Between the two, we hire 'Big Four' type firms at a functional level and second-tier players on operational issues. Middle managers do use them to fill resource or knowledge gaps; at this level there is more risk of an overlap between what different consulting teams do."

Tillotson's role means that he is generally looking to hire consultants who have experience of the telecoms sector, in-depth expertise of a particular field and "raw talent". The brand of a particular consulting firm is less important than the people. "We want consultants who are genuinely committed to the success of our business, people we know and trust." But that does not mean he would prefer to buy from smaller players: "If we have a particularly difficult problem, then a global firm may be more likely to be able to help, not so much because of its breadth of expertise but because its brand has enabled it to attract the best people." Indeed, like many others, he is wary of firms that try to offer too many services. "I don't see the value of buying strategy work from an IT supplier. To have the best people in a particular field, a firm has to have a specialist reputation."

Although Tillotson is convinced consultants add value, he also believes Vodafone UK should continue to do more things in-house. "The level of engagement with the business is higher," he says, "we also retain the knowledge better and, of course, it is cheaper." Perhaps as a result of these aspirations, he has seen some changes in the way consultants behave over the past three years. "They are trying much harder to work with clients, rather than impose a process on them. There is more engagement, more combined client/consultant teams. While these things often make it harder for the consultants – they find it more difficult to articulate the specific value they bring – the client team members accelerate the learning curve and allow the consultants to get to the heart of a problem more quickly."

The procurement professional

Alan Gotto, procurement manager for Aviva, an insurance company, and a former consultant, believes that if they are employed intelligently, consultants can bring tremendous benefits to a business. "Having been on both sides of the fence, I've a realistic understanding of the pressures both sides are under and how to mitigate these to ensure successful service delivery," he says.

One of his main concerns is that consultancy is generally bought and sold badly. "Companies engage consultants for three broad reasons: brand, bodies and brains," says Gotto, "but often they don't take the time to understand which of these they need and end up paying for one when they wanted the other. You shouldn't be using global blue-chip suppliers to work on projects which could be delivered by one-man bands." At the same time, some consulting firms pay their consultants a commission, based on the new business they bring in, and this encourages both the firm and the consultant to focus on one-off sales rather than the long-term investment. "At Aviva," he says, "we've looked at how we can remove these inefficiencies and develop supplier relationships for the benefit of both parties."

Gotto thinks that the purchasing department has a crucial role to play: "As many internal budget holders are only occasional users of consultancy, purchasing can ensure that as a client you remain as joined up as the consultants." This must be about more than just "policing consultancy" and "picking fights over rate cards". "While consultancy fees are significant, and must be managed, the outputs, such as a future strategic direction of a business, can be far more significant. Purchasing's role is to bring best value consultancy to the business; enlightened consultants recognise this and bring us best value to sell to the business." A classic case would be where a consulting firm has delivered an outstanding solution for a client in one business unit which it could use again in another if a similar solution is required.

To achieve this at Aviva, when spending on a project is expected to exceed a certain amount, group purchasing must be notified, so that it can decide on its level of involvement, whether that is helping select the right firm, managing the relationship or evaluating success. "A mistake the purchasing department often makes", Gotto says, "is to adopt a classic procurement process, providing support up to the point where a contract is signed, then disappearing – which, of course, is exactly when the consulting sales machine kicks in and it is needed the most to avoid unnecessary dependencies developing. While some consultants may claim to be one-stop-shops, none are market leaders in all areas, so an important part of our role is to capture feedback so that consultant firms can be graded by capability, rather than as a whole."

Gotto believes that as clients increasingly question the value added by consultants, it is essential for consultants to develop mature, trust-based relationships with their clients. "Often they don't even seem to trust their own products as they excessively limit their liability," he argues. "The challenge they must now meet is that if they want to call themselves professionals, and be paid as professionals, they should be prepared to be held responsible as professionals."

The managing director

Unimills is a Dutch subsidiary of Golden Hope, a Malaysian agricultural products business. Jan van Driel is its managing director: "We hire consultants when we do not have the in-house expertise to do something for ourselves. For example, we are in the middle of a project to increase the entrepreneurial skills of our staff, and we have used consultants for this. We have also launched a new energy-saving programme and have hired some consultants to benchmark it."

If anything, Unimills has seen its use of consultants grow, as it has become clearer about what is and is not core to its business. Cost is a factor in selecting consultants, as are experience and references from other clients. Brand counts for less. "I don't care about names," says van Driel. "Big names usually come with big price-tags." For some types of work, experience in the food industry is preferred – "otherwise we end up teaching the consultant, and paying for it" – but for others, such as organisational redesign, where the issues are usually common across all sectors, it is much less so.

Van Driel has noticed a marked change in the behaviour of consultants since 2000: "The downturn in the economy has been felt by consultants too. There is more willingness to work with us, rather than impose a standard process on us." However, he is wary about becoming too dependent on a single source of advice: "We like to keep our thinking fresh by switching from one consulting firm to another, otherwise there is a danger that the consultants will become too used to our way of working and will not challenge it."

How do good consultants add value? "They provide you with new thinking," says van Driel. "They can act like a spark within your organisation and force you to challenge your assumptions. Not-so-good consultants just confirm what you already know and do. It is then a matter of imitation and not adding any value, a waste of energy and money."

The entrepreneur

Jan Quant was head of royalties at the Chrysalis record group before he and a couple of partners set up Screendragon, a company developing desktop-based communications software used in marketing and internal communications campaigns, in 1999. It is a relatively small business that has survived the fall-out of the past few years, partly with the help of an angel investor who stepped in during the darkest days of 2001.

"We are a lean and mean organisation," says Quant. "Where we can outsource our needs, we do so: we want to be as virtual as possible." This might mean, for example, hiring the former finance director of an advertising agency to help with developing some new accounts. But the effort to be flexible sometimes means the company is caught out and needs help in a hurry. Because it is small there is not much cash to spare for consultants' bills, except that which they help generate. "Fees have to be contingent on success," he points out. "Our scale means that we are a comparatively low-risk client – we are not looking for armies of consultants – but we are potentially high-reward. We will pay people according to their success: a percentage of new sales, for instance. If consultants are good at what they do, they will succeed. If I was a consultant – if I thought I had a particular skill that people were interested in – this is how I would want to be paid because it shows I am an entrepreneur and that I believe in my own product. It gives clients confidence. Of course, consultants have to pay the bills like the rest of us, but this is about having a portfolio approach, mixing some more speculative work with more mainstream activities."

This attitude has suited Screendragon well in a market where there is plenty of competition among consulting firms. "Lots of people are now having a go on their own, as independent consultants, and I think that is pretty healthy," says Quant. "It means they are more responsive and flexible than they were when we started up; it's also kept prices down." Does that mean Screendragon's use of consultants will increase as it grows? Quant is sceptical, if only because of the wealth of information now readily available to clients over the internet. "Five years ago, we would have hired a lawyer if we wanted to know how to set up escrow accounts," he says. "Today we don't need to because the information is at the end of our fingertips." The image of consulting does not help either: "We are always looking for people who can do things. The term consultant implies that is all they do – consult. The successful consultant gets on and does stuff."

The CIO

Ahmad Abu El-Ata trained in Egypt as an electronics engineer before studying for a doctorate in digital signalling in the late 1960s. Moving into industry was the obvious next step, especially as large-scale financial institutions were just beginning to wake up to the potential of computing. Even so, Abu El-Ata always meant to return to academia; instead, he ended up as head of the group IT office at Credit Suisse Group, and later as head of IT for Europe, the Middle East and Africa at Credit Suisse.

"As a chief information officer (CIO), you have to use consultants," says Abu El-Ata. "There are some projects you simply cannot get done without the specialist know-how consultants bring." Experience of previous projects – failures as well as successes – is especially valuable. But he sees a significant shift in the way in which CIOs buy consulting. "Consultants were used as the extension of in-house resources when there were headcount restrictions and/or skills shortages, in effect as a pseudo-variable cost," says Abu El-Ata. "CIOs used consultants as a means of balancing fixed and variable costs: on-the-spot outsourcing." That could still – indeed, often – mean a long-term commitment: "We ended up working with the same group of consultants for years. The project manager got promoted as the size of the business grew. Whenever there was a new project in the offing, you would call the partner or senior manager and carry on from there. That is how it was."

The change happened slowly, almost imperceptibly. Increasingly, the idea of the blanket relationship began to disappear. There were still areas where skills shortages or pressure on headcount occurred, but these became far more focused. This is a change Abu El-Ata attributes to the rise of the central procurement department: "Large organisations have tried to develop technology purchasing divisions, much as they already have office supply purchasing divisions. There has been a huge reduction in consulting fee rates as a result, but this is not a uniformly good thing – lower price is not always synonymous with the best value."

At the same time, Abu El-Ata believes consultants do not particularly help themselves: "Too many sales pitches are still treated as showcases, putting their best people on display, and you know you will never see them again. Sometimes the skills and experience of those left are not markedly different from in-house staff, and that sows seeds for difficult working relationships at all levels. Our people would make salary comparisons and see the plum jobs going to the consultants, all of which can be quite damaging. You have to educate the organisation as to why it is necessary to bring consultants in and create mixed client–consultant teams; the tendency to backbite goes down when both sides work together. You also have to break projects down into controllable tasks and ensure there is transparent governance and decision-making, so that no one can think you are in a supplier's back pocket. Finally, you have to ensure expertise is retained internally: what is the point of using consultants, if all your best staff decide to leave to become consultants as a result?"

The HR manager
Michelle Morgan has worked in human resources for more than 20 years and is now the HR director of Boy Scouts of America.

"The real change for HR professionals was when the year 2000 pushed companies into buying packaged software rather than building their own. It was easier to buy than to build, but we needed consultants to come in and help because we were not familiar with the technology. In other words, we use consultants because we do not have sufficient resources internally and/or we need specialist expertise. But using consultants more has also made us better at managing them. In the past, HR directors were as guilty as the next director of hiring consultants, then walking out and leaving them to it. We're more in control now: we use them to support what we're trying to do, not to take things off our hands. Like others, we're also concerned that consulting firms should bear fiduciary responsibility for getting things right. As clients, we know what we're doing now; our expectations are higher and we intend to hold consultants to a higher standard."

Morgan sees the differences between firms boiling down to price and personality. "There are only a handful of premier firms left," she believes. "The majority have become systems integration and software companies." Brand is important, especially if she is looking for a firm with a good reputation which will see a project through successfully, on budget and on schedule. "But you don't always get what you pay for," she says. "The most expensive firms are not always the best: there are perfectly good freelance consultants who subcontract their services to the larger firms."

The chief executive

"I spent 17 years incarcerated at McKinsey," jokes Dick Cavanagh, "but I liked it enough to chair one of its alumni groups." As poacher turned gamekeeper, he is now president and chief executive of the Conference Board (an independent membership organisation which carries out and publishes research, and brings executives together to learn from one another), the non-executive director of several companies – and a client of consulting firms.

"A lot of business people have the same schizophrenia about consultants that they have about other professional firms. They begrudge how expensive they are and are concerned that they're getting advice without accountability. I suspect some also envy them, because the consultants get to work on the most important, politically charged issues – and then get to walk away. But consultants will continue to prosper because people like me need independent advice. Indeed, if you consider all the corporate governance changes we're seeing, most of them are aimed at increasing the level of independent thinking in a company – and that's one of the most important things consultants bring. Consultants should not be part of the political fray; their career does not rise or fall on whether they do or do not introduce a new model of a car. The other thing they bring is experience. You are always encountering problems in business that you have not met before. Entering the Brazilian market, for example, is probably a once-in-the-lifetime experience for most senior executives, but you can hire a consultant who has done it many times before."

Being able to focus on a specific problem for several weeks, as consultants can, is a luxury most executives do not have. Consultants' ability to be able to deal with a corporation's outside constituencies is also an important factor. "There are times when it is critical for a business to demonstrate to shareholders and other stakeholders that a particular decision or strategy has been verified externally. Corporate downsizing has shredded the number of analytical staff available in many organisations. But clients have to manage their consultants effectively; they should be as critical of the consultants' work as of their own, and they should not abdicate responsibility."

Cavanagh divides consultants into two groups: people who bring expert knowledge and focus to bear on a specific problem; and – the much rarer breed – people who bring wisdom and judgment, who are counsellors as much as consultants. "Some firms have some people who can do the latter," he says. "I wish they all did, but they do not. Every time there's a crisis in corporate management it creates a cottage industry in consulting: people go from being a specialist in one type of crisis to the next, just following what is hot. That's a very sad situation; basically, they're charlatans." Not surprisingly, the crucial thing Cavanagh would look for in a consultant, in addition to competence and candidness, is professionalism: "Consultants should serve clients rather than sell more consulting assignments."

Categorising clients' needs

Despite the disparity of their needs, talking to clients yields many common themes. Indeed, you can ask almost any organisation in the world about their use of consultants and be reasonably sure that they will focus on the same points.

Consulting projects, they will say, fall into three broad categories:

- **Specialist projects.** Specialist knowledge has always been high on clients' must-have lists, but it is especially so now, since most remain unpersuaded by the idea of the integrated, multidisciplinary firm touted by many consulting firms in the 1990s. A client seeking to resolve a specific issue will hire a consultant with special expertise in that area. The work may vary in length, from a few days to a more long-term commitment, but it rarely involves more than a handful of consultants, all of whom will have to work closely with the client's own staff. Specialisation is a great leveller, putting the smallest consulting firm on a par with the largest. What counts is not breadth or even global reach, but having genuinely world-class expertise in a narrow field.
- **Integrated solutions.** There are occasions when specialist knowledge is not sufficient, such as when an organisation is facing especially large-scale change, perhaps following a merger or acquisition, or associated with the implementation of new technology. In such circumstances, hiring a group of discrete specialists from different firms will not provide the type of joined-up service or the number of people that is required. For many organisations, hiring a large team of consultants is something they do only reluctantly. Most would prefer to do at

least some of the work in-house as a means of ensuring they retain control over what can be enormously invasive changes and to control costs. But circumstances may dictate otherwise.

- **Strategic advice.** Falling somewhere between specialist services and integrated solutions is the help clients want in generating new insights into their business and formulating new ways to respond to threats and opportunities in the marketplace. The remit here is too wide for this to be classed as a specialist service, but focusing on advisory work rather than implementation means that clients do not need the large teams of consultants associated with integrated solutions.

Categorising clients' needs in this way, however, does not answer more fundamental questions. Why are they hiring outside consultants at that moment? Why not do the work in-house? Why bring consultants in now, rather than next month or next year? What is it that external consultants can do which their organisations cannot do for themselves? It follows that there are three broad categories of client needs:

- **People needs.** Clients hire consulting firms for their consultants, people who have specialist skills or a level of knowledge they lack internally. Clients need people who are experts in their sector (industry-specific knowledge), perhaps to assess the implications of a regulatory change, to respond to a move by a competitor, or to help decide whether they should adopt a new management idea. Alternatively, they may be looking for people who are experts in a particular issue (issue-specific knowledge). For example, two banks seeking to set up a shared services centre to process their combined back-office administration might view the initial decision as strategic. They might want to talk to experts in the financial-services sector to learn what their competitors have done and to assess the likely benefits in their case. Once that decision is made, they might well look to external consultants who have prior experience of setting up such processing centres. Lastly, to implement their plan, they may need extra pairs of hands – bright, energetic and informed people who can help get the new initiative up and running, simply by being flexible and rolling up their sleeves to do whatever it takes to get the job done.
- **Thinking needs.** Even in the smallest organisations it can be difficult to stand back and understand what is happening.

Opportunities are missed; threats are ignored. Consultants, like therapists, can provide clients with an invaluable perspective because they are looking at an organisation objectively, from the outside in. Sometimes that independent opinion is enough, but there are many occasions when managers need hard information and consulting firms can be better equipped to gather and analyse this. Lastly, there may also be occasions when someone wants access to creative thinking – consultants who can generate fresh insights about intractable problems and challenge long-standing assumptions.

◪ **Process and technology needs.** Organisations may have sufficient knowledge and information to know what it is they want to do, but they may lack the wherewithal to convert their idea into reality. It might be that they do not know how to: they may never have implemented a particular idea before; they might want to avoid the pitfalls of past failures; or they may wish to follow best practice. Either way, they need consultants to provide a roadmap, a plan they can follow. It might also be that they need a consulting firm to provide momentum, to keep a difficult project going despite inevitable setbacks. Clients may look to consultants to ensure that a project, once started, is finished. Consultants can dedicate all their time and effort to this one project, whereas employees of the client organisation usually have other responsibilities to distract them.

Put the types of consulting projects and the fundamental reasons for hiring consultants together (see Figure 4.2) and the underlying shape of today's consulting industry becomes apparent.

Clients hiring consultants may be motivated by one or more of these reasons; those looking for information and analysis often want an independent view. But some drivers are becoming mutually exclusive. As those quoted at the start of this chapter illustrate, many clients feel uncomfortable with the notion of mixing independence with momentum. They are not sure that they can trust a firm to be objective about the approach they should take when that firm might have an interest in selling them large teams of consultants later on.

Specialist services, strategic advice and integrated solutions are bought by clients for different reasons. Clients who use consultants to provide specialised services lack (and are therefore looking for) information on and analysis of a particular issue, an in-depth knowledge of

Business consulting needs and projects map `4.2`

	SPECIALIST SERVICE			
Content		STRATEGIC ADVICE		
	Information and analysis	Independent view Innovative thinking		
People	Industry-specific knowledge	Generalist resources	INTEGRATED SOLUTION	
	Issue-specific knowledge			
Process	Roadmap		Momentum	

that issue and/or of a particular sector, and a tried-and-tested approach to tackling the issue, honed through extensive experience. Clients who use consultants to provide an integrated solution also lack (and are looking for) industry and/or issue-specific knowledge, but they do not particularly need more information or analysis. They know what they want to do; it is more a question of getting it done. This is why they will also use consultants to provide a plan and, crucially, to inject momentum. By contrast, clients who use consultants for strategic advice will be looking for independence, innovation and expertise, but not a process for doing things.

The question is, as a client, what results do you need and how do you get them?

5 Projects

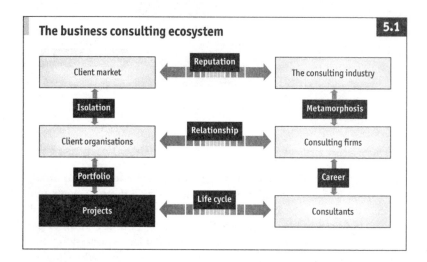

The business consulting ecosystem   `5.1`

Client market — Reputation — The consulting industry

Isolation — Metamorphosis

Client organisations — Relationship — Consulting firms

Portfolio — Career

Projects — Life cycle — Consultants

WHEN IS A CONSULTING PROJECT not a consulting project? The answer is when it does not seek to improve business performance. Consulting projects, like pieces of string, come in different lengths, so it is hard to generalise about their focus, duration, size, scope, complexity, and so on. Programmes are generally longer and more complex, while projects are shorter and more straightforward. But if they do not aim to make a positive difference to a business, they should not be called consulting.

The Children's Mutual has been helping parents in the UK provide financial security for their children for more than 50 years. But in 2003, poor stockmarket performance had adversely affected the market for savings, making conditions difficult for selling the company's flagship product, Baby Bonds. At the same time, the UK government had unveiled its Child Trust Fund, whereby every child born on or after September 1st 2002 will receive a lump sum for investment, aimed at building up a stock of assets for the young person to reinvest or use when they are 18, giving them added security and opportunity in adulthood. The phasing in of the fund means that the number of new customers processed by The Children's Mutual could rise from a typical 4,000 to 120,000 per month. "It will be a totally different market, where every new child has an account," says Graeme McAusland, chief operations officer of The Children's Mutual.

Succeeding in this new market required the one thing The Children's Mutual did not have: scale. Together with David White, the chief executive, McAusland hired a small team from Troika, a consulting company specialising in providing outsourcing advice to financial institutions, to help them decide how best to respond. "We put together a presentation, showing the status quo and what would happen when the 'bow wave' of demand hit the company in early 2005, which had an enormous impact," recalls Andrew Stewart, Troika's managing director. "Although it brought home the scale of challenge, it also highlighted a potential opportunity: creating a 'utility', using The Children's Mutual's existing business and specialist expertise as the foundation of a much larger, more sustainable business." "But with charges capped by the government at 1.5%, the only way to run a profitable business was to secure efficient distribution alliances based on an efficient platform," continues McAusland. "We were bringing our specialist knowledge of children's savings products, but we needed a partner capable of handling high volumes of transactions."

Clearly, not just any partner would do. Rather than the conventional mountains of paperwork involved in a standard selection process, Troika ran a series of interactive workshops to help the shortlisted partners refine their proposals and to agree the main commercial principles upfront. "We split the sessions into two parts," says Andy Colvin, Troika's project manager. "We gave a series of briefings describing the company's current operation and the impact of the fund on its future economic model and service requirements. We then gave the potential partners a few days to think about how they would respond: how they would do the administration and the pricing, and how they would want to structure the arrangement and deliver it." But the key was to break up the work into components, enabling both sides to see what would be required for each part with absolute clarity. "The result," says Colvin, "was a much higher quality of bids and a swifter negotiation process." The UK's largest life and pensions outsourcing contract (worth around £430m over 20 years) was signed in July 2004 between The Children's Mutual and Capita after just three months of negotiations.

Troika's small team worked side-by-side, 12 hours a day, with White and McAusland. "They were a fantastic client with a clear idea of where they wanted to take their business," says Stewart. "What we did was help find a strategy that took them where they wanted to go." This was not a case of the client handing over the problem and saying come back when you have developed a strategy. The project team was based in the same office, and team members went on fact-finding trips to India, even to football matches, together. "We were trusted advisers for them to bounce ideas off," says Stewart. "Our role – whether it was as part of their management team, or on the phone in the evenings and at weekends – was to help them select the best option. We saw ourselves as extra brain capacity, putting another head on the client's shoulders in order to take half the weight off them."

The respect is mutual. "This felt quite different from the other consulting projects I've been involved with," recalls McAusland. "It was far more hands-on. The people from Troika aren't arrogant and don't pretend they have an instant solution to every problem. They're real people who roll up their sleeves and get on." "These are bright guys with a good understanding of the financial services market," says White. "Given that we were also taking a major strategic decision, Troika brought something else that was crucial: their good judgment. It has been a genuinely collaborative effort. Without it, our ambitions for the new world of the Child Trust Fund would have been much diminished."

The three Es

Consulting starts (or should start) at the point where managers want to improve the performance of some part of the business but recognise that they cannot do at least some of the work involved. There are, of course, business improvement projects which are done wholly internally, using only the skills and resources an organisation has in-house. But when it comes to ensuring it gets the best result, an organisation should at least consider the input of consultants.

The scale and scope of that input vary considerably. Managers may hire a single consultant to carry out a particular task: to advise on a market the client knows little about, or to help select the best supplier from a crowd of bidders, perhaps. The larger the issue and the more important it is to the business, the more likely it is that the size of the consulting team will grow and that the style of work will become more collaborative. Rather than the consultant reporting to the client like any other employee, the consulting team will work alongside the client's own staff, jointly allocating work, sharing ideas and information. There comes a point, though, where the balance of responsibility for completing the project shifts from the purchaser to the consultant. In such projects, the consultants are no longer advisers but implementers, doing the lion's share of the work.

Every business improvement project is concerned with three things:

- effectiveness – getting the desired result (doing the right thing);
- efficiency – getting it quickly (doing the thing right);
- economy – getting it at a reasonable market rate.

Although all three should play a role in every project, one or more factors may predominate. A chief executive who is looking to take a new product to market more quickly than the competition is unlikely to be particularly price-sensitive. In a perfect world, the three factors would also be cumulative. The number one priority should be to get the job done. When a client and/or consulting firm is confident that this will be the case, the emphasis will shift to efficiency and to using the appropriate level of resources, to doing the job, but doing it more quickly. That is certainly one of the changes Alan Kantrow, chief knowledge officer at Monitor, a consulting firm, has seen in the past few years. "The willingness of clients to undergo extraordinarily lengthy interventions has largely gone," he says. "They want consultants to work distinctly faster, and that puts many aspects of the conventional consulting process under enormous pressure."

Lastly, where clear processes and methodologies exist for delivering the desired result quickly, the focus will be on price. We know all these firms can do this work, thinks the client, so which one will do it most cost-effectively? The same thinking can apply to consultants too: we know that there is nothing to differentiate our services in terms of what they will achieve or speed; if we want to win this work, we will have to cut our fees. Sometimes, in less successful projects, the balance may go awry: the programme manager, worried about meeting a tight deadline, may be tempted to sacrifice effectiveness in the name of efficiency; the manager, who is already over budget, may try to cut corners.

The level of consulting involvement and the motivation underpinning a project are interrelated (see Figure 5.2 on the next page). Projects which predominantly focus on effectiveness are more likely to involve either consultants acting as advisers or both sides working collaboratively. Efficiency-oriented projects may also involve collaboration, but they will encompass occasions when the consultants say to their clients: "We do not have time to involve you in every stage. There are some processes we will have to do for you if we are to meet our deadline."

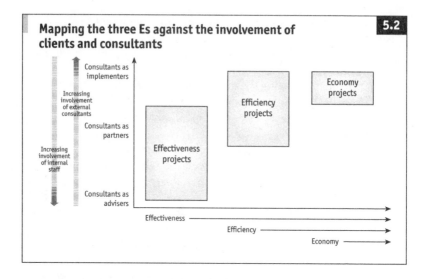

Mapping the three Es against the involvement of clients and consultants

`5.2`

Consultants as implementers

Increasing involvement of external consultants

Consultants as partners

Increasing involvement of internal staff

Consultants as advisers

Effectiveness projects

Efficiency projects

Economy projects

Effectiveness ————————————→
Efficiency ————————————→
Economy ————————→

Consulting firms are even less likely to invest in working "in partnership" where the pressure on the fees they charge is intense.

Clients using consultants have historically put effectiveness at the top of their agenda. They use consultants to help them do what they were planning to do better. This kind of project is typified by the work Troika undertook for The Children's Mutual: being a second head on the client's shoulders. However, that the project had to be completed within a very short time frame indicates the pressure consultants are under to be efficient as well as effective.

Max Wideman is a past president and chairman of the Project Management Institute. "The first step to managing a consulting project effectively is for clients to be clear on whether they are bringing in someone to achieve a specific objective or hiring bodies on an hourly basis – in essence glorified employees to augment an in-house team. For the former, they have to spell out exactly what they are looking for, either in qualitative terms or more quantifiably: return on investment, for instance. For the latter, the right balance between clients and consultants is crucial." He cites research by PricewaterhouseCoopers that concluded that the highest performance is achieved with consultants making up around 25% of the total team. More than this does not guarantee higher performance; indeed, the client may lose control to the external consultants. Fewer than this and the external consultants may lack the critical mass to make a genuine difference.

But the most important differences, Wideman argues, are less to do with a project being an external consulting project, an internal project or a joint client–consultant project and more to do with the underlying differences between organisations. "An organisation based on a rigid hierarchy with deep vertical divisions between its functional departments will have a different style of project management from a matrix-based organisation. The first will be more command-and-control, whereas managers in the latter must put more effort into ensuring buy-in and using teamwork to solve problems."

A project should be divided into two separate periods, the first for planning and the second for execution. Planning is about effectiveness, "doing the right thing", and execution is about efficiency, "doing the thing right". Interestingly, these require different mindsets and whether consultants are brought in for the former or the latter may be largely determined by the underlying culture of the organisation and the personal disposition of its managers. Using the Myers-Briggs typology, which tests individual preferences, he argues there are four distinct types of project managers which coincide with the four corners of the Myers-Briggs 4x4 matrix. These can be described as follows:

- The driver manager gives orders and expects things to be done. Such a person is good at making sure things are done within a budget but is less able to handle the political sensitivities that are so often a part of large-scale projects.
- The co-ordinator thinks of all the options in order to come up with the best solution. Such a project manager is good at managing projects, but will not necessarily have all the specialist skills required to complete the project.
- The ideal administrator is excellent for tidying up the loose ends.
- The entrepreneur, by contrast, excels at getting things off the ground. But few entrepreneurs are able to follow the initial idea through to a successful conclusion. They need the other three types of project manager to complete the entire work.

Dennis Christmas has been a consultant at Twynstra Gudde, a Dutch firm specialising in the management of large-scale, complex projects, for seven years, before which he was an internal consultant in the public sector, so he understands project management from both a client and consultant perspective. "We do not work for clients but with them," says Christmas, "taking them from the drawing board to completion."

Twynstra does not take on sole responsibility for finishing a project ("it's a group effort," says Christmas), but the firm believes that by focusing on five aspects – time, costs, quality, information and project structure – it can substantially increase the probability of success.

So what difference does the presence of external consultants make when it comes to project management? Ironically, Christmas believes that external consultants have most to add in the early days of a project, when everything is new. "One of the problems with long projects is that those involved become an organisation within an organisation. They develop their own culture which makes it hard for them to be truly objective." But the real barrier is the client. "Clients are often the most unprofessional party," says Christmas. "Consultants know what they are there for. They do project work all the time, so it is easy to discuss what is expected with them. But clients may be dealing with a large project for the first time and be much less clear about their role."

This inexperience surfaces in four ways.

- Clients do not always make decisions at the right time or in the right way. They may involve too many people, and they may try to fudge or defer decisions.
- Clients do not always give their consultants important information. Even though the latter have specialist expertise, they still need information. Often clients do not know what information is required or where to find it.
- Clients may lack a coherent vision of the desired outcome of the project. They may think of it in process terms (launching a new product) at the expense of the end that the process is designed to achieve (to improve the company's image). This can mislead those involved in the project, sometimes to the extent that they focus on the wrong objective.
- Clients ignore the dynamic environment that is true of most large-scale projects and can derail a project if it is not carefully monitored and managed.

The roots of the consulting industry are in effectiveness projects, such as the lengthy projects typical of business process re-engineering. But enterprise resource planning and preparing for the year 2000 taught clients that effectiveness was not enough and that you needed efficiency too. An emphasis on speed was compounded by the dotcom boom, when consulting firms competed on the basis of how quickly they could take their clients' ideas to market (sacrificing effectiveness into the bargain). The internet bubble may have burst, but that perception has not changed. As one client said at the time, "You can't put toothpaste back in the tube." Having demonstrated to clients that they could expedite their work, the consulting firms could not very well slow it down again.

This is the consulting equivalent of choosing to compete on price or on quality. Manufacturing companies used to be able to compete on one or the other; now they have to do both. Similarly, consulting projects have to be not only effective and efficient but, increasingly, cost-efficient as well. Despite the recent recovery in the consulting sector, client budgets continue to be tight. Furthermore, residual oversupply, ferocious competition and a growing army of experienced freelance consultants mean that consulting firms are not well placed to resist pricing pressure. Into the melting pot can now be thrown a new ingredient: offshoring.

Is consulting the next manufacturing?

"Certainly from an IT outsourcing point of view, offshoring has become standard for large corporations," says Tom Weakland at DiamondCluster. "Not long ago it was viewed as an agonising decision. Lots of time was spent finding a qualified partner; there were lots of cultural issues. Those concerns have pretty much gone away. Virtually all our clients are either offshoring already or thinking about it." Although offshoring currently accounts for a small proportion of outsourcing revenues, most people accept that, barring a backlash or protectionist legislation, we are at the beginning of the curve.

Organisations, says Weakland, do not go to offshore companies just because of the price differential. "We have found that clients feel they get more value from offshore than onshore relationships. Offshore firms put a huge amount of effort into ensuring their processes are rigorous. Sometimes too much so – there are cases we've seen where a process has been followed religiously, so that a poor-quality specification from a client was not challenged and resulted in poor-quality code. But offshore firms are getting better at developing their understanding of how clients work. Five years from now we'll be hard pushed to see the difference between 'onshore' and 'offshore' firms. Look at Infosys: it's already doing IT strategy and design work, neither of which is generally thought of as an offshoreable activity."

For anyone who knows London, the suburb of Croydon conjures

up images of 1970s office blocks and litter-blown concrete, not a place where you would expect to find one of the world's fastest-growing outsourcing and consulting firms. B.G. Srinivas joined Infosys in 1999, having spent 16 years with ABB in Europe and India; he is now responsible for the company's operations in Europe, the Middle East and Africa. "Of course, Infosys was not so well known then, just 3,000 people compared with ten times that today." Infosys's size may have changed, but its culture, says Srinivas, has remained remarkably constant: "We are an entrepreneurial organisation that encourages initiative. As a growing company, we benefit from an exciting, individualist environment, but at our heart lies a deeply held belief in excellence."

Making that belief a reality is especially difficult when only one-third of the work you do is on clients' sites, the rest being based in almost 20 development centres around the world. Like other offshore firms, Infosys sets great store by its accreditation by various international project management and software development standards bodies. External benchmarks such as these are underpinned by continuously assessing and improving the way it works internally. "If something moves, we process it. Everyone is behind this from our most senior executives to our newest recruits," says Srinivas. "Our values define our culture and how people should behave. They are the means by which we have been able to do what we have done."

Despite appearances, Srinivas says the company has been cautious about growth. "When we were hit by the post-ERP slump in the late 1990s, we could have just sent people out and told them to sell anything. Instead, on the basis that fortune favours the brave, we invested in adding new services and thinking. Now more than one-third of our business comes from services we have introduced in the last five years." According to Srinivas, Infosys is more likely to find itself competing against big-name western consulting firms than other offshore companies. "Even where they win the work, it will usually be at a lower than usual price. At the same time, we don't want to be seen as a commodity player, fighting on price alone – hence our focus on delivering value to the client and the quality of that delivery." The company is right not to be too bullish. One important challenge of the next few years will be how to fulfil clients' demand for face-to-face interaction (the effectiveness component of consulting projects) with a low-cost structure. "The world is not one market," says Srinivas. "We know local knowledge of our clients is hugely important, but we do not want to increase our onsite costs. We operate with the bare minimum of overheads. Indeed, we practise what we preach by offshoring our back-office operations; even our business cards are printed in India."

Hubris will undoubtedly be another challenge. In 2005 Infosys UK was looking for new accommodation. There were two buildings on its shortlist, both in the heart of London's financial district, both being vacated by big consulting firms.

The limits of offshoring?

Offshoring – or, more broadly, the relocation of consulting resources to different countries – is the next challenge to a client's project management skills.

Face-to-face contact is important to client–consultant and customer–supplier relationships because it increases effectiveness. Clients who are looking for effectiveness are more likely to want their consultants and IT service providers to work onsite with them and are less likely to countenance the work being done offsite, let alone offshore. Clients' desire for effectiveness, and consequently interaction, is therefore one of the main reasons offshore companies believe they have to build their own onshore (onsite) resources if they are to move up the supplier pecking order. Similarly, onshore companies have derived comfort from what they see as a clear line over which offshoring cannot cross.

The point at which face-to-face contact ceases to be essential and starts to be merely nice to have is a fluid one. In the recent downturn, efficiency and economy became more important than effectiveness and the proportion of a consulting or IT services project that required face-to-face interaction shrank. But in better economic conditions this trend may be reversed: think back to the internet mania of the late 1990s to see how comparatively unimportant cost (economy) can be (see Figure 5.3 on the next page).

In shifting the balance from effectiveness to efficiency, and from efficiency to economy, two factors predominate:

- the availability of alternative ways of working;
- the extent to which clients feel there is scope for cutting costs.

These two factors also indicate how important (or not) face-to-face interaction is likely to be in the client–consultant, customer–supplier relationships of the future, and therefore the balance of onshore/offshore resources a supplier will need.

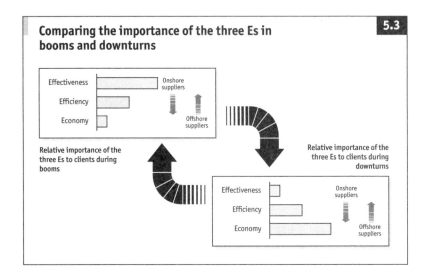

Comparing the importance of the three Es in booms and downturns `5.3`

From effectiveness to efficiency: the end of end-to-end processes?

People working side-by-side are better able to exchange information; they can plumb each other's experience and challenge each other's assumptions; and they are more capable of handling complexity and being flexible. With interaction, there is more trust and less bureaucracy.

Or so we think. A decade ago, at the height of the business process re-engineering frenzy, the focus was on breaking down internal barriers in order to see processes end-to-end. Today the opposite is true: efficiency comes from breaking down processes into their component parts. The opportunity to reduce labour costs may have initially sparked the demand for offshoring, but we have had to wait for technology capable of handling complex processes for the market to really take off. But although it is hard to believe that every process can be offshored in its entirety, the more organisations break down a process's components so that each stage can be handled by highly specialised, comparatively independent teams, the more likely it is that some of the process can be offshored.

Greater segmentation of processes also raises questions about the global delivery model which most large-scale suppliers espouse. First, clients themselves will be more widely distributed. But a second, more significant trend will be the rise of centres of excellence in supplier organisations, too. Success in the future will come from seeing the patterns in complicated pictures, and knowing which part of the value chain or which industrial sector you should specialise in and how you are going to deliver that service. Process segmentation is particularly important because it is not confined to particular types of process. All processes, instead of being divisible into clear-cut categories (added value versus commodity, onshore versus offshore), are in fact hybrids (added value and commodity, onshore and offshore).

From efficiency to economy: the scope for cutting costs

While breaking a process down into its component parts is seen to create greater scope for efficiency, clients will move into economy mode only if they believe there is scope to cut costs. Indeed, clients who are wholly focused on negotiating the lowest possible price will not set much store by something as intangible and apparently ephemeral as interaction between themselves and the consultant. They want the job done, and they want it done cheaply. Interaction may be important if a consultant or service provider is to do their job effectively, but it is icing on the cake when they have to do it economically. The wage differentials look even more attractive when placed against the scarcity of qualified labour in many western economies. Even in 2005, when more than 200,000 computer and maths specialists were unemployed, it had been estimated by the US Bureau of Labour Statistics that there would be a shortfall of more than 10m workers in the United States by 2010. Of course, such predictions rely heavily on growth in GDP; the truth is that nobody knows how big the actual shortfall will be. However, offshore suppliers are likely to benefit from:

- the increasing use of contractors in IT departments (the Meta Group, a research company, predicts that 50% of IT employees could shift to contract work by 2007, analogous with the shift in manufacturing jobs 30 years ago);
- increasing specialisation, which in turn is driving IT managers to look for a flexible mix of skills;
- the growing preference to buy rather than build IT applications (which requires fewer in-house programmers).

Barring major political and social upheaval, it is hard to see the supply of qualified labour in countries such as India and China drying up in the foreseeable future. The sustainability of the wage differential is, however, more questionable. Although conventional outsourcing allowed organisations to cut costs in two ways (by reducing both the number of people required for a particular activity and the average cost per person), offshoring has delivered savings purely in terms of the average cost per person.

These two factors – clients' willingness to trade face-to-face interaction where there is a clear economic rationale for doing so and the unabated pressure on costs – mean that the location of suppliers' resources (whether these are consultants, IT implementation teams, contractors, or outsourcers) will be an important decision in every large-scale project.

The management of consulting projects has just become even more complicated.

3
THE CONSULTING WORLD

"The test of a good consultant is not whether he or she has generated a unique insight, but whether that insight can be applied to produce positive results. Consultants can't just be smart; they have to be capable of delivering a business outcome."

6 The consulting industry

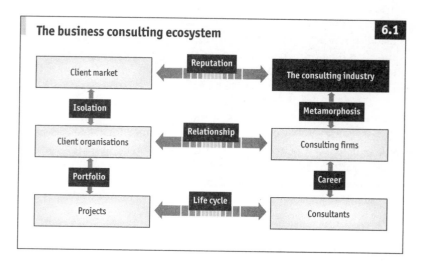

The business consulting ecosystem 6.1

Client market

Reputation

The consulting industry

Isolation

Metamorphosis

Client organisations

Relationship

Consulting firms

Portfolio

Career

Projects

Life cycle

Consultants

THERE ARE PROBABLY MORE WAYS to segment the consulting industry than there are to skin that infamous cat. As noted in Chapter 5, the demand for consulting falls into three broad categories: specialist services, strategic advice and integrated solutions. At its most fundamental level the structure of the consulting industry reflects this. There are specialist firms focusing on a particular industry or type of work, strategy firms that primarily offer advice and firms that implement integrated solutions, such as putting in new technology or outsourcing a business process. But, of course, nothing is that simple.

Put six consultants in a room and you will end up with six different approaches, maybe more. Why is it so difficult? People in the fast-moving consumer goods or banking sectors do not put so much time and heartache into segmenting their industries, so why has it become so complicated?

No industry ever fits perfectly into the boxes analysts attempt to put it in, and the consulting industry is no exception. Somewhere between the specialist, strategy and integrated solutions firms are those with a foot in each camp. This is what consultants call the "middle ground". Some firms deliberately steer clear of the jack-of-all-trades mentality they believe it typifies. Those that occupy it live in hope that their combination of services will differentiate them in a crowded and homogeneous marketplace.

But another reason for the fuzziness in what consultants do is genuine complexity. Consulting is a broad church, and the traditional ways of segmenting the industry – by size or services offered – fails to capture stark differences at other levels: in the type of interaction and relationship consulting firms have with their clients; in ownership structure; in the way in which consulting firms organise themselves to deliver their services; and in their approach to global clients.

The messy side of consulting?

A lot of myths surround the middle ground in consulting: that it is better to be in it; that it is better to be out of it; that it will be squeezed out by a small number of large firms on the one hand and a large number of small ones on the other; that it is poised for growth. Some firms seem to have thrived in it for years; others barely make it before being swallowed by a larger player or breaking up again. New entrants come and go.

The pressure from specialists

No one knows exactly how many specialist consulting firms there are, let alone how many sole practitioners.

Anecdotal impressions are that the number of small consulting firms and sole practitioners is at an all-time high, boosted by a combination of lay-offs from consulting firms, people in industry choosing to go into consulting after retirement, and people who want to work as consultants without the plane-hopping lifestyle. Certainly, middle-sized consulting firms complain they are competing against – and losing to – this group more than they used to. Clients understandably find the fee rates of independent consultants, which do not carry such high overheads, attractive. A middle-sized firm employing experienced project managers on salaries of $120,000 might expect to charge them out to clients at between $1,500 and $2,000 per day. But if clients expect to pay only the daily rate of an independent project manager – probably more like $800 – the consulting firm cannot make a profit. Consultancy is not an industry that is driven by economies of scale. It is possible to run a small, profitable consulting firm specialising in a particular field in a way that would not be possible for a small manufacturing company.

Indeed, many of the larger firms that call themselves consultancies do not deserve the name, says Mark Leiter, who runs a consulting firm specialising in the professional services sector. "There is enormous confusion about what 'consulting' is today," he says. "Very few are pure consulting firms: their economics are driven by technology and have little to do with consulting." This has created an opportunity for independent firms that have a clear proposition and that can still add immense value to clients. "The market has become tougher," says Leiter. "Clients, many of whom are veterans of consulting firms, have higher expectations; the bar for consultants has gone up by an order of magnitude. Clients are looking for specific expertise. It is high-class labour: clients want to get leverage out of using the consultant, rather than vice versa. And clients are finding it in a smaller and smaller number of firms. Sometimes it comes down to finding an individual expert within a firm. The other factor for this more sophisticated generation of clients is price. The buyers are often former consultants who understand your economic model inside and out, which enables them to be extremely talented negotiators who can easily unbundle your offering or poke at your underlying assumptions of what it will take to get the work done."

Obviously, not all start-ups remain small; niche firms diversify. The middle ground of the consulting industry is constantly fed by specialist service firms which have grown organically or – more commonly – merged with or acquired firms working in complementary areas. The best examples of sizeable but still specialist firms are those that focus on human resource issues, including administration, training and development, advice on organisational structure and, increasingly, the outsourcing of parts of the HR function. However, in recent years there has been a wave of new players specialising in particular industry sectors rather than particular services, such as First Consulting Group, which concentrates on the health-care, pharmaceuticals and life sciences industries.

Pressure from strategists
Strategy firms are also eating into the space middle-sized consulting firms have to play with, albeit for different reasons.

As with the niche end of the consulting industry, reliable figures are hard to get, primarily because none of the largest strategy firms – Bain, Booz Allen Hamilton, the Boston Consulting Group and McKinsey – release much information on their performance. Unofficially, however, strategy consultants say that in 2003–04 there was a marked recovery in their market after two very tough years. Figures for smaller strategy practices are less encouraging. If public-sector strategy work is stripped out, the strategy consulting industry overall appears to have experienced negligible growth. If sourcing strategy work (advising companies on whether activities should be internally or externally sourced has been an area of significant growth for strategy firms) is also stripped out, this part of the consulting market may well be shrinking. What seems to have happened is that the leading strategy firms have retained a strong hold on the market and, although the level of traditional strategy consulting is declining, clients are more likely to turn to the big name firms for this type of work.

"If you look at strategy consulting, Bain and Monitor are the only new entrants in the last 30 years to have reached sustainable presence and scale," says Leiter. "Why? Because clients know who these firms are and there is no room for anyone else. McKinsey has a brilliant, enduring value system which regards consulting as a 'higher calling' – it treats clients the way doctors treat patients – and has created a privileged position that is not going to disappear. It takes enormous patience to build a firm like McKinsey."

David Barrett has worked for both Bain and Capgemini and is now a director at Corven, a consulting and private equity firm, so he is in a good position to view these changes with detachment. "Two factors have really shaped today's consulting industry," he says. "The mass hysteria of the e-business boom meant that plenty of consulting firms lost control of the quality of the people they hired. Lots of people were sucked into the industry who didn't know what they were doing. The difficult past two years focused their attention on survival; they have not been thinking about whether clients need the services they're selling. The net result is that clients have had six years of very mixed experiences. There have been some sound consulting projects but also plenty of others that just shouldn't have happened. The top strategy firms have used the last two years to strengthen their position and brand in the marketplace; they have become clearer about what they do well and pulled out of areas where they are not so good. Clients, meanwhile, think less and less in terms of 'strategy consulting' but perceive each firm to have areas where they are particularly strong. Smaller strategy firms are therefore increasingly seen as specialists, not generalists."

"There has been a gigantic sucking sound as the big IT-oriented firms have focused on big outsourcing and government projects, and have in essence vacated the strategy consulting space," says John Donahoe, Bain's worldwide managing partner. "The IT firms may give a strategy project away, but increasingly their work is not seen by clients as objective because in the end they need to win more work downstream, and so their recommendations may be biased (for example, the answer is 'to outsource'). At the same time, a greater distinction has opened up between the largest strategy firms and smaller ones that lack global coverage. Demand for strategy consulting remains relatively healthy: senior managers are under greater pressure than ever to deliver results, but obtaining those results is increasingly complicated."

Hans-Paul Buerkner, chief executive of the Boston Consulting Group, agrees. "Companies are facing an enormous number of challenges. For the past 20 years, people have been saying that the pace of change is accelerating and that business is becoming more complex. But it is true: regulation and deregulation; new entrants from Asia; new markets opening up in China; merger and acquisition activity going up again; governments putting more pressure on business. Companies are having to make larger bets more often. Every decade the number of companies that move in and out of the *Fortune* 100 grows. You have only to look at some sectors – automotive, airline, high tech and financial services – to realise how much has happened and how quickly."

Ken Favaro, Marakon's chief executive, argues that the distinction between advisory and systems integration work became blurred during the late 1990s, but it is now becoming clearer as clients recognise the importance of independent advice. "It is almost impossible to put advisory and systems integration work under the same umbrella. You can't make the cultures mesh; you have to give up one side of your business to be an expert in the other, and clients will see this and unbundle it. We get calls all the time from outsourcers who want to work with us and get access to our clients. At the same time, the study-and-recommend model for advisory work is dying, if it is not dead already. Clients need to know that, in the process of working with their adviser, it will be easier to get results in the future, and that there will be some sort of legacy that improves the way they are able to handle similar problems, challenges and opportunities as they inevitably arise. This requires higher levels of involvement on both sides and a step-by-step 'repeatable' process from the adviser/consultant. Strategy firms like Marakon have to be able to offer a combination of fresh advice (much of what is out there is stale) and lasting impact (by generating tangible business results and instilling new capabilities within the organisation)."

The pressure from new entrants
The consulting practices of Deloitte Touche Tomatsu's member firms were classic general management consulting firms until the mid-1990s. Like the other Big Four firms, Deloitte shifted its focus in the late 1990s

and early 2000s and concentrated more on tailoring the implementation of large-scale software systems to meet the needs of individual clients. Unlike its rivals, it did not follow this strategy through to selling or spinning off its consulting practice. The Deloitte member firms' consulting practices therefore remain part of multidisciplinary organisations that also provide audit and assurance, tax and corporate finance services. "Our old incarnation as a package-implementer was just that: old," says Paul Robinson, Deloitte's global managing partner, consulting. "We realised that continuing to operate in this mould would not lead to success. We looked at what services would fit within our brand and recognised that we could not, for example, offer transformational process outsourcing on any scale – it was simply something that clients did not expect from us. What we do have is a very strong advisory focus and an ability to execute; essentially, we operate at the intersection of thinking and doing. We are different from a strategy firm because we offer a wider range of services, particularly when it comes to implementation. We are different from the technology firms because we offer an objective viewpoint. We are different from the other Big Four firms because we have kept our sizeable consulting practices."

With the ending of the non-competing arrangements which prevented the other Big Four firms offering consulting services, there is every expectation that they will invest more in advisory work. Rebuilding their substantial practices will take time and will be expensive, although they will have the advantage of being able to start with a comparatively clean sheet of paper rather than redrawing an existing practice. All four firms, however, face constraints about the types of services they can sell to audit clients. "Regardless of any regulatory prohibition, we are not likely to do any consulting work for 'attest' clients (those to whom we have given a specific opinion)," says Robinson. "Clients themselves are saying it has become too difficult. That creates a very different marketplace because the attest relationships used to be an important channel to market for us."

The pressure from systems integrators, outsourcers and technologists

Who is the second largest employer of doctors in the UK, after the National Health Service? Is it one of the burgeoning private health-care companies? No, it is Atos Origin Medical Services. "It began when we won a contract with the Department for Work and Pensions to assess entitlement to disability benefits," says Paul McDonald, head of new business, sales and marketing at Atos. "We have worked well with the

DWP to clear a backlog of assessments and improve the quality. We took over the entire process." A much bigger business has been built on the back of this initial contract. It carries out 800,000 medical assessments each year, does all the medical work involved in compensation claims for the Department of Trade and Industry compensation schemes for former miners, and is now the largest provider in the occupational health field. Asked how business process outsourcing of this type fits with a consulting firm, McDonald argues that each plays a distinct but complementary role. "Consultants define the need – they diagnose the problem – and the systems integrators and outsourcers fix it. The contracts we sign typically cover between seven and ten years, but no client will want the same service in ten years' time as they receive today. They want to see continuous improvement, so it makes sense for us to integrate the process of outsourcing with change management and business process improvement. No one would go to a supermarket that sells just one kind of beans, and that is equally true for consulting firms. Our clients see the advantage of buying a full range of services from a single service provider because it is easier to integrate all the activities involved. When you have multiple subcontractors, you can end up stepping on each other's toes."

Integrated solutions firms with a voracious appetite for acquisition challenge middle-sized consulting firms in a different way. Their continuing development of practices or acquisition of firms specialising in emerging markets is predicated on these firms being able to offer an end-to-end service. Integrators also seek to combine consulting with hardware and software sales and outsourcing. Thus technology firms such as IBM have acquired consulting firms (PWC Consulting), and consulting firms such as Accenture have launched outsourcing services (see Figure 6.2 on the next page).

Several factors are driving this convergence: the need to be able to deliver an end-to-end service for clients seeking to make substantial changes to their systems and business processes; the desire among hardware and software suppliers to move into higher-margin services; and the need of consulting firms to have "annuity" income streams (discussed in more detail later in this chapter). "For the first time there's one company – IBM – straddling all three segments here," points out John Condon, executive vice-president at BearingPoint. "None of us really know how this will play out, but it's something we all need to watch."

But integrated solutions firms have problems of their own. Most people accept that there will always be a role for end-to-end services,

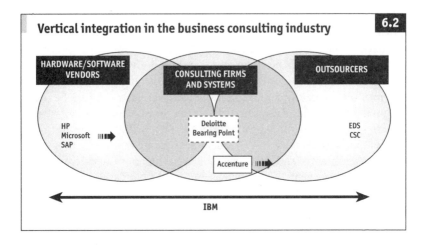

Vertical integration in the business consulting industry 6.2

HARDWARE/SOFTWARE VENDORS

CONSULTING FIRMS AND SYSTEMS

OUTSOURCERS

HP
Microsoft
SAP

Deloitte
Bearing Point

EDS
CSC

Accenture

IBM

especially among clients undergoing large-scale change resulting, for example, from a merger or acquisition. But is the market sufficiently big to generate the profits expected by the likes of IBM, and attractive and interesting enough to motivate the people it acquired from PWC? The skills, culture and remuneration associated with technology vendors, consulting firms and outsourcers are famously different, and there are plenty of highly visible examples of uneasy unions.

"The challenges firms like IBM and Capgemini have faced in bringing together different cultures don't mean there won't be more mergers and acquisitions in the consulting industry," says David Barrett. In particular, he expects to see firms reconfigure themselves around horizontal services, such as human resources business process outsourcing, rather than industries. "The top of the market is characterised by illogical purchases. People sell consulting businesses (that is how they get their money out), rather than buy them. But the potential economies of scale in business process outsourcing, the need for offshore companies to build up onshore businesses and the shrinking margins from technology implementation will all combine to drive these companies together. Different business models are required across the advisory, systems integration and outsourcing businesses; companies need to be clear where their focus will be and commit to that. Accenture is a good example of a firm that is already doing this. It has an utterly single-minded focus on business process outsourcing and has seized the initiative. Where does everyone else go now? Firms that have been less clear on where they are going are facing greater challenges."

"We do not have that much to do with EDS any more," says Michael Traem at A.T. Kearney. "EDS thought it could manage each part of its portfolio in the same way, and that was very difficult. You can't treat consulting and outsourcing businesses in the same way; they have different clients, processes, ways of selling, intellectual capital and people. If we can help EDS, then of course we do so, but the main focus of our business is on serving our clients and managing our people."

Pigs in the middle?

Easy to enter, the middle ground is hard to graduate from with honours. It is continually fed by specialist firms which grow and diversify, only to be acquired by the integrators or to fall apart as the market evolves. The firms that dominated the consulting industry 30 years ago are still largely the firms that dominate it today, albeit under different names. Even during the heyday of the dotcoms, only one firm, MarchFirst, came within an ace of hitting the $1 billion revenue mark, but it disappeared the subsequent year. What goes wrong? Some, like MarchFirst, expand through merger and acquisition on the back of a rapidly expanding market only to collapse when demand does. Others come unstuck when they try to move outside their original specialisation. Costs go up, the proportion of time spent on billable work falls as more time is put into selling and building a reputation in the new markets, and clients become confused.

Of course, the definition of a middle-sized player varies from market to market. A large consulting firm in, say, the Nordic region may be only a small player on the international stage. But looking purely at the global business consulting industry (worth over $400 billion in 2004), around 25% consists of small firms, over 60% of large firms and less than 10% of middle-sized firms (see Figure 6.3 on the next page).

The problem with the middle ground is not so much that it is shrinking (in practice it is larger than ever, at least in terms of revenue) but that the rate of revenue growth in consulting is largely a factor of size. Big firms are getting bigger more quickly than smaller ones. If your consulting company had been ranked number 40 in the world in 1986, its revenues would have grown tenfold by 2003. But if your company was number one in 1986, its revenues today would be more than 30 times higher. In other words, the largest consulting firms have been growing at three times the rate of smaller ones.

Logica and CMG were founded within five years of each other in the late 1960s. International expansion and a trail of acquisitions by both firms culminated in their merger, in 2002, to form LogicaCMG. Listed in

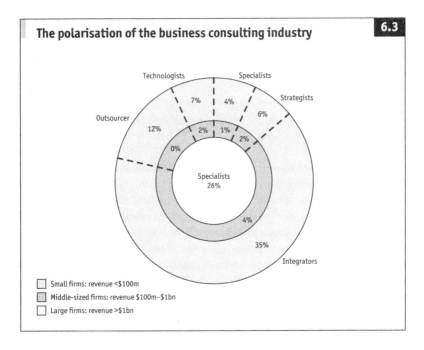

The polarisation of the business consulting industry   6.3

both London and Amsterdam, the combined company employs more than 20,000 people, four-fifths of whom are in Europe. LogicaCMG works in some of the worst-performing areas of the consulting industry (IT consulting and systems integration, telecommunications and financial services) and its revenues, like those of its competitors, have been hit (6% lower than in 2003). Even so, the firm has had some spectacular successes.

"I don't believe in luck, bad or good: people create their own luck," says Mike Zehetmayr, who heads LogicaCMG's global risk management practice. The realisation that, despite the merger, the firm is still not one of the top ten global players forced it to think long and hard about the kind of luck it needs. "We recognised the need to have a clear focus on what we do well," says Zehetmayr. "We've reduced the number of global competencies we focus on from nine to just three where we know we can do well. Management consulting is not our forte, and we do not pretend otherwise, and our size means we can't afford to invest in managing as many client accounts as the very large firms can. But what we can do is concentrate on those areas where we are a world leader, such as payment methods, and build relationships and global coverage around that expertise."

Understanding what it is good at has also helped LogicaCMG be clearer about the gaps in its services and how it can use alliances with other firms to fill them. "Service organisations like ours have traditionally been prolific partners," says Zehetmayr. "Often partnerships have been pursued at the expense of clients, not on their behalf. We have cut the number of alliances we have to just four because of the time and commitment it takes to build knowledge about and trust in another organisation. We are also aware that some of our competitors have a propensity to partner too prolifically. It has been a big shift for us not to think we ought to be doing that. We have had two difficult years, but we have fantastic skills in specialist areas. We have to be incredibly focused."

BearingPoint began life as KPMG Consulting. It acquired Andersen Business Consulting in the United States in the spring and early summer of 2002 and followed this up with Andersen's businesses in Scandinavia, Spain, France and Switzerland in August and September of that year. KPMG Consulting in Germany was acquired in August 2002. "In retrospect it wasn't the best time to create an enlarged firm through European acquisitions," says John Condon, executive vice-president in the UK, Netherlands and Ireland. "Within six months of acquiring the KPMG Consulting business in Germany, we had to make a quarter of the people redundant. Demand had shrunk significantly and we didn't have the right skills. Like many of our competitors, the cultural shock of this was immense. We had a generation of managers who'd only ever seen good times and found it difficult to understand what was happening. You can't go through this kind of experience without being changed in some way."

One of those changes has been the introduction of a formal account-management structure and the recruitment of a professional salesforce. "There was some resistance to this," says Condon, "but we had to do it. We now have a rigorous account-planning process and business development managers who are responsible for building our client relationships. They're not just administrators: the best can earn as much as or more than our managing directors. In theory, they could earn as much as the chief executive."

The results are seen in areas such as the public sector, which is growing at a rate of more than 20% a year and accounted for around 40% of BearingPoint's $3.5 billion revenue in 2003–04. "We've relationships in the US military going back 20–25 years and have recruited ex-military people who have the skills and understanding of the issues to maintain these," says Condon.

The challenge now is keeping pace globally with IBM and Accenture. "To be a long-term player in the consulting industry, you need scale of operations," says Condon. This may mean limiting the regions in which you operate rather than dissipating your efforts over too wide an area. One strategy has been to set up BearingPoint's Global Technology Services, which has lower-cost development centres in Canada, Mexico, New Zealand and Spain as well as in more conventional locations such as China and India. It may well be that clients will not want a one-stop shop but will value the objectivity that the pure consultants and systems integration businesses can bring.

Segmenting the consulting industry

Apart from size, there are five distinct, but interrelated, ways to carve up the consulting industry:

- relationships and income streams;
- ownership and objectives;
- consulting philosophy;
- delivery model;
- geographical coverage.

Putting these together creates a more realistic and meaningful way of understanding the differences in today's consulting industry.

Relationships and income streams

"Trust is still terrifically important in the consulting industry, more so in the advisory segment of it," says Corven's David Barrett. "A client will ask a consultant they already know if they can recommend someone who is knowledgeable about a particular issue, and will trust the consultant's recommendation. Where IT implementation services and outsourcing are concerned, it is more transactional. Given the size of many systems and outsourcing contracts, the overall reputation and credibility of a firm – the way clients judge it from the outside – become more important. This has been reinforced by the behaviour of the players themselves; as big consulting and IT firms have come together in recent years, they have tended to concentrate more on chasing transactional business, not building relationships. This has been compounded when, having historically relied on relationships, they have made many of their most senior people (and relationship-builders) redundant."

This is how one executive with more than 25 years' experience of dealing with professional services firms put it: "There are two really fundamental dynamics as far as I can see. The first is whether the consultants are up to the job I'm asking them to do. Sometimes that's easy to judge, other times it's much harder. But the thing that makes you pick up the phone and say 'I've got a problem, come and talk to me' is a personal relationship. I've employed the same consulting firms maybe half a dozen times. Why? Because I understand what their process methodology is, and I believe I can get more from them because of that. They have benefited by tapping into a valuable revenue stream. I've also worked with strategy firms where your experience is much more dependent on the individual you are working with at a given moment: different strokes for different folks. But there is one person in particular that I'll ring up, even when he isn't doing any work for me, just to ask his advice, and I know he won't send me a bill. That's where a relationship gets you: it doesn't mean that you automatically win work, but you're more likely to be on the shortlist in a fiercely competitive market. It's the web of relationships that is critical."

At one end of the consulting spectrum are long-term relationships, where individual consultants become "trusted advisers" to their clients, working for them on a continuing but irregular basis as and when their input is required. At the other end of the scale are transactions – large-scale, one-off pieces of work where there is no commitment from the client to use the firm once the contract has finished. Falling between these two extremes are consulting "products". These resemble transactions in that they are discrete pieces of work, but they are smaller in scale: auditing a bank's exposure to regulatory risk or implementing a particular software package, for example. Having a relationship with a client can be important when it comes to selling products as it helps to know what products will be appropriate to which people in an organisation, but it is depth of specialist expertise that counts most.

Whether a firm has relationships, products or transactions dictates how it organises itself. Relationship firms are more likely to be structured around individual clients or markets, product firms around particular services, and transaction firms around individual transactions, the scale of which might well mean that a single contract occupies the lion's share of the firm's resources in a particular country.

Relationships and transactions determine the predictability of a firm's income stream. Reacting to clients' needs as they arise can make it more difficult to predict income more than three months ahead. Both the volume and value of the projects they undertake vary. Product firms generally have a better idea of the average value of their projects (even where they are managing a portfolio of several projects) but find it harder to forecast the volume of work. Transaction firms, which are signing contracts for as long as ten years, have "annuity income": they know how much they will be billing and when they will be billing it.

Predictability (or otherwise) of income has its own ramifications where the structure of consulting firms is concerned. Relationship firms have to be more flexible, able to reconfigure their resources to fit clients' changing needs. Because their planning horizon is so close, they cannot afford to be too big; having too many consultants can leave them dangerously exposed to overall downturns, as many large relationship firms found to their cost in 2001. Caution also means that relationship firms do not usually grow rapidly. Both product and transaction firms have a much clearer idea of the specific skills they need, although transaction firms will also have a good idea of the numbers of people they require with those skills.

Ownership and objectives
Greater predictability of income also paves the way for the single biggest organisational change a consulting firm can make: the transition from private to public ownership. Historically, the overwhelming majority of consulting firms were private partnerships, but a combination of factors – the need for capital in IT and outsourcing work, mergers and acquisitions, the desire for a corporate decision-making structure and transparency – has meant that private partnerships have become limited to strategy or new niche firms. Through either an IPO (initial public offering) or acquisition by a publicly traded company, most consulting firms are now listed.

BearingPoint was launched on NASDAQ in February 2001, just before the dotcom bubble burst. "Being publicly owned has brought much greater discipline to our business," says John Condon. "Because we have to deal with quarterly reporting, we have had to become much clearer about our objectives and improve our internal reporting. The world we operate in is harsher than it was, and the reality of a partnership structure is that it is a comfortable, clubby environment. Now, all our people are focused on client work, whereas the partnership meant that we carried a fair number of people who were not delivering." Although new objectives and metrics have not made people feel uncomfortable, changes to decision-making have: "Partners are now called managing directors, their role is different; they do not always feel they have the same breadth of authority they had before the IPO," says Condon.

Many believe that this switch has provoked a shift from long-term to short-term thinking in which revenue booked is more important than clients helped. "The consulting industry of the 1990s was a highly attractive market," says Bain's John Donahoe. "There was a boom in technology consulting and the boundary between that and management consulting became fuzzy: it became hard to say when consulting finished and software implementation started. At the same time, many consulting firms became publicly owned. The pressure on these firms to maintain predictable earnings growth is relentless; keeping shareholders happy has to take precedence over keeping clients and, after clients, employees happy. Because we are a private partnership, we can say 'no' to work if we believe it is not in our clients' best interests. That builds trust and loyalty over time although it can be tough on short-term economics."

The official line from the firms which have become publicly quoted in the last few years is that it has, of course, made no difference to their commitment to putting client service first. Clients themselves, and perhaps even more tellingly employees of these firms, would beg to differ. "Every quarter we get an e-mail saying this is the most crucial quarter ever and to raise as many invoices as we can," is how one insider described the change.

Laura Empson, of Saïd Business School and the Clifford Chance Centre for the Management of Professional Service Firms at the University of Oxford, has spent the last three years looking at the impact of public ownership on the governance of professional firms. As part of a larger study of governance in professional service firms, her research included a comparison of two consulting firms which had formed an alliance in 1995 in order to integrate their services and offer a unified image in the marketplace. From a client perspective it was one firm, but internally there were two very different governance structures: one was an American-based private firm which floated in 2000; the other was a UK partnership which became a limited liability partnership in 2004.

"Any professional firm has to deal with three potentially competing sets of stakeholders: shareholders, professionals and clients," says Empson. "If you take away the combination of personal ownership and personal liability offered by the traditional partnership model, you threaten the equilibrium and the needs of shareholders may become dominant." But it is not, she argues, inevitable: "Everything comes down to a firm's underlying beliefs about governance – how managerial authority should be channelled and constrained, whether professionals' need for autonomy is recognised, and the extent to which creating long-term value is allowed to take precedence over short-term profits. Economic efficiency does not necessarily equate to client satisfaction. Systems and structures which embody partnership principles can be put in place, even within a publicly owned company."

The chief executive of the American company that Empson studied had invested considerable time, before its IPO, instilling the discipline of accurate forecasting. "No one would be happy if the company did not make a profit, but he recognised that getting a forecast wrong was the worst thing that could happen in analysts' eyes. He was not aiming at rapid expansion, but at steady growth," says Empson. "Moving to public ownership does not inevitably change behaviour." What will change it is a focus on growth at all costs, and a private partnership can have this just as much as a public company. "Going public can be used as an excuse for setting and pursuing aggressive targets. Executives can use shareholders to justify taking all sorts of actions."

Consulting philosophy
The impact consultants have on the organisations they work with varies in two respects.

The first is the way in which firms approach clients' issues. This can be didactic: a team of consultants is commissioned by a client to examine a particular problem and, in resolving it, the consultants mainly rely on gathering data on the problem and analysing it in relative isolation from the client on a highly objective basis. Or it can be facilitative: consultants work with members of the client's staff to discuss, investigate and design solutions to the problems. This can range from working closely with a small number of individuals to engaging the collective intelligence and enthusiasm of a much larger group. A key component is that the consultants use the relationships and trust they build to gain a more profound understanding of the issues, rather than accepting information at face value. Facilitative consultants will therefore look at the underlying causes of a problem rather than its symptoms, and explore options rather than follow a pre-specified methodology. The didactic and facilitative models are at opposite ends of the same spectrum, and most consulting involves elements of each. However, consulting firms position themselves quite consistently at points on the continuum – strategy firms usually

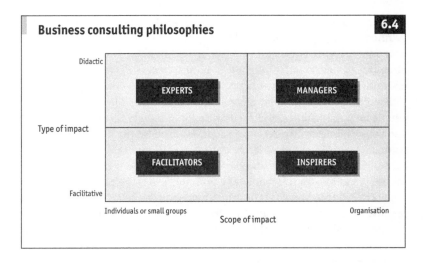

Business consulting philosophies   6.4

operate at the didactic end, but smaller, specialist firms often adopt a more facilitative approach.

Facilitative consulting has proved invaluable over the past decade as it has been seen as the industry's response to the frequent criticism that consultants do not engage with client organisations and try to impose preconceived ideas in very different situations. But there is a significant drawback to this approach. The best facilitation is also the least perceptible, and consultants who tease out ideas based on the client's thinking may be accused of adding nothing of their own. As a result, most consulting in today's market is didactic, taking the form either of intensive data gathering and analysis (among strategy firms) or of outsourcing (among IT and operational firms).

The second dimension of a consulting firm's philosophy is the scope of the impact it seeks to have. Some firms concentrate on individuals or small teams of people: a strategy consultancy might deal with the board of directors; an independent consultant might coach a business unit manager. At the other end of the scale are firms whose work involves taking over the running (outsourcing) of part of such functions as finance.

Putting these two dimensions – type and scope of impact – together means that you have four choices when it comes to selecting the type of firm that is most appropriate for your circumstances (see Figure 6.4).

"Experts" provide a small number of people with the information they require to make a decision or effect a change. They have a direct but comparatively limited impact. They are excellent at marshalling large volumes of data and identifying courses of action (move into this new market, withdraw that product, ignore this threat but react to that one), but not necessarily so good at letting clients think for themselves or engaging with a wide audience throughout the client's organisation.

By contrast, "facilitators" have an indirect impact. Their role is to help clients help themselves, and their attention is largely directed to individual client managers, as executive coaches or mentors. This type of consulting is now almost exclusively done by small, specialist firms, often by independent consultants who have themselves held senior positions in industry and can therefore identify with the issues their clients face on a daily basis. Large firms find it much harder to replicate the skills profile required to do this kind of work on the quasi-industrial scale they require.

Rather than trying to act through a team of senior executives, "managers" have a direct impact on an organisation by taking over part of its operations – running a particular business process, or a specific business unit. Again, there are consulting firms that excel at this type of work; rather than offering to work in partnership, they provide an opportunity to offload a particular problem.

"Inspirers" are the rarest of all: firms or people that can facilitate on a grander scale, trying to galvanise an organisation to act by presenting it with certain catalytic experiences or ideas. This is essentially a leadership role, providing an organisation with a sense of purpose and direction without being overly prescriptive about the means of achieving it. It is rare in consulting: first, because the majority of people capable of playing this role are doing it in industry, not talking about it in consulting firms; and second, because it would be a high-risk activity for a consulting firm to be involved in. This is not to say that consultants never do this; there are specialists, usually small firms experimenting with different communication and change management models.

Sourcing models

The massive lay-offs by consulting firms in the early 2000s taught them a lesson their clients already knew: the importance of having a cost base that can grow or shrink in line with revenues. Scalability is the word on everyone's lips. The traditional model of a consulting firm, with armies of full-time junior consultants leveraging the superior experience of senior partners, proved inflexible in a shrinking market. Even though better times seem to have returned, few firms want to repeat the mistake. Most are looking at alternative structures: alliances, offshore services, using freelance consultants rather than full-time employees.

Consulting firms traditionally organised themselves along similar lines, with pyramid structures in which the valuable time and experience of the most senior people were leveraged through less valuable and less experienced junior people. The width and depth of the pyramid varied. A small strategy consultancy might have two or three partners at the top and between ten and 15 consultants. A large IT consulting firm would have more intermediate grades and a ratio of perhaps 25 junior consultants to one partner.

There are, however, serious problems with this model, all of which have been highlighted during the past few years. Clients have never liked feeling that they have been palmed off with junior staff for most of the day-to-day work, only seeing more senior people at occasional meetings. They are increasingly looking for world-class input, and they want it from the horse's mouth. "Clients will pay a premium for senior people but not junior analysts," says Mark Leiter. "What can junior people really do? Gather information, analyse numbers, prepare presentations? They do not have the broad-based experience of senior partners. Clients want to unbundle the pyramid." Moreover, clients' persistent search for specialist skills means that junior, less experienced consultants were most vulnerable to downturns in the market. What use are armies of IT consultants, when no one is implementing new IT systems?

Different parts of the conventional organisational pyramid have always served different functions, which roughly equate to the three Es (see pages 50–5). Thus firms were able to accommodate clients' preferences by offering teams that combined small amounts of senior partner time (effectiveness), some project management input (efficiency) and lower cost resources (economy). However, the pressure from clients for specialist input and lower prices has made this combined model harder to sustain: junior consultants are seen to dilute the input of senior partners; the role of project managers is compromised by having to keep more junior consultants utilised; and consulting firms employing expensive senior people cannot offer the lowest prices. The pyramid is therefore starting to breakdown as clients go to "effectiveness" firms for effectiveness, and so on.

Where leverage is still taking place, it is not so much from senior to junior staff, but from onshore (expensive) to offshore (low-cost) locations. "Everyone is trying to change the cost model," says John Condon. Most large consulting firms have in-house facilities in countries where labour is much cheaper; those that do not are forging alliances with companies based in those locations. "We are adopting an 'any shore' principle," says Condon. "We have set up a separate business, Bearing-Point Global Technical Services, which is building a pool of technical resources, not only in China and India, but also in Spain, the UK and Ireland, Mexico, Canada, Australia and New Zealand, so that we can provide the appropriate balance of resources, whatever a client needs."

The first phase in offshoring growth was the result of temporary shortages of skilled labour in the West. But the current, and perhaps more permanent, phase has been driven by cost-cutting: having travelled to India in search of skills, western corporations have stayed to take advantage of lower labour rates at a time when domestic IT budgets are depressed. With budgetary pressure unabated, more functions have been deemed "offshoreable", such as package software implementation, systems integration and customer contact centres. The National Association of Software and Service Companies (NASSCOM) in India estimates that exports of IT software and services will total almost $19 billion by the end of 2004 (see Figure 6.5)

Thus although low-cost suppliers have benefited at the expense of their high-cost counterparts, price alone is not enough to ensure a long-term competitive advantage.

The slowdown in IT expenditure has affected the low-margin end of the market too, and the first generation of suppliers faces competition from even lower-cost producers such as China. With rivals snapping at their heels, Indian firms are seeking to move up the value chain, using quality as a key differentiator in winning longer-term, more complex deals. But brand recognition, especially among western companies considering offshore alternatives, remains poor. There are challenges, too, on the demand side. Stories of problems with cultural issues, unrealistic service level expectations, transitional costs and the expense of relationship management mean that cautionary tales are becoming more common.

In recent years, offshore suppliers have been recruiting sales and marketing staff in western countries where their clients are located, and forging alliances with onshore firms which have established access to the main markets. Now the talk is of acquisition, giving these firms their own business consulting skills and experienced client relationship managers. In a mirror image of this activity, onshore firms have hired offshoring experts or sought alliances with offshore service providers to bolster profits in the face of increasing price pressure.

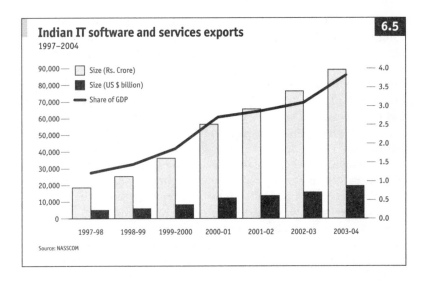

Indian IT software and services exports
1997–2004

6.5

- Size (Rs. Crore)
- Size (US $ billion)
- Share of GDP

Source: NASSCOM

Onshore firms, too, are increasingly looking at the acquisition of low-cost offshore facilities.

Convergence between high-cost onshore and low-cost offshore firms is inevitable. But which will be easier: onshore suppliers shedding their legacy of high-cost software development staff, or offshore suppliers building exclusive client relationships? Onshore suppliers' problems centre on current levels of onshore staff and how to recruit, develop and retain people in the future, together with the willingness of senior managers to drive through necessary changes. For offshore companies, the critical issue is how to increase their onshore presence without compromising their overall cost advantage.

The principal challenge is one of scale. Suppose that an IT consultant based in India can be charged to a client at roughly 25% of the onshore rate, and that a consulting company employs 10,000 people, 80% of whom work in IT services which clients would now like to see delivered from an offshore location so they can take advantage of the 75% discount. If the consulting firm moves 8,000 jobs offshore, it will lose 60% of its revenue. Another way of looking at it would be to say that, to maintain its existing revenue, the firm would have to employ three times as many people offshore and win three times as much work. Of course, margins might improve, but consulting firms have historically rated themselves against each other in terms of revenue growth (some do not release figures on profitability).

The transition to this model will be difficult enough. How will consulting companies cope with making so many of their onshore staff redundant? How will they make sure that they recruit offshore staff of the right calibre? What are the implications for managing a company that may go from being 100% onshore to 80% offshore? Global suppliers, accustomed to reconciling different agendas and perspectives, will have an advantage, but how many genuinely global firms are there?

Many firms say that their organisational structures look more like diamonds (see Figure 6.6). Leverage (the process by which the time of senior people is spread across teams of subordinates) is usually far more between senior partners and the next level down. Fewer firms recruit junior consultants, and if they need this type of labour, they increasingly look to lower wage-rate economies to provide it.

But the diamond-shaped firm has its own drawbacks. Although it reduces the costs and increases the overall level of expertise a firm can field, it lacks flexibility. It is still hard to reduce staff numbers when times are hard. When times are good, it is difficult to grow because other firms are competing for the same limited pool of experienced people. Moreover, the past few years have shown that people businesses, such as consulting, can be just as inflexible as manufacturing ones. Consultants cannot be retooled, any more than they can be rebranded, overnight, at least not in a way that is credible in clients' eyes.

Global coverage

Another factor dividing the consulting industry is its approach to globalisation. Many of the larger firms claimed to be global in the 1990s, but few could truly be said to have anything more than international networks of autonomous offices. This half-way house is being challenged from three directions. For some firms the expense of maintaining offices in different locations has proved prohibitive, and for some it has become irrelevant as clients have become more willing to go to where world-class expertise is, rather than expecting to find it on their doorstep. Others have found themselves having to field genuinely global teams to meet the increasingly complex needs of their multinational clients.

The new challenge is China. Norman Sze has many years of experience of working as a consultant and a businessman in Asia, and he is now the managing partner of Deloitte's consulting practice in China and Hong Kong. "Consulting is quite new here," he points out. "Like the majority of Asian companies, Chinese businesses have relied on their

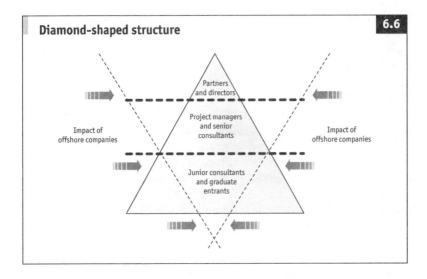

Diamond-shaped structure 6.6

Partners and directors

Project managers and senior consultants

Junior consultants and graduate entrants

Impact of offshore companies

Impact of offshore companies

ability to change themselves. However, the more these companies start to compete with western multinational corporations, the more they're starting to realise they need to make more radical changes – and this transformation agenda is driving up demand for consultants."

The regional consulting industry is still small, however. Sze estimates that around 2,000 "premium" consultants (that is, employed by established western consulting firms) are based in the region, primarily providing a mixture of strategy, technology, process improvement and human resources management services. "Chinese clients have a very different understanding of consulting," says Sze. "They treat consultants as doctors and expect them to write out prescriptions guaranteeing a cure, not as people who provide tools and resources. When they don't get that cure-all, they question its value. Moreover, like Asian clients generally, they are wary of young consultants. They want to work with experienced consultants in their 50s, not recent MBA graduates."

Sze reckons that fees, too, are a hurdle. Almost all work is done at a fixed price, and average rates are between 50% and 70% of their American equivalent. "Salaries are lower," says Sze, "but the fee rates are nevertheless indicative of the perceived lack of value of consultants. China is potentially a great opportunity for consulting firms, but how fast their business grows will depend not only on the overall rate of economic growth but also on the extent to which China's home-grown multinationals change their views about consultants."

"Everyone thinks China is a big opportunity, but it is by no means clear exactly where those opportunities will be," is how Sze's colleague, Paul Robinson, sums up the situation. "A lot of consulting firms have spent money investing there, but the jury is still out on how successful these ventures will be. Unquestionably, China is a huge market in terms of the potential volume of consulting work, but the rates clients expect to pay are still much lower than those in the West. The value part of the code has not yet been cracked, but it needs to be."

Not every big consulting firm needs to have the same approach to globalisation. In the past consultancies have adopted one of two approaches. Some subscribed to the burger model: opening lookalike offices and practising common methodologies in a wide range of increasingly unlikely locations. What they lacked in terms of sensitivity to local issues they made up for with discipline. Others opted for the spaghetti strategy: forging increasingly vacuous alliances with largely unknown, untested partners across the globe. The spaghetti approach has been thrown out as confusing to all those involved but the burger one still has merit, although it is no longer the only item on the menu.

"LogicaCMG is a very strong regional player with global reach," says Mike Zehetmayr. "Although assessing organisations' exposure to regulatory risk means that, at least in my practice area, we have to be able to work across the entire world, this is relatively unusual within the consulting industry as a whole. There are few organisations that have the resources and cash to invest in global relationships. We have one investment bank as a client which wanted to work with just one global consulting firm on the grounds that 15% of any supplier's time was always spent simply getting up to speed on a client and it did not want to have to keep paying for this. The problem was that it couldn't find any consulting firms that it considered to be genuinely global. Instead, it has built relationships with regional players like us."

Global firms offering clients a coherent and consistent approach irrespective of location are what multinational clients turn to when they want to impose coherence and consistency on their own businesses. Above all, global firms can help enforce new processes, drive compliance to new procedures and implement global systems. But global firms are at a disadvantage when they encounter local problems, such as particular cultural sensitivities and differences in employment law. To deal with these, they need the input of local consultants who are able to speak to the people affected by the new IT system in their own language

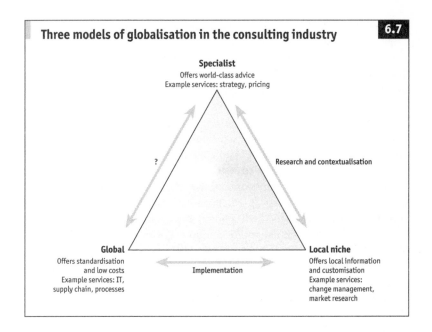

Three models of globalisation in the consulting industry `6.7`

Specialist
Offers world-class advice
Example services: strategy, pricing

?

Research and contextualisation

Global
Offers standardisation
and low costs
Example services: IT,
supply chain, processes

Implementation

Local niche
Offers local information
and customisation
Example services:
change management,
market research

or who are conversant with the regulatory environment (see Figure 6.7).

Similar opportunities exist between local consulting firms and firms that are international specialists in a particular field. Simon-Kucher (see Chapter 8), for example, is an internationally renowned expert in pricing strategies. Clients do not expect to find such expertise on their doorstep and they will travel to find it. Thus a company based in Amsterdam interested in, say, chaos theory will be prepared to go to Albuquerque if that is where the world's experts on chaos theory are based. Specialist firms may have networks of international offices, but they do not need them. Indeed, it makes far more sense for them to concentrate their scarce resources in a small number of locations, rather than spread them too thinly. Specialist firms also need input from local consulting firms, not so much in HR issues, but in contextualisation. What good is pricing theory if it does not take account of the behaviour of local consumers?

The crux, though – as always in the consulting industry – comes when a local or specialist firm wants to expand and/or diversify. "There is a clear limit to our growth as an independent firm," says Mihai Svasta, who runs his own consulting firm in Romania. "If we are to continue to grow, we have two options: either to enter long-term partnership agreements and strategic alliances with other suppliers, or to sell to a global player entering the Romanian market. Global consultants come with brands, solutions and global networks and relations. The only advantages a local firm can offer are price, flexibility and, sometimes, innovative solutions."

In conclusion

Defining, let alone segmenting, the consulting industry is complicated by two factors. First is the "messy" end of consulting, the changing boundaries between large, medium-sized and small firms, between integrators and specialists. Second is the consulting industry's genuine complexity, which makes it impossible to categorise consulting firms against any conventional framework. Client relationships, ownership structure, consulting philosophy, delivery models and geographic coverage all play a role.

The key is to combine these factors in a single, overarching framework which encapsulates the current structure of the consulting industry – and this is the focus of the next chapter.

7 Consulting firms

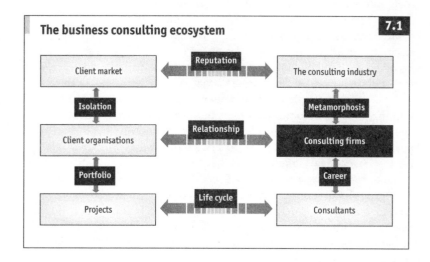

The business consulting ecosystem `7.1`

Client market ←→ Reputation ←→ The consulting industry

Isolation | Metamorphosis

Client organisations ←→ Relationship ←→ Consulting firms

Portfolio | Career

Projects ←→ Life cycle ←→ Consultants

"IN THE PAST TEN YEARS, the consulting industry has evolved from being a profession to being an industry encompassing everything from pure strategy firms to outsourcing companies," says Paul Robinson of Deloitte. "One of the results of that evolution was that it became difficult to see where the boundaries between different kinds of consulting fell. Today, this is changing: the different models of consulting are becoming more distinct."

How do the different ways of segmenting the consulting industry, described in the previous chapter, translate into particular types of firm?

In the past, it was possible to draw simple but meaningful distinctions between firms at a high level, but this has become harder as the lines separating advisory, implementation and outsourcing work have blurred. The main differences between consulting firms fall into two categories: their income stream; and the way in which they deliver their services. Income stream is largely a function of the extent to which a firm relies on relationships, which produce irregular revenues, or annuity products, such as outsourcing deals, which guarantee income for a fixed period. However, income stream tends to reflect, and may even drive, ownership structure: in general, relationship firms are privately owned while annuity income firms are publicly owned.

Similarly, a delivery model is closely linked to the services a firm provides. Advisory work (conventional management consulting) is usually the preserve of "integrated" firms, those that rely almost exclusively on their internal expertise. This used to be the model for all consulting firms. Organic growth, acquisitions and mergers were the primary means by which firms responded to new skills requirements and emerging markets. However, the more a consulting firm becomes involved in implementation, the less likely it is to have all the skills required in-house. A firm specialising in organisational design, for instance, may have plenty of experts in the design process, but few in training, internal communication or performance measurement. Moreover, the variety of skills needed for a project continues to grow in proportion to its size and complexity. The point has been reached where, for the largest deals, almost all of which will involve advisory, implementation and outsourcing work, it is difficult to envisage a single firm providing all the services required. Indeed, clients are increasingly reluctant to trust one firm to do everything, partly because they do not expect one firm to have a monopoly of the world-class skills they need, but also because they want to be able to spread the risks involved in such projects across several suppliers.

Thus three distinct delivery models emerge: traditional, integrated firms, which have almost all the skills they require in-house; what could be termed "hub-and-spoke" firms, which specialise in a particular field or function and rely heavily, sometimes exclusively, on third parties (individuals and/or firms) to deliver their services to clients; and integrators, which have a wide range of skills internally but also subcontract to, or partner with, other suppliers in order to deliver an end-to-end service.

The business consulting revenue/delivery matrix

Combining revenue and delivery gives six distinct types of firm in the business consulting revenue/delivery matrix (see Figure 7.2):

- Relationship firms, which survive and thrive on the basis of their client relationships.
- Broker firms, which co-ordinate the resources required to deliver services to a client.
- Product firms, which focus on a single or small number of markets and/or services.
- Diversifying firms, which are product firms attempting to move out of their original niche.

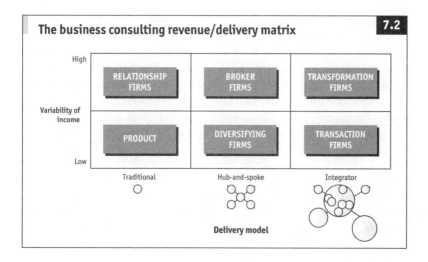

The business consulting revenue/delivery matrix · 7.2

- Transaction firms, whose business depends on winning a small number of big implementation and outsourcing contracts.
- Transformation firms, which depend on large-scale projects but are trying to use those projects to make substantial changes to the performance of their clients' business.

Relationship firms

Relationship firms largely work on effectiveness projects (see Chapter 5). This work – strategy consulting is the best example – focuses on conceptual problems, finding the right answer to a question and developing a high-level view of how to act on that answer, rather than becoming involved in the minutiae of implementation. Although a plethora of tools exist to ease the process of finding the right answer, the way in which they are applied will differ from project to project. It is inherent in the nature of "effectiveness" work that it may be unstructured, sometimes inefficient and often expensive. If it were easy to work out the answer, clients would not need the help of consultants.

Precisely because the process of finding the right answer cannot always be mapped out in advance, industry knowledge is more important to relationship firms than product knowledge. "The top strategy firms have never really depended on the next 'big thing'," says Bain's John Donahoe, "although we have certainly benefited from them in the past. Where we can really add value is in taking ideas from one sector to another, when we bring a partner who is an expert in, say, consumer products, high tech or retail distribution to talk to the chief executive of a bank."

Relationship firms' duration of assignments vary widely, and because uncertain revenues sit uncomfortably with stockmarket expectations, most of these firms are privately owned. "Without shareholders to worry about, we can put our clients first," says Donahoe. "If our clients are happy, we'll earn a good return." It is a model focused on the long term – and by having a range of smaller-scale projects relationship firms can spread their risk and be less dependent on a small number of very large projects. "Every assignment should be able to deliver real value – by which we mean real results," says Donahoe. "Through our private equity group, we have been taking equity stakes in private equity clients' deals, on which we helped conduct due diligence, for more than 15 years – way ahead of the rest of the market. We didn't do this because we wanted to make more money, but because we wanted to ensure we shared our clients' aspirations and because we wanted to weed out clients who were not fully committed to the project."

The most important way in which relationship firms mitigate the risks they face is by developing and maintaining personal relationships with senior executives in client organisations. Some, like McKinsey, have elevated this to an art form, making astute use of an alumni base that is an important source of future income. However, the business model of a relationship firm needs to accommodate short-term fluctuations in revenue. One way to do this is to reduce the variability of income by having a powerful, well-recognised name, which makes it more likely that the firm will be shortlisted for new work. This strategy is paying off. The top tier of strategy firms has emerged much more distinctly since the millennium as clients have abandoned the smaller firms that sprang up in the late 1990s. Chief executives are more aware that there are not many consulting firms offering the combination of global coverage and unyielding independence they require. "Demand is robust," says Donahoe. "Senior executives are under more pressure to deliver real results than ever, and getting these results is more complicated – industry boundaries are shifting, new technology is constantly emerging, and the options for allocating resources are more diverse. Chief executives can't know everything."

Strong relationship firms tend not to feel under pressure to collaborate. The combination of strong brands and deep relationships in their niche, large or small, means their clients are familiar with the scope of their services and they are less likely to be asked to undertake other types of work. Indeed, collaboration – becoming more involved in delivery – might easily appear to compromise a firm's independence. "I'm sceptical about alliances with other consulting firms," says Marakon's Ken Favaro. "Clients put objectivity and expertise first and they are wary of firms that might combine in-depth knowledge in some areas with mediocre skills in others, because the latter tends to muzzle the former." "Close collaboration is difficult," adds Hans-Paul Buerkner of the Boston Consulting Group, "because people work in very different ways and firms spend a lot of time jockeying for position. If you don't get the people and the chemistry absolutely right, combined consulting teams are a very tough undertaking."

Established relationships have also helped firms in this category withstand some, but not all, of the encroachment of corporate procurement departments (see Chapter 13). "Some large companies believe that all advice and consulting has been commoditised, and have turned buying consulting services over to procurement teams who hire ex-consultants to beat the hell out of suppliers," says Donahoe. "Frankly, we try to focus on clients who recognise that good advice is not about getting the lowest possible price. Our clients want the best advice in the world. They want to hire intelligently and form a relationship, a win-win collaboration, in which they trust that our relentless focus on value will deliver results for their business."

High-profile brands bring their own problems, however. If Enron had been advised by a two-bit firm of undistinguished consultants instead of McKinsey, it is unlikely that the role of consultants would have been exposed to so much speculation and opprobrium.

Moreover, the impact of advisory work is notoriously hard to quantify. "2001 was a very challenging year," says Buerkner, "and we have not gone back to business as usual. We have to be more proactive. Our role is to help clients achieve a competitive advantage, but we need to ensure that the clients we work for can see measurable value. In the short term, we can look for increased market share, higher revenues, better quality of recruits, improved retention and/or lower costs. But some of the changes will play out over a much longer time frame, so we have to be careful that there are tangible interim milestones. It is a discipline from which both sides benefit."

Broker firms

One way of coping with a variable income stream is for a consulting firm to increase the variability of its cost base either by using associates, through alliances with other firms, or by having a distributed structure, allowing it to link several product firms without being dependent on one. Broker firms depend on their "core" – which might be a collective brand or a small number of employees – to forge relationships with clients. But they have no aspirations to use that core as the main channel for service delivery.

Like other strategy firms, Eden-McCallum believes that it must have only the best people working for it: almost half are former employees of Bain, the Boston Consulting Group and McKinsey; two-thirds have an MBA; and three-quarters have more than ten years' consulting experience. The difference is that they are not employees.

Dena McCallum, Eden-McCallum's co-founder, used to work at McKinsey, but it was as strategy director at Condé Nast in Europe that she spotted a gap in the market: "My time as a consultant had been spent surrounded by people who loved consulting but did not relish the pressures of being in a big firm. Now I was working for a relatively small organisation which wanted to use McKinsey consultants but could not afford them." Eden-McCallum, which was founded in 2000, has directly employed just a handful of people responsible for building relationships with clients, winning and resourcing new work, and quality assurance. Projects are staffed from what McCallum calls a "talent pool" of around 200 people (associates), all of whom are vetted as thoroughly as full-time recruits would be. "Eden-McCallum does not deliver the content, but helps structure the work. We identify likely consultants so that clients can interview them. We also help get projects started and stay in touch with the consultants to make sure everything is going well," says McCallum. Consultants are attracted primarily through word-of-mouth, although the firm does tap into other consulting firms' and business schools' alumni networks. "The majority of consultants are attracted to us because they don't like selling. This is also attractive to clients because they don't want to be sold to. Everyone can just focus on getting the work done." To make the point, remuneration is not based on sales, and the firm is open about how much it charges and what the client's expectations are. It also makes it clear that it does not guarantee consultants' work, so there is no pressure to oversell to keep people utilised. Without the overheads of the large firms, its fees are lower; 30% of fees go to the firm, the rest to the consultants. Turnover in 2003 was $4.5m. "Transparency is hugely important," says McCallum.

However, Eden-McCallum is not trying to compete on its alma mater's home turf. Although concentrating on FTSE 250 companies, its relationships are usually with business unit heads, not chief executives. "We don't try to compete with the top firms," says McCallum. "We can't offer their scale or global cover." Work focuses on discrete issues, such as turning a poorly performing function around and assessing new markets, rather than long-running projects. Teams are generally small, averaging between two and four people.

The idea of brokering or body-shopping is not new to consulting, but what is unusual is the way Eden-McCallum attempts to compensate for the weaknesses of the associate model. Hub-and-spoke relationship firms find it difficult to replicate the collegiate environment and sense of camaraderie of conventional firms. They can also lose out when it comes to developing their expertise because they may lack the opportunity to exchange ideas with people working in different areas and may not be able to afford access to expensive market research.

"We hold networking events and put a lot of effort into staying in touch with people," says McCallum, "and we have relationships with market research companies that are also spin-offs from McKinsey. We encourage cross-fertilisation so that, for example, someone who is an expert in a particular technique would offer to train others. We also have grades, just as a traditional firm would have, and expect people to progress through them. From the individual's point of view, we're an attractive alternative to being wholly freelance. Because we're bigger we can attract more interesting and diverse work; we also take away some of the frustrations of working by yourself – the administration, the constant need to sell, and so on. The only thing we can't do anything about is the uncertainty about how much work someone gets."

Monitor was founded in 1983 by a small group of people with strong links to Harvard Business School, largely focusing on Michael Porter's work on competitive advantage. It now employs around 1,000 consultants in 29 locations worldwide. "We began with the idea of commercialising Porter's intellectual property and still maintain strong links with several academic and research institutions," explains Alan Kantrow, Monitor's chief knowledge officer, "which makes us disproportionately comfortable with working with outside experts." Although most of the firm's work focuses on strategic advisory services, the Monitor group of companies – the Monitor "family", as Kantrow describes it – includes (among others) businesses specialising in management education, consumer analysis, logistics and supply chain strategy, venture capital funds and advice, and not-for-profit and public organisations. "From the very beginning, the vision has been of a set of related firms, each focusing on a particular area," says Kantrow, "the logic being that we have certain core assets – people, knowledge and financial resources – but that we should be willing to combine and reconfigure them to suit different client situations and not be constrained in what we do by imposing a conventional strategy model that does not necessarily fit. Many consulting firms approach projects in the way Henry Ford approached cars: clients can have any project they like, as long as it is black. We are channel indifferent. Clients should not have to organise or shape their needs around the way we work."

Chris Meyer, co-author of *Blur: The Speed of Change in the Connected Economy* and *Future Wealth* and now a partner at Monitor, has a further take on the hub-and-spoke model. He is in the process of launching a new business unit at Monitor which aims to help clients get access to world-class expertise. "Today's scarce resource is human capital," says Meyer, "so it follows that this is where all the innovative ideas will be. We have the opportunity to make Monitor the equivalent of Goldman Sachs, but dealing in human, not financial, capital." Every organisation has to decide what balance of resources it wants to dedicate to exploitation activities (farming) and which to exploration (hunting). Most have historically put most of their money into exploitation, which is why so much consulting has been focused on how to optimise an existing business. But Meyer believes this is changing. "The world's most successful businesses are those which are innovative, they adapt quickly and seize opportunities when they are presented." It follows that the consulting industry will have to offer exploitation services too. "Previous attempts to do this – scenario planning, for instance – all share a common structure," says Meyer. "Ideas are pulled together from a diverse set of sources, and this is followed by a selection process to identify which are useful. Consulting firms that focus on exploitation services will therefore need a variety of inputs and a means of aggregating and filtering them." He hopes to put Monitor in the forefront of this activity, pulling world-class experts in different, non-consulting fields together into a network which clients can tap into.

But why should business school professors be prepared to be a node on this network, rather than pursue their own independent consulting careers? "Individuals do not scale well," says Meyer. "There's lots of motivation to go straight to the market, but most people are not very good at managing their own back-office, so it makes sense to combine this with others'. It's also difficult to market an individual as a business, and, if you're good at getting work, you face constant difficulties in resourcing it. Fundamentally, though, these people need to be able to talk to each other. We are therefore looking to build a community, with the right exchange mechanism – emotional as well as economic – and we have to be able to accommodate different needs."

Product firms

Which consulting company do Porsche or Mercedes turn to when they want to work out the best price for a new model? Which consulting firm has worked on four of the five best-selling drugs in the world today, or with 23 of the world's top 25 pharmaceuticals companies?

Simon-Kucher is the world's leading pricing consultancy. "You can divide consultancy into two industries," says co-founder Hermann Simon, "cost-cutting and revenue enhancement. We work only in the latter field. Our core business is improving profitability through top-line growth. A typical project would be our work on Mercedes A Class. Mercedes initially suggested one price but we recommended a higher one, based on analysis that showed the potential market for the car was smaller than Mercedes had envisaged but less price-sensitive – and we were right."

This kind of clear, directly attributable return enabled Simon-Kucher to grow by 20% year on year in 2004 to $45m and to recruit more consultants than any of the major strategy firms in Germany. When competing for pure pricing work, Simon claims the firm beats McKinsey 75% of the time and the Boston Consulting Group 90% of the time. "But clients do not come to us when they have a big strategic problem," he says. Track record is hugely important in clients' eyes, but so too is the firm's sheer intellectual power. It employs 50 people with PhDs, mainly in economics, pricing and related marketing issues, and eight people with PhDs in physics. "We have a very high level of competence," is how Simon puts it.

Although the firm may have a continuous stream of business with its largest clients, companies like Pfizer and Siemens, it does not have relationships in the conventional consulting sense. "These are discrete projects and the decision to hire us is made by different people in the organisation," says Simon. "Repeat business is based on past performance, not wining and dining."

The firm pays considerable attention not just to recruiting experts but to developing their expertise even further. "We do not feel cut off from our academic roots," says Hermann, "because most innovation in this area comes through client work, from applied not theoretical work. We run a big internal training and development programme and put a lot of effort into continuing research. Our clients are very sophisticated in this market, which is better because they are more discerning. They judge people on their knowledge rather than by looking at what they say on paper. Clients expect us to know more than they do." Not surprisingly, Simon-Kucher has no alliances with other consulting firms; even the subsidiaries it has set up overseas are 100% owned by the firm.

Product firms generally specialise in one or a small number of areas and, unlike relationship firms, are less dependent on who they know than on what they know: they win business on the back of their technical expertise, not their strength of relationship. Because they are more specialised, doing similar work over and over again, their income streams are more predictable. The crucial challenge they face is how to grow and whether to diversify.

Immediate growth is less of a worry for Simon-Kucher than raising brand awareness and reputation. Ironically for a firm that specialises in pricing and that can demonstrate such an unequivocal return on the cost of its services, Simon-Kucher is hard-pushed to work on anything other than a conventional time and materials basis. "Contingency fees sometimes make it easier for middle-sized clients to buy our services," says Simon, "but larger corporations are sometimes put off by the amount of money they could end up paying us." This is a problem because the firm's daily rates are around 20% cheaper than those of McKinsey and the Boston Consulting Group. "It brings home the importance of brand value. A recent survey in Germany put Simon-Kucher in the top five consultancies in four of the seven industries the study looked at in terms of reputation, and we were by far the smallest company to feature on the list." But it is not an urgent problem, and Simon-Kucher prefers to take the long view. "If we have a good reputation, awareness will follow," says Simon. "We try to make a lot of noise in the marketplace. We spoke at a lot of conferences in the pharmaceuticals industry five years before we launched our business in that sector. We're currently making speeches in China in the confidence that we'll start winning business there in three to five years' time. There is still huge growth potential in the area of pricing – we have no need to look elsewhere."

Diversifying firms
Some product firms take the slower route of organic growth, usually because they have no desire or pressure to move beyond their existing

niche; but others are looking for a faster track, seeing their specialist heritage as the launch pad for larger, more diverse businesses.

That is certainly how Tom Dolan, president of Xerox Global Services, sees it. "We're bringing Xerox into the world of professional services, where consulting becomes our common front-end," he says. The company had the classic, product-focused approach. "We had accounts and sold them products. We did not try to understand their business."

Although Xerox has ground to catch up in adapting to this new way of working, it also has advantages. "Consulting firms have a tendency to come in and describe or plan the future state, and then walk out. Xerox, by contrast, can design, implement and manage better business processes because that's how we run our own business. We can go into a mortgage firm and halve the time they take to process an application by using imaging technology. We have just helped a car rental company save millions by imaging new contracts overnight. We are applying our core competency to other organisations." This strategy was successfully followed by IBM in the 1990s, when the company used its own turnaround – from one of the largest corporate losses in history – as a means of demonstrating both its credentials and its empathy with other corporate behemoths. Xerox currently earns around $300m from professional services and it is aiming to increase that to $1 billion by 2007. Its outsourcing business already generates $2.7 billion in revenues and employs around 10,000 people.

Part of that growth will come from increased specialisation. "We have reorganised our salesforce by industry and are recruiting people who are experts with years of experience who will be credible in the eyes of more senior people," says Dolan. "We're also building practices around very specific ideas – the rental car solution is a good example." But the rest will come through ensuring these specialist offerings fit into a broader set of services. "We have a three-pronged strategy for growth. We intend to grow organically and via direct recruitment, and we are planning to expand the number of alliances we have, not only with the largest, most established consulting and outsourcing companies, but also with small consulting boutiques where we think there are specific opportunities. Some of these may be candidates for acquisition in the future."

Diversifying firms often have more problems with brand than product or broker firms. For product firms, brand will be built on their reputation in a specialised field. For broker firms, brand strength lies in the hub and the spokes: the hub may provide the name that secures client relationships but the spokes have the reputation for delivery. Diversifying firms, as they move away from the single focus that has previously defined their identity, have to challenge clients' existing assumptions. In Xerox's case, it is hard to find a better-known corporate brand, but it is not a name that managers will immediately link with consulting. "We have an advantage in that we do not have to come in and win on a generic professional services ticket," says Dolan, "but overcoming clients' preconceptions is not trivial."

Transaction firms

Transaction firms have products too, but they are much, much bigger. This is consulting as corporate finance: income is derived from a small number of very large deals. But unlike corporate finance, the actual income stream is spread over a period of years, sometimes unevenly, so that the consulting firm may earn less in the early years when it has improvements to deliver and more in later years when the situation has reached a steady state. As this implies, transactions are focused on large-scale systems delivery or outsourcing. There may be an advisory component to the project, such as change management, but it forms only a small proportion of the overall deal. Transaction firms are therefore much more geared towards implementation and delivery than relationship or even product firms. "Transaction firms do not do consulting for consulting's sake," says Bjorn-Erik Willoch at Capgemini, "it is not their function. They want to use their consulting practices to create opportunities for outsourcing and technology. Business process outsourcing and transformational outsourcing are both symptoms of this. The best BPO suppliers will take over a client's messiest processes, fix them and then run them on their behalf."

Because these large deals can absorb the cash that a consulting firm might have earmarked for other uses, transaction firms have to be of a certain size. "Some projects are so large that they almost merit an individual line on the supplier's balance sheet," says Alan Russell, head of consulting at LogicaCMG. "Even the largest firms have to adopt a portfolio approach, spreading their risk across several projects; second-tier consulting firms would get corporate indigestion. We will also see consulting firms using more special-purpose vehicles, even those that are time-consuming and costly to set up."

For the past ten years, the assumption has been that transaction firms require a high degree of vertical integration so that they can offer an end-to-end service to their clients. However, with the number of large-scale outsourcing contracts cancelled early appearing to rise daily, the single-supplier model is giving way to consortia deals. Although some firms hold to the integrated model, many more now see the future in terms of project-specific collaboration.

Ten years ago, BT (British Telecom) created Syntegra, a systems integration offshoot. "Systems integration was not part of BT's focus at the time," recalls Paul Hayes, who is responsible for BT's consulting and systems integration technology transformation team, "so we concentrated on being seen as a completely separate entity." That decision was reversed in early 2004. "BT recognises that its core offerings around voice, data and networking are becoming increasingly commodity-based and it is looking to create a much broader set of services for its customers." Syntegra's skills and approach – its familiarity with deals that spread the risks and rewards involved between customers and suppliers, for example – are seen to be crucial to success. "We've now rejoined the BT family," is how Hayes describes it. "We have a complete change in strategic focus, management team and branding – we're now known as BT Consulting and Systems Integration. More importantly, the Syntegra model, in which we were one step away from being an external partner to BT, has changed. Internal corporate barriers have come down, and we're getting to a position where we have a single account-management structure selling an integrated set of end-to-end services, from consulting to outsourcing, with everything else in between." The transition has not been without tears – some parts of BT have found it harder than others to adapt to the new environment – but it is one Hayes thinks is long overdue and marks a shift away from BT's product-dominated history to a complete end-to-end services culture. It has already helped the company win major projects for the UK's National Health Service, catapulting it from relative obscurity in the services domain to the top tier of consulting and IT services firms.

Paradoxically, BT has simultaneously recognised that it should not try to do everything. "Clients want to work with suppliers who understand their own strengths and weaknesses and who therefore choose to work with other suppliers whose skills complement theirs," says Hayes. "They judge us as much by the company we keep and the quality of the firms we partner." Having both the cultural maturity and the management capability to operate effectively in this environment, he believes, is one of the factors that will separate success from failure in the future. "It needs a sophisticated mindset. If you had looked at BT a couple of years ago, that characteristic would have been hard to find. There is still a long way to go, but BT is uniquely placed to help other organisations make the same transition because of the way we have successfully exploited technology to transform our own business and work in a more distributed world. The BT transformation story is a compelling one and excites and surprises the people who hear it. Nonetheless, some people still see us as a staid 'holes, poles and phones' company – but they used to see IBM as just a hardware manufacturer." The aim is to create a £10 billion ($15 billion) revenue services business within three years (ten times the size it is today).

The difference between the way in which hub-and-spoke firms and integrators deliver their services lies in the size of the centre. Transaction firms have a much larger "core" and are more likely to play the role of a prime contractor than an equal partner in a consortium. Indeed, although some transaction firms have a long history of collaborating with other suppliers, many others have their roots in the one-firm model of the 1990s, which they have abandoned only reluctantly because of the size and complexity of deals. Working with other suppliers is an important way to maintain operational flexibility; a firm does not need to rely wholly on its own resources, but can bring experts in from other suppliers when required. On the down side, integrators can end up expending substantial time and effort reviewing the governance and contractual arrangements around these types of projects.

Innovative payment structures and continuing price pressure from clients mean that keeping costs down is a priority for transaction firms. "These firms will be the big users of offshoring, their own or that of third parties," argues Willoch. "That is the game: the industrialisation of consulting."

Dependency on a small number of high-value deals and offshoring are already driving changes to the organisational structure of transaction firms. "Offshoring kills the pyramid model because most of the junior staff will be based thousands of miles away," says Willoch. "It also means, as a western-based firm, you have to recruit more people into more senior positions, and that's always higher risk. Consulting firms really need to grow from underneath, but that underneath is disappearing."

Transformation firms

Drawbacks of the transaction model for consulting firms are that it:

- almost exclusively involves technology or outsourcing deals;

- is predicated on one-off deals, focused on moving from A to B, rather than continuous improvement;
- reduces the opportunities to establish a long-term relationship with a client; once the job is done, contact with the client may be lost.

Two firms, IBM and Accenture, are unquestionably leading the way in changing this model, shifting their attention from transactions to transformation. "We talk about business performance transformation," says Eric Pelander, a partner at IBM's Business Consulting Services responsible for the firm's strategy and change practice globally. "It's an expanding market, driven by clients who want to achieve a radical improvement in performance and realise that they need a combination of consulting, outsourcing and technology services to help them do this. Looking at the speed with which big businesses have switched from trying to do everything themselves to relying on external parties, we estimate the business performance transformation market is worth something like $500 billion per year."

Pelander argues that three factors will drive success in this market. The first is the ability to deliver results. "Business performance transformation depends not so much on what you can do, but on what you can achieve. It's about scale. Some of that scale is organisational – having the range of skills and experience required to work on hugely complicated projects – but some is financial – being able to offer the kind of payment terms and contingent fees which clients in this market expect." Scale, of course, represents an almost insurmountable barrier to entry. "One of the advantages IBM has is our experience of running a $90 billion company, and that gives us extra credibility in the transformation marketplace. We've just won a contract to outsource all the after-sales servicing and technical support for a major consumer electronics company. We wouldn't have had the capability to do this if we hadn't already had our own world-class warranty and repair service."

Most middle-sized consulting firms and even some transaction firms would find it hard to marshal the capabilities and skills required. Just one very large business transformation project could occupy the entire resources of such firms. The need for scale will undoubtedly drive further consolidation among outsourcing, consulting and technology firms. According to Pelander, IBM is looking for potential acquisitions to strengthen its hand in markets where clients need help to transform their business processes; for example, IBM recently acquired Liberty

Life, a life-insurance processing and administration company. But middle-sized firms may also be tempted to try to buy their way into this part of the market by merging with firms of a comparable size.

The second is a firm's depth of knowledge in a particular industry and/or business process, such as how to set up call-centres in the insurance sector. "This is more critical than ever," says Pelander. "Before they are prepared to turn over a business process to an outside organisation, clients have to be utterly convinced by the latter's track record and expertise in that precise field." Lastly, argues Pelander, business performance transformation requires a fusion of business and technology thinking. "It's not enough to have just business acumen or technology skills, something people have been aware of since the business process re-engineering era. But it has proved difficult to bring the two sides together. Business process re-engineering put the process first and made the technology an afterthought; technology suppliers have put technology first. What is different now is that in some cases the technology, such as telematics (combining computers and telecommunications, such as wireless data applications in cars) and grid computing (applying the resources of many computers in a network to a single problem at the same time), may unleash new business possibilities for a client. IBM spends over $5 billion annually on research, much of which has shifted from pure technology research to looking at how we can apply science to our services business."

Critical for any transformation firm is to get consulting, technology and outsourcing people to work together, which has eluded these industries in the past. "We have to be able to bring all our capabilities together without diluting the expertise in any of them," says Pelander. "We have to be a bit like a supermarket, able to offer the range of products but also have bread of a similar quality to that of a specialist bakery. Just having the capability is not enough: we have to be world-class." Squaring this circle has meant reorganising around client sectors rather than service lines, making sure internal metrics drive collaborative behaviour, and building bridges between the firm's research capability and its consulting practice. "Communication has also been crucial," adds Pelander. "We are well positioned in this market, and nothing breeds success like success."

Positioning in the business consulting revenue/delivery matrix

The revenue/delivery matrix (see Figure 7.2 on page 91) provides a definitive way to map the new business consulting landscape. While some firms survive, indeed thrive, in the conventional relationship model, many more occupy positions that are radically different, in terms either of their more predictable revenue streams or of their delivery model. Inevitably, firms will try to gravitate towards those cells in the matrix where profits and/or long-term growth seem highest. For some, this may involve returning to their traditional consulting roots; for others, the challenge will be how to diversify without compromising their specialist reputation and cost base; and some will be seeking to graduate from focusing on transactions to enjoying a more transformational relationship.

Each cell has its advantages and disadvantages. Each represents a sustainable business model, although never one without challenges. Success for consulting firms lies in understanding their position within the matrix, and the specific threats and opportunities this brings.

8 Consultants

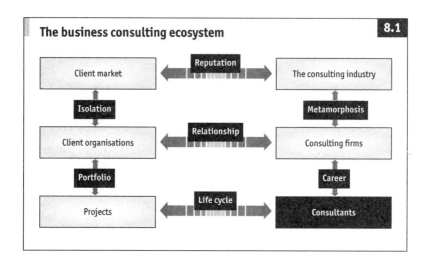

The business consulting ecosystem 8.1

Client market

Reputation

The consulting industry

Isolation

Metamorphosis

Client organisations

Relationship

Consulting firms

Portfolio

Career

Projects

Life cycle

Consultants

LOTS OF PEOPLE BECAME CONSULTANTS who should not have in the late 1990s," says John Kopeck, North American president of Compass. "I believe there are two fundamentally valid reasons for a client to hire a consultant. The first is to gain access to specific knowledge, experience, tool-sets, frameworks and expertise in an area the client chooses not to build internally. I'll willingly hire a licensed electrician to rewire a fuse box in my home rather than go to electrician school to learn how to do this task myself. I'm also scared of electricity, making the decision that much easier. I'll listen to the electrician's advice and probably follow it, since he has the knowledge and experience to back up his words. Is this consulting? You bet it is. But I am not going to ask the electrician for investment advice, or anything else beyond his acknowledged base of expertise.

"The second reason for hiring a consultant is to allow an unbiased outsider to focus on a specific issue or problem the client has. The client could use his own resources to tackle this problem, but (hopefully) the client's people already are occupied with their full-time jobs, and therefore could not focus as efficiently as an outsider can. For this task, smart ambitious generalists, unaffected by internal company politics, may be able to identify a sound solution and make actionable recommendations for the good of all. The people who should not have become consultants in the 1990s were the electricians who tried to sell investment advice and the generalists who tried to rewire fuse boxes. Good, solid consulting is tough work, hard on body and mind."

This is a pertinent reminder, given that consulting firms, after three years in which most have frozen recruitment, are now hiring again. "We have seen a fivefold increase in the level of recruitment," says Tony Restell, who runs Top-Consultant.com, a leading online recruitment website specialising in the consulting industry. "If we go back to 2003, consulting firms tended to talk about individual shortages – a project manager with experience in the telecoms sector, for instance – but since Easter 2004, they have switched to looking to recruit entire teams for a particular practice area." Research in the UK suggests that two-thirds of a typical consulting firm's costs are people costs. And these are rising, according to Restell. "A year ago, no one had any expectations of a pay rise or bonus, now they are expecting double-digit growth."

Consulting firms depend on the quality of people they employ. A big-name brand or word-of-mouth referral from a colleague may get a consulting firm on a client's shortlist, but it is the individuals the client meets who will win – or lose – new work. "I go for individuals and the value they bring to the table rather than the organisation they represent. Individuals are more important than the reputation of the firm," was how one client put it. "You have to meet, vet and specify the individuals who will work on the team for you. The expertise of a consulting firm changes with departures of their key people: you have to approach them afresh for each new project." "I buy the individuals, not the firm," said another.

Of course, consultants come in all shapes and sizes (see Table 8.1 on the next page). There is no such thing as an "average" consultant any more than there is an "average" project. Indeed, the range of work consultants undertake means that consulting firms need diverse backgrounds, perspectives and skills.

However, there are two fundamentals:

- Business consulting is based on the notion that consultants – unlike interim managers, contractors or other forms of temporary staff – work to improve the business performance of their clients. So consulting firms need people who are committed and able to make a positive contribution to their clients. They need people who know that their reputation and long-term success are based

Table 8.1 **The consultant spotter's handbook**

The trusted business adviser	What every consultant yearns to be but few manage: the consultant engaged in armchair conversations with chief executives, offering solace as well as solutions, being coach and mentor rather than technician
The good sales angel	The consultant able to discern and analyse client needs; the "shaper" who can formulate propositions that clients find valuable and relevant, who can articulate the issue and craft an appropriate solution
The bad sales angel	The consultant who is able to offer only stock solutions, who has a product-push mentality more geared towards talking at clients than listening to them
The experienced farmer	The bedrock of consulting as far as many clients are concerned: the specialist who can draw on in-depth technical knowledge and a wide experiential base and who has been there and done that
The scientist	More than a number cruncher, the highly rational analyst who goes to a greater level of detail than most clients think possible in order to generate insights
The marathon runner	The implementation specialist who wants to get in the trenches; ironically, although they see projects as a battle to be won, these are the best collaborators
The pointy-head	The laboratory or desk expert in the true geek tradition, taken along by a colleague to wow clients with their technical knowledge

on doing the right thing for their clients, people who know not to let their egos and arrogance, in-bred by an industry whose reason for existence is telling people what they are doing wrong, get in the way of making a difference.

◪ Consulting firms are not charities. They need people who know how to do the right thing without breaking the corporate bank – the firm's or the client's. They need people who understand that the duration of their work is finite – whatever contribution they make has to be made within a specified number of days or hours – that projects cannot drag on, that their skills are valuable and they have to be well used.

Are these facets in-bred? Or do they stem from experience? It all comes down to the old chestnut of nature versus nurture.

Nature

Yesterday's consultant focused on process; today's focuses on results. "We have thankfully lost the silly distinction between strategy and implementation," says Monitor's Alan Kantrow. "The test of a good consultant is not whether he or she has generated a unique insight, but whether that insight can be applied to produce positive results. Consultants can't just be smart; they have to be capable of delivering a business outcome." The word "outcome" is important: it is something clients are talking about more and more. Yesterday's consultant might have satisfied his or her client by writing a report analysing how the company might target its promotional activity more effectively; today's consultant will also be expected to liaise with the client's buyers, marketers and designers to ensure that this analysis translates into higher sales.

Jules Beck is an associate director at CSC Computer Sciences. "One thing that has always been – and still remains – relevant is passion about what you are doing for clients," he says. "Consultants need to understand their clients at two levels: organisational and personal. They have to know what their collective and individual ambitions are, and to translate this into something they, the consultants, can deliver."

Delivering results means that today's consultants have to have a much better understanding of what makes organisations act, rather than just listening. "Consulting should not be gathering data for data's sake," continues Kantrow. "You have to understand how to convey information that is both appropriate and appropriately shaped to convince them to make the decisions they need to make and to move them to action on those decisions. That requires an unprecedented level of engagement. We now start every assignment by challenging clients to think whether the question they have asked – 'tell us how we should respond to our competitors', for instance – is the right one. Once we are clear about the fundamental choices they face, we can identify what information they need to have in order to believe the answer. We have to know we can meet their burden of proof, otherwise there is a risk that they will not accept the logic and findings of the analysis in which they have been involved."

Good consultants genuinely want to do good. Accenture's staff survey consistently shows that although money is important, it is by no means people's prime motivator. "Top of the list is always interesting work," says Sue Rice, Accenture's HR director for the UK and Ireland. "They want the ability to develop themselves through involvement in a wide variety of work. There's also a big interest in being seconded, at a lower rate of pay, to our own charitable organisation that provides business, management and IT skills to the developing world. Corporate social responsibility is a big concern for Accenture and among its employees, and critical when it comes to attracting new graduates. They want to know that we take our responsibilities in society seriously and that we do the right things."

At CSC, Jules Beck believes that delivering results means consultants have to be better at handling organisational ambiguity than used to be the case. "When you first walk into a client's office, you will not be aware of the dynamics of the situation or the political undercurrents. You will often be challenged. People will claim that your ideas won't work, that they have tried that before and that you don't know what you are talking about: all the classic signs of resistance to change. As a consultant, it's important you can work your way through that ambiguity. And it's becoming more complex because organisational boundaries are more blurred. You don't always know where a process or line of responsibility starts and finishes, making it harder to define the scope of what you do and the levers you can use that will actually make a difference."

"Relationship skills also matter," says Jeremy Franks, an HR director at Deloitte. "In complex environments, you have to be able to win a client's trust – it makes projects run more smoothly and is fundamental where there are problems to be untangled. Flexibility is important too. Consultants can't pitch up with a prescribed solution and expect clients' problems to fit it." "Open-mindedness and a willingness to learn would certainly be top of things Accenture looks for in a new consultant," agrees Sue Rice. "Our range of projects is diverse, so we expect our consultants to be flexible. That means harnessing their natural enthusiasm and ensuring they have a questioning mind." There is a temptation, she argues, to put too much emphasis on the way consultants present their results. "Listening and adapting to what you hear are the real keys to success."

Of course, delivering results takes more than the commitment and good will of a single individual. As consulting work becomes more specialised and projects – even small ones – more complex, it is rare for a consultant to work alone. Even if he or she is the only one based at the client's site, it is now almost inevitable that there will be experts back at the office whose input will be required. Teamwork matters, too, when it comes to the client–consultant relationship. Probably the greatest compliment a client can pay a consultant is to say that they are one of the team; that they do not look or behave like consultants.

This adaptability is now being stretched in a new direction, as consultants from different firms increasingly find themselves working together on collaborative projects. "This is an important aspect of what CSC does now," says Jules Beck. "Multi-sourcing – what we call 'smart-sourcing' – is central to our value proposition. But we are also aware that genuine collaboration is a difficult trick to pull off. There is always the temptation, especially if you are a large firm, to try to take a disproportionate level of operational control and to undervalue the input of people from other firms. This can lead to friction at a personal level and can potentially destroy the relationship. We therefore need people who can be mature and professional about situations where they may be working closely together one day, only to be competing for another client's business on the next."

Lastly, everything has to be done at speed. One of the main differences between a client and a consultant is that the latter will be working on an issue for a limited amount of time (even a two-year contract is limited). This can be a double-edged sword. On the positive side, the ability of a consulting team to focus absolutely on the problem in hand and not become distracted by their day jobs is tremendously valuable to clients. However, it also puts the consulting machine under ever greater pressure. "The willingness of clients to undergo extraordinarily lengthy interventions has gone," says Kantrow. "They want consultants to work faster, and that's quite different from a few years ago. Consultants have to be careful that they don't cut corners or skip steps in their effort to meet a tight deadline."

As people are under greater stress, it is more difficult for them to build relationships. Focused entirely on finishing a piece of work by a given date, consultants are likely to be less tolerant of clients who want to work with them; flexibility, even relationship-building, become something of a luxury.

Teamwork, open-mindedness and speed are greatly helped by leadership. But, while the shelves of book stores are sagging under the weight of celebrity business autobiographies, where are the lions of the consulting industry? There is certainly no shortage of good stories to tell: we could have been treated to *McKinsey in the Era of Enron* or *Deloitte to Braxton and Back Again*. The possibilities are endless, so why the deafening silence?

Marvin Bower joined McKinsey in 1933, when it was a nearly defunct accounting and engineering firm; when he formally retired in 1992, it employed around 2,500 consultants. Bower believed that McKinsey's reputation would come from "putting client interest first, conducting themselves ethically at all times, only taking on work where they knew they could provide true value, and maintaining their independence by always telling the truth". Pursuing his commitment to work only for chief executives, he turned down work from presidents of business. He refused to work for Howard Hughes because he did not agree that the problem highlighted by Hughes was the most pressing one facing his business. Rather than take the firm public (as Booz Allen Hamilton had done in 1970), he sold his stock back to the partnership at its book value: "My purpose," he said later, "was to establish a firm that would live on after me."

In a 1953 presentation, he said: "We are what we speak – it defines us – it is our image. We are management consultants only. We are not managers, promoters, or constructors." It was always "we" with Bower, never "I"; he even spoke of the firm as having a personality into which the egos of individual partners were subsumed. Outside McKinsey, Bower's impact has been, if anything, even more profound. The way in which the consulting industry, in contrast to other professions, evolved around professional firms rather than professional individuals can be traced back to him. Of course, the irony is that the well-known and influential Bower resisted all attempts at a personality cult, famously refusing to change the name of McKinsey & Co because he did not want to give clients an incentive to demand his input, rather than that of his colleagues.

Consultants have historically been advisers, not doers – the power behind the throne rather than the person sitting on it. Moreover, in an industry where collegiate culture remains strong, there is a tension between individuals' desire to promote themselves and the need for a firm to ensure it is not overly dependent on a small number of star performers. Puffing up your personal brand provokes criticism from your peers and invites failure. Thus the great names in consulting are largely unknown outside their small circle of colleagues and clients.

But this model remains tenable only in the rarefied environment of strategy consulting. Clients who have put faith and a great deal of money into a consulting firm's ability to deliver a time-critical project want to put a name and a face to the process. They want leadership from consultants; they want them to stand up and be accountable for the results of their ideas. Obviously, this is important if you are delivering a high-profile, multimillion-dollar new system or are engaged in the transformation of an entire enterprise, but it is equally important for smaller, advisory projects. Modesty may have got the consulting industry to where it is today, but it will surely need leaders to take it to where it has to go tomorrow.

"We have seen many instances where the senior management of a consulting firm has become introspective in the aftermath of a merger or major acquisition," says Alan Russell of LogicaCMG (itself the product of a merger). "The consulting industry needs inspirational leadership to keep an outward-looking perspective."

Nurture

Where do consultants come from? Do they emerge fully fledged from the bowels of a consulting firm or are they drafted in from industry? The provenance of Accenture's consultants is probably typical. "We have a two-pronged approach to recruitment," says Sue Rice. "We recruit graduates from universities and business schools, but we also recruit experienced people, mostly from industry, who have specialist skills and experiences."

Graduates are brought into consulting firms at a junior level and inculcated with not just the skills they will need in their careers but also the values of the firms. It is the Jesuit model applied to business: get them young and you get them for life. Crucially, this type of labour is also the most flexible. Bright, young and energetic, these consultants can switch from project to project and from sector to sector with little difficulty, precisely because they do not have the specialist expertise which would take them into any one in too great a depth.

The ratio of generalist to specialist consultants varies from firm to firm, but by and large small firms are almost wholly staffed with specialists (that is the definition of niche, after all), whereas larger firms have the infrastructure and spread of projects which make having a generalist pool economically viable. However, that ratio is also sensitive to market conditions. Generalist consultants are more in demand in boom times when there may be a short-term scarcity of specialised skills. Thus the larger firms have been well-positioned historically to take advantage of emerging ideas – business process re-engineering, enterprise resource planning, customer relationship management, and so on – as the few niche firms specialising in those fields could not cope with demand once client interest had taken off. Consequently, during the bear market of the past few years specialists have predominated.

This trend may be partially reversed as demand bounces back, but it is unlikely to disappear altogether as specialist skills are always at or near the top of a firm's agenda when it comes to selecting consultants. However, something else is becoming just as important in clients' eyes. "Specialist knowledge is necessary but no longer sufficient," says Monitor's Alan Kantrow. "Some of the things that used to be in the final report of a consulting engagement are now in the letter of proposal – the knowledge is still important but it's been commoditised. The value consultants bring has to come from elsewhere." It has to come from experience, and this is in short supply.

"It's a situation that will only get worse," says Richard Granger, at the UK's National Health Service's National Programme for IT, who is already having problems finding people with sufficient experience to help him. "Recent cutbacks by traditional consulting houses and offshoring have reduced the pipeline of graduates, so that next year's project managers are simply not coming through in sufficient numbers." He draws a parallel with oil engineers in the United States, where a shortage of skills means the average age of engineers is 49–52 (this demographic time-bomb is a result of the upsurge in oil exploration in the 1970s). "It's the same in the consulting industry. We're rapidly returning to an environment in which the consultant of choice is an experienced person in his or her 40s or 50s, but that's exactly the kind of person consulting firms and clients are now struggling to find."

The challenges to consulting at a personal level

But if everyone agrees about what the ideal consultant should be on paper, why is it, when they walk through the open-plan offices typical of a consulting firm, that clients may be impressed by the modernity of the art on the walls or the cost of the technology on the desks but are not swept off their feet by a wave of energy focused on improving organisational performance?

Ironically, the opportunity to make things better is one of the main reasons people move into consulting in the first place. Indeed, if you question individual consultants, this is something that remains close to their hearts. Moreover, ask individual clients about the consultants they have actually worked with (as opposed to those whose ideas they are told to implement), and they are usually (though not universally) positive. Part of this is self-interest: if they have hired the consultant, admitting he or she has not added value is tantamount to questioning their own skills as managers. But part of it is genuine. So why is it that it seems to be lost in aggregation? Why does the business equivalent of racism seem to apply, in which you like the consultant at the next desk but not consultants en masse?

The problem is that not everything called "consulting" is aimed at improving performance. Sometimes the fault lies with clients, when they ask consultants to resolve the wrong issue or to rubber-stamp decisions already taken. Sometimes it lies with consultants, when bright young things, eager to work on a high-profile strategy assignment, give scant attention to the operational project they are currently assigned to. Arrogance and ambition blind many a consultant to the small things that can have a big impact on clients. It is not realistic for a consulting firm to expect its consultants to work on genuine consulting projects all their chargeable time – human nature is simply not that perfect. What matters, though, is that there is a critical mass of business improvement projects sufficient to set the standard for consulting overall, the bar to which all consultants – and projects – at least aspire.

In many firms, two trends have shifted the balance away from business improvement work: outsourcing and the sales imperative.

Opposing cultures?

Outsourcing and consulting are very different businesses. Outsourcing projects are concerned with efficiency and economy, not necessarily continuous improvement. Consulting projects can take months, whereas outsourcing projects last years. The background, skills and remuneration of those involved in outsourcing and consulting are different, as is the resulting culture. Consequently, attempts to bring consulting and outsourcing business together are fraught with difficulties, as EDS's uneasy marriage to A.T. Kearney illustrates. Accenture keeps the two parts of its business separate.

However, where a business earns most of its revenue from outsourcing, and where the majority of its people are employed in outsourcing services, there is always a risk that the values of its consulting practice – the focus on business improvement rather than cost reduction – may be overwhelmed. "There is too much focus on process, such as authorising expenses claims, too many overheads and not enough trust," was the complaint of one insider. "Micro-management might suit an outsourcing culture, but it demoralises a consulting one. The corporate survivors are those who are prepared to bend with the wind. There's been no attempt to define a new culture – our stated values keep being updated, but that's not the same as having a cohesive culture." "A firm that carries out consulting and outsourcing work has to be careful," agrees CSC's Jules Beck. "In building up an outsourcing business, as many big firms have done in the past few years, there's a danger that you will end up missing some of the more traditional consulting skills. You have to think how you will replenish this side of your business – and that's particularly important now, as the market picks up, when creating value for clients is more important than basic cost control. The real skill is to ensure you bring both together in an integrated way so that clients cannot see the gaps. It's when this does not happen that problems arise."

At Xerox, Tom Dolan is one of many senior executives faced with the challenge of combining outsourcing and consulting practices in an effective way. "The cultures of consulting and managed services are very different," he concedes, "but they have to work together. Each has its own perspective and a clear sense of demarcation – something we are trying to change by combining both businesses into a single one." At Capgemini, Bjorn-Erik Willoch has seen a greater proportion of people leaving the firm choosing to work for clients rather than other competitors, and argues that this says something about their aspirations. "These are all people who are looking for the opportunity to run something for a couple of years, to see a project through. Perhaps consulting firms are missing a trick by underestimating the extent to which outsourcing – particularly business process outsourcing – may offer their staff a chance to do this without leaving the firm. Such deals offer consultants a chance to do something real and tangible. If they want a change later, they can rotate back into the consulting practice." Indeed, if a firm cannot make outsourcing strengthen its consulting culture, it may well end up being cannibalised by it. "An outsourcing practice, if it is not turned to the consulting practice's advantage, can suck the latter dry," says Willoch.

One way in which consulting firms are seeking to close the gap between their consulting and outsourcing business is to redefine outsourcing.

Sales person versus adviser

The differences between outsourcing and consulting have an impact on how a consulting firm wins new work.

Consulting firms have always needed individuals with commercial acumen, but the form it takes has become increasingly complex. "Today's consultant can't go to a client and say that a project will take 20 people 20 days at $2,000 a day," says Beck. "Cost-plus, even 'value' pricing, is not adequate in a world which demands you calculate the risks associated with complex, multi-supplier deals." "Complexity also means consultants have to be that much more aware of what their firm has to offer," says Deloitte's Jeremy Franks. "Good consultants leverage the resources of the firm to their full advantage. They go and find experts, rather than rely on what they know personally. They understand the process of intellectual arbitrage involved in taking ideas from one situation to another, rather than constantly reinventing them."

The classic model for selling a consultant – the trusted adviser who barely had to pitch for business because his relationships all but guaranteed him a steady stream of work – is not applicable in a market populated by sophisticated clients whose needs/requirements are increasingly polarised between a small number of large-scale projects and a large number of specialist assignments. Some firms have responded by establishing a professional salesforce; others have adopted an account-management structure, giving one individual the responsibility of co-ordinating all the selling to one client. "We don't have the traditional sales model," says Beck. "We don't have highly paid senior partners out there focused on new business. What we do have are people who are responsible for long-term relationship building. CSC needs a pipeline of new work – we can't depend on opportunistic or small-scale projects. But we don't expect our consultants to be blue-blooded sales people; we want them to spend time understanding clients' needs, to link them back to the capabilities of CSC and its partners, and to articulate all that in a smart way." Beck argues that clients expect consultants to bring them ideas. "They want consultants to come into their room and do more than say: 'How can I help you?' They want them to have a strong opinion about where real improvements can be made and how to achieve them. Chief executives are human, they have all these challenges on their plate, and they are always looking for help."

However, oversupply since the millennium has put unprecedented pressure on consulting firms to win new business to keep their people occupied, and, in clients' minds, this is sometimes translated into overly aggressive selling tactics. "Cross-selling is never a comfortable experience," said one consultant. "You try to do the right thing for your client, but you have colleagues breathing down your neck asking if you've got the hardware deal sorted yet."

The irony is, for an industry that likes to parade its "our people are our greatest asset" credentials, that many consulting firms have yet to

find a business model which comfortably balances the potential con-
flicts between employer and employee on a sustainable basis. "Consulting has not been an easy place for staff to be," acknowledges Deloitte's
Paul Robinson. "After the early 2000s, when most firms froze recruitment and many had to lay off staff, some of the glitter has gone off the
industry, and other careers are looking equally attractive. The premium
that consulting used to command, in the eyes of both potential recruits
and employees, which justified the fact that this is a tough profession in
the first place, has been eroded. Consulting firms have to rebuild that.
They need to put the mystique back if they are to attract and retain the
right people."

4

THE WORLDS CONNECT

"The pressure on consultants will, if anything, grow. Clients have been to the same business schools as their consultants and are equipped with the tools and techniques that used to be the preserve of consultants; many are ex-consultants. They are more discerning and demanding, and better able to recognise quality when they see it."

9 Seven themes of interaction

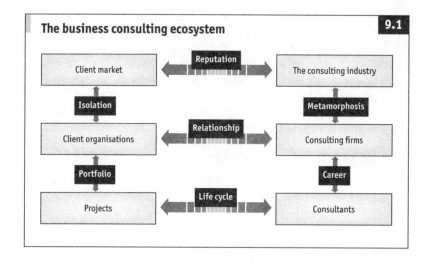

The business consulting ecosystem   9.1

Client market — Reputation — The consulting industry

Isolation — Metamorphosis

Client organisations — Relationship — Consulting firms

Portfolio — Career

Projects — Life cycle — Consultants

THIS PART OF THE BOOK has seven sections, each one focusing on a different way, or theme, in which clients and consultants interact.

Reputation

Chapter 10 looks at the reputation of the consulting industry as a whole. Starting with the impact Enron has had on the accounting industry, it questions whether individual consulting firms can isolate themselves from the collective reputation of their industry. It argues that the industry's reputation is perilously close to being damaged by corporate scandals of its own making, and that the conventional means consulting firms might rely on to defend themselves will be ineffective.

Isolation

Chapter 11 argues that the likelihood of the consulting industry being hit by corporate scandal is increased by a lack of reliable, objective information about what consultants offer. In a world characterised by information overload, it seems ironic to be talking about its scarcity. But it is true that clients today are not much better informed than they were ten or even five years ago. This matters because it makes the managers who buy consulting services less able to make the right decisions. Most consultancy users rightly point out that their decisions are discretionary. They do not have to use consultants, and when they do, they are responsible for the decisions they take – in other words, *caveat emptor* (let the buyer beware). However, most would also say that it is hard to exercise that responsibility where they cannot make informed decisions. If consulting firms do not provide sufficient details and explanation of their services or their specific approach, clients may be misled. Even worse is when they sell services a client does not need. Nowhere is this more clearly illustrated than in the business media where new management ideas are promoted every year. Some will be genuinely useful, many (if not most) will not and some may be positively dangerous. But how is a client to tell them apart?

Metamorphosis

Chapter 12 looks at the threat to the consulting industry from another angle: is there anything consulting firms can do to improve their collective image? The main problem is the ability of separate firms to act in unison. Consulting firms have been driven by their own corporate agendas. They need to work together more in order to improve the consulting industry's reputation. This will involve quite radical change – but to what extent is this metamorphosis occurring?

Relationship

The theme of Chapter 13 is complex relationships. Clients hiring consultants used to enter into self-contained, comparatively simple agreements aimed at managing discrete projects. Every project would be looked at in isolation. Three factors have changed this: procurement has been professionalised; clients are choosing to "multi-source" (using several suppliers where they previously used one); and new governance rules and contractual terms are being put in place to cope with the widening of consultants' roles from advisers to implementers.

Portfolio

For clients, complexity is translated into a need to manage a portfolio of consulting projects (Chapter 14). As the pace at which businesses want to change increases and the number of activities considered to be core shrinks, the proportion of work undertaken by business consultants will grow in both volume and importance. The challenge of deploying consultants in the most effective way will demand a new way of thinking.

Career

Chapter 15 looks at the relationship consulting firms have with their people. Being a consultant used to be a job for life, but in recent years many consultants have left their firms – through choice or redundancy – to join other firms or clients or to go freelance. At the same time, client demand for specialist skills means that older consultants with decades of experience are now some of the most sought after individuals in the industry. Accommodating this in a comparatively low-growth environment means that consulting firms have to look at other ways of building their businesses: by using associate consultants or subcontractors, or through alliances rather than acquisition. The bonds that used to exist between consulting firms and their consultants have become increasingly fluid and uncertain.

Life cycle

Interactions matter, too, at the most detailed level, when it comes to client and consulting teams working together on a specific project (Chapter 16). It is here, after all, that consultants have to make good on their promise of adding value. Yet clients' objectives are usually pedestrian – ensuring that a project "delivers" on time, within budget and to a satisfactory standard. By focusing on the early and final stages of consulting projects (procurement and handover), both clients and consultants are guilty of ignoring the way projects change during the course of their life cycle. Governance, management style and mindset need to be adaptable, not set in stone at the outset.

10 Reputation

The client market and the consulting industry

MOST CONSULTING FIRMS will argue that their individual reputations – their ability to differentiate themselves and their brand – are strong enough to set them apart from the industry. But is this still the case?

It is the kind of question that would have alarmed Marvin Bower, the *eminence grise* behind McKinsey's rise to power in the 1940s and 1950s. Bower's philosophy combined two important strands: individual integrity and collective professionalism. He would have had no truck with the apparent excesses that bedevilled the consulting industry in the 1990s – the bottomless expense accounts, fast cars and exorbitant salaries. The guardians of these ethics were consulting firms. It is largely due to Bower and his counterparts in the other leading firms in the 1930s that consultants do not have to be "qualified" as lawyers or accountants do. Quality assurance came instead from the recruitment, training and development procedures of the top consulting firms.

This model served the industry well while firms' reputations were based on the quality of their work alone, not on that of others. It may be less effective in a world where clients are more sceptical about the value consultants in general can add.

This chapter examines the way in which individual consulting firms have sought to differentiate themselves from the industry, and the factors which suggest that an additional, more collective response is increasingly important.

Building the big brands in consulting

In the early 1990s, strange things started happening in cities around the world. Billboards appeared showing creatures changing shape. Television adverts showed snails turning into frogs. "Metamorphosis in a world of change" was the message; Andersen Consulting was the name.

The origins of this lay in the formation of Accenture, then known as Andersen Consulting, which in 1989 was established as a company independent from Arthur Andersen, an accounting firm. "We had to establish Andersen Consulting as a separate legal entity," says James Murphy, Accenture's chief marketing officer. "From day one, we had to treat marketing as a business function, not something you did on weekends, which is how other firms tended to see it. We had an enlightened management team that recognised that if we wanted to be successful in the business we were in, we needed to build our brand and communicate our services to clients aggressively. We moved away from the traditional model where, for the most part, each partner did a lot of their own marketing, to an integrated strategic, organised and sophisticated marketing approach. We were the first firm to apply the best principles of consumer marketing to professional services, and we continue to do this today." Accenture now employs around 400 marketing people throughout the world, but it is not just the number that is unusual. "They are a very cohesive group," says Murphy. "They have been trained in the same processes, and they work on the same messages."

Conventionally, consulting firms have tended to conduct stop-start marketing campaigns, with each part of the firm doing its own thing. "Technology firms have done much better," says Murphy, "but consulting firms rarely invest enough and often lack clarity when it comes to the messages they are trying to communicate – and we benefit from this."

According to Murphy, the results of the campaigns ("Go on – be a Tiger" in 2004 cost $75m) are impressive. "Our primary objective is to build awareness and to increase the likelihood that we get onto clients' shortlists. Buyers who experience our advertising are three times more likely to put us on shortlist than those who have not."

Of course, brand is not just about having a clever tag-line. Accenture's message of "high performance delivered" would fall decidedly flat if clients' experience did not match the expectations it sets. "It is not just a slogan," says Murphy. "We invested a huge amount of time identifying what makes companies successful, industry by industry, and documenting the data we had to support this. We have to have an integrated approach: all of our people have to deliver in practice, as well as on paper." The point is reiterated by Dave Higgins, consulting marketing director for Europe, the Middle East and Africa at Deloitte. "Success lies in delivering sustainable value for our clients. Good brands do this some of the time. Great brands do it consistently. The doing requires embracing the art of listening, seeing the world from our clients' perspective, walking the mile in their shoes. Understanding, however, is only half the battle: it is when you come to solve the problems that the rubber meets the road."

Higgins argues that some professional services firms adopt an inside-out approach, proving the adage that people who are only good at using hammers see every problem as a nail. The opposite – looking from the outside in – involves reconfiguring everything, from service delivery through to the marketing messages, in a way that reflects clients' own priorities. "A brand is a very transient thing if it's not offering consistent value to clients," says Higgins. "Business leaders are continuously faced with increased scrutiny and pressure to enhance shareholder value. Investors are becoming more demanding, forcing companies to focus their attention on strategies and processes that add value to the shareholders. As a consulting firm, we need to ensure there's consistency between what we say and what we deliver, otherwise we'll fall into the value gap. From a marketing point of view, this is about getting to what matters most first and about ensuring that everyone in the organisation understands and is able to deliver consistently. In essence, everyone needs to be a chief marketing officer. It's a big task, but a high-class problem for any marketing team to have. At Deloitte, these principles are reflected in our tone of voice, a straight-talking style. We believe that great relationships create lasting value for everyone involved and, in our experience, those relationships always start from good conversations. We identify the ulcer-inducing issues our clients face and go out of our way to encourage clients to talk to us."

From 1998 to 2002, Tony Tiernan was director of marketing for Europe, then global director for The Boston Consulting Group. He now runs his own firm called Authentic Identity. Tiernan argues that there are two dimensions to a consulting brand: what a firm does and what it is. Both are essential and valuable, but most firms' attention is skewed towards the former. This is ironic, because it is generally the latter that distinguishes firms from each other. "The key differentiator in clients' eyes has always been the relationship they have with a particular firm," he says, "but consultants are more comfortable with the rational, even when the emotional value is so important." The type of people recruited by consulting firms and the training they go through exacerbate this, as does consultants' desire to reassure clients that there is a concrete value to their service.

This imbalance has three consequences for consulting firms when it comes to external marketing and communications:

◪ They confuse positioning with brand, adopting a "let's find a hole in the competitive landscape and convince the world we can fill it" approach, which is essentially manipulative and ignores what the firm is.

◪ Their external communication centres on describing features of a firm's consulting process in exhaustive detail.
◪ They focus on what a firm does, resulting in a one-dimensional, uncreative approach.

"Despite the big marketing budgets, consulting is very self-absorbed," concludes Tiernan. "It's a crowded and undifferentiated industry, but we're missing a trick by ignoring the emotional side of what we do, the client experience, how meetings are conducted, the physical environment, and so on. It has enormous influence on how clients see us; indeed, clients will usually identify this, but we do not take it into account." Nor do brands provide much in the way of protection. "When a big brand runs into trouble, it reflects on the whole category. A strong, well-developed brand will buy a consulting firm time and a second hearing, but not magical immunity."

Branding has become the continuation of Bower's strategy – the consulting firm as guardian of professional standards – by other means. But there are potential drawbacks. It is easy for a brand to take on a life of its own. The link between what a firm says it does and what it actually does is by no means umbilical, and in the hands of less responsible marketers, a consulting firm's advertisements can become an exercise in corporate hypocrisy. A second drawback is the irony that although marketing campaigns may be aimed at differentiating individual firms, they inevitably contribute to broader perceptions about the consulting industry as a whole. They set a standard not just for the firm concerned but for every consulting firm, whether they subscribe to it or not. Lastly, and perhaps most importantly, the more successful the campaigns are, the more they create a focal point for attention. The consulting industry used to be anonymous; it is not any more.

From small acorns, giant oak trees grow

In *The Tipping Point*, Malcolm Gladwell identifies three factors that "tip" a small change into a big change, for example an obscure book into a bestseller or a few occurrences of a virus into a full-blown epidemic:

◪ The power of context – when the timing of a change makes it more or less likely to be significant.
◪ Stickiness – the extent to which the impact of a change is lasting.
◪ The law of the few – where a small number of people behave in a way that, intentionally or not, increases take-up of a change.

127

The impact of Enron's collapse in 2002 was akin to a social epidemic, gaining the kind of media and water-cooler coverage usually reserved for blockbuster movies. All three of these factors were apparent:

- **The power of context.** It is doubtful that Enron would have riveted the world as it did if there had not already been a recessionary environment complicated by international tension and the threat of war. Although the scale of Enron's collapse was remarkable, its prominence was increased as it filled the role of convenient public scapegoat for the crash in stockmarket values and the impact this had on personal pensions and investments.
- **Stickiness.** Massive corporate losses have happened before, but when Enron collapsed it passed a point of no return. No amount of cost-cutting or restructuring could restore the damage done to those who worked there or who were dependent on the company's fortunes. Moreover, the "stickiness" of Enron was also a result of the corporate culpability perceived to be involved. It is alleged that the company's collapse was not just an instance of managerial negligence, but of a determined attempt to hoodwink stakeholders. Similarly, in the case of Arthur Andersen, it was revelations of document-shredding that destroyed the firm's reputation, not its incompetence.
- **The law of the few.** The resonance and scale of the Enron scandal ensured some level of public interest, but it was only when the cause of its investors and other stakeholders was taken up in the US Senate that prominence was guaranteed.

Enron was not unique. The same three factors are evident in other prominent business scandals, from the belief that irresponsible speculation by banks precipitated the Wall Street Crash in 1929 to the fears that the failure of Long-Term Capital Management Fund in 1999 would bring down the world's capital markets. A combination of context, impact and the interaction among those affected resulted in a groundswell of public opinion sufficiently great to precipitate external interference of some form (notably government regulation).

For the consulting industry to experience a scandal equivalent to that which engulfed Andersen as a result of Enron, the same three factors would have to be in place. In other words, the timing would have to be such that clients, perhaps even the general public, were looking for someone to blame; the problem, when it surfaced, would have to be beyond salvage; and some organisations or individuals would have to be sufficiently motivated to publicise the issue.

Are these factors already in place? The only people who can answer this question are clients themselves.

The power of context

Most criticisms of the consulting industry are long-standing, and none will come as a surprise to experienced consultants. They do not add value; they are short of new ideas; their suggestions are impractical; they tell you what you already know and, worse, what they know you want to hear. So far such carping has remained a sideline activity, never gaining the critical mass to push it up the agenda of more than the occasional, isolated client. Two factors suggest this may not continue to be the case: over-aggressive selling by consulting firms; and the impact of a generation of client managers who have grown up working with consultants, rather than just hiring them.

Consultants and clients have learned different – and contradictory – lessons from the economic strictures of the early 2000s. Consultants have learned that it is no longer possible to rely on traditional ways of selling their services: clients rarely call them, so they have to take the initiative. They have invested in training their people to be more effective business developers; they have hired professional sales people; and they have set up account-management structures. Above all, they have changed the way in which people are rewarded, putting more emphasis on individual sales targets. Clients, meanwhile, have learned to suspect the motives of consultants. If someone's career depends on winning new business, they may be tempted to sell clients services they do not need. The problem is exacerbated by the difficulties in quantifying the contribution consultants do – or do not – make. In the absence of any rigorous and far-reaching analysis of where and how consultants add value (whether, in hard terms, by increasing their clients' shareholder value, or, in softer terms, by improving their management capabilities), the idea that consultants are poor value for money has gained widespread acceptance.

Many surveys of consulting clients focus on the person who foots the bill, the all-important budget-owner whose influence over the decision to hire consultants and the choice of consulting firm is critical. This approach ignores the fact that tomorrow's budget-holders are the people who, today, are working with the consultants their bosses bring in. What senior executives perceive to be valuable consulting input often translates into disenfranchisement and disappointment among those who work with the consultants on a day-to-day basis. One such manager summed up the experience: "My use of consultants has left me with a pretty jaundiced view of their experience and usefulness. Setting aside the situations where they are used simply as pairs of hands, under in-house management, to supplement the workforce, consultants should be able to offer real experience of the subject they are advising on, when in fact they are often recent graduates filling in until they can get a proper job. Bright as they may be, they cannot add to the knowledge of experienced in-house staff. The term 'consultant' has been devalued."

That consulting firms are sometimes perceived to be putting their own interests above their clients' and that some managers have grown up feeling pushed aside by consultants suggest that Gladwell's first "law" – the context in which a financial scandal takes place – applies to the consulting industry.

Stickiness
But context is not the only factor. Financial scandals are more likely to be prominent where they have a lasting impact: in Gladwell's terminology, where they stick. For a scandal to acquire sufficient stickiness to warrant government intervention it needs to:

- affect large numbers of people in a substantial way;
- be seen as symptomatic of a wider problem;
- involve a prominent individual or corporation that acts as a focal point for criticism and who can stand indicted for the perceived misdemeanours of an entire sector.

The principal difference between any putative scandal in the consulting industry and the one that brought down Arthur Andersen is that consulting projects are discretionary. Unlike audits, clients do not have to hire consultants. Because clients believe that their proactive management of consulting projects is crucial to determining success, they believe the main barrier to preventing a large-scale consulting disaster is the market's judgment in choosing to use consultants in the first place. "The implementation of a consultant's recommendations is always (even if by default) a company management decision," comments one executive. "This is very different from an auditor's scrutiny of accounts, which is meant to be independent, unbiased and in adherence to professional standards." In other words, even if a consulting project (a new strategy, a major IT implementation, an organisational restructuring) went so badly wrong that it was unquestionably implicated in the bankruptcy of a company, the buck would still stop with the company's management.

But this does not mean consultants are off the hook. "I could see a major scandal occurring in the consulting industry if a consultant was brought in to manage a big enough and critical enough project and was not subject to sufficient monitoring," says another manager. "All of a sudden, big money is committed to something that can be delivered only by spending more than can be afforded. The client goes under, and the consultant becomes a pariah." Some clients simply do not accept the philosophy of *caveat emptor*. Many believe that it is possible for a failed project to generate industry-wide shock waves if it can be shown that the consulting firm involved had knowingly and deliberately sold work a client did not need or could not afford.

The risk that a consulting firm will be tempted to sell unnecessary services increases as its range of services grows. "I'm amazed there have not been problems with this already," says one client. "The old Chinese Walls idea has never been particularly convincing. Going forwards there will need to be a much clearer understanding of who does what if the consulting industry is to remain credible."

For a failed consulting project to have a serious impact people would have to perceive a pattern. Most clients have their favourite consultants-as-cowboys anecdotes, but few have an overall view because they do not talk to each other. Thus it would be possible for a consulting firm delivering an atrocious service to go from client to client without any one client seeing the pattern. Ultimately, of course, the consulting firm would run out of new clients (repeat business would be impossible) and go out of business, but lots of organisations would waste money in the interim.

Almost universally, clients believe that the consulting firms they work with are the highly differentiated ones, otherwise their authority in selecting them would be suspect. It follows that clients are unlikely to believe that these firms will be vulnerable in the event of a large-scale scandal. At the same time, the existence of such brands provides public opinion with a lightning rod should a major scandal occur. A contradictory picture emerges. "Yes, I believe that the consulting industry has a collective reputation which could be severely damaged. But I like to think that the consulting firms we work with are comparatively immune to such a problem," a client might say.

The law of the few

Media criticism of the consulting industry is unlikely to drive change unless there is a clear agenda for change and a coherent voice in the form of a pressure group or a small number of influential evangelists.

To what extent is a coherent agenda emerging among clients? Clients are remarkably consistent about the kinds of changes they would like to see in the consulting industry:

- ◪ Information. It often looks as though consultants are only too keen to regurgitate the latest solution or package without trying to take into account a client's specific situation. This means that there may be lots of impressive presentations but little substance. It is not just the consulting firms that are at fault; clients should demand better information.
- ◪ A code of practice. This would correct the distortion many clients see, particularly during a recessionary period, in which consultancies, under pressure to maintain the growth rates of the previous decade, are tempted to sell clients work they do not need and cannot afford. In other words, clients need reassurance that consultants are genuinely acting in their interests.
- ◪ Accountability. Many clients feel that consultants should have a similar level of professional liability as, say, lawyers and accountants for their advice. The underlying concern is clarity of ownership. The majority of clients accept that there are consulting projects where the buck unequivocally stops with them. They also believe that there are other projects where responsibility can reasonably and unambiguously be assigned to the consultants involved. Their main concern, therefore, is when accountability is unclear, when they think consultants are ducking the issues.

The consulting industry has begun to respond to this agenda. Trade associations like the Management Consultancies Association have codes of practice which their members must abide by. Contractual structures, which share the risks and rewards of projects between clients and consultants, are becoming more prevalent. However, the problems in exchanging information and the intangible nature of consulting services constitute formidable barriers to making the industry more transparent.

These barriers are also part of the reason there has been no collective pressure from clients for change. Many of the companies surveyed for this book noted that there are user groups for software companies but no equivalent for clients of consulting firms, and most felt the effectiveness of such groups would be seriously compromised by the need to protect confidential information. Although understandable, this stance severely limits meaningful debate.

From differentiation to common purpose

"The underlying problem with both brand promotion and public relations is that they paint a veneer," says Geoff Dodds, who was until 2002 the global director of brand at PWC Consulting (now part of IBM). "What counts is not what people say or claim about themselves, it is what really happens." With so much negative publicity – failed projects, exorbitant fee rates and disenchanted middle managers who feel pushed aside by their bosses' use of consultants – rehabilitating the reputation of the consulting industry is, according to Dodds, "like pushing water uphill".

Success, he believes, will come down to three things. First, consultants do not spend enough time finding out how they have done. "Clearly, the intangibility of consulting makes client satisfaction hard to measure, but consulting firms have been at fault for being reluctant to get under the skin of this issue. By taking a more systematic, rigorous and objective approach to surveying clients' reactions, they would force clients themselves to think about it more deeply and have better feedback to act on. As a result, the quality of work would improve." If groups of consulting firms do this, there will be a basis for some effective peer pressure and the opportunity to raise the standards of all involved.

Second, having got its report card, the industry would be in a position to defend itself. "People in senior positions in the consulting industry need to weave messages about the contribution consultants make into everything they say," says Dodds. "The positive value of consulting has to be at the top of their agenda when they talk in public, not just promoting a particular aspect of their firm." The media would be one way to do this, but a viral approach, with senior consultants talking to influential clients, would be far more effective. It would have to be bottom-up as well as top-down. New consultants would need to understand from the start how they add value to clients. It would also have to be outside-in as well as inside-out. Consulting firms should take some responsibility for improving the way in which clients use them, perhaps through workshops with the client team, effectively training people to be good clients and to get the best value from their consultants.

Ultimately, though, it is a question of changing people's sense of priorities. "Consulting firms have become fixated on differentiation," Dodds argues, "and marketing departments are at fault for banging on about unique selling points, an old-fashioned concept that doesn't often apply now, especially in an environment where competing consulting firms are increasingly working together and the distinctions between them are already blurred. If you look at some of the companies that have done well over the past few years, they are not hung up on differentiation but are focused on simply delivering the best possible value to their customers. And they are relentless in their efforts to increase that value year in year out. If consulting firms, too, were to concentrate on delivering better value to their client, the industry as a whole would find itself in a better place than it is today."

11 Isolation

The client market and client organisations

THE PEOPLE WHO HIRE CONSULTANTS tend to see their needs as different from their neighbours' and every project as unique. In one sense they are right: no organisation faces the same set of pressures or has identical resources at its disposal. But at another level, they are ignoring the undeniable fact that their decision to use consultants is influenced by what they see going on in the wider market. They may have heard about initiatives competitors have undertaken, or they may have read an article about a new technology they think they could use. No firm takes decisions in an airtight environment, even if they believe that they do.

Moreover, some organisations think they must keep their use of consultants secret because the projects the consultants are working on are a source of competitive advantage, or perhaps because they are afraid that if they confer with competitors, they may be accused by consumer groups of collusion, which would open them up to the scrutiny of the regulatory authorities. There is an element of truth in this, but it is by no means the whole picture. Some consulting projects, such as preparing a hostile takeover bid, are genuinely highly confidential, but most are not. If they provide a sustainable competitive advantage, it is in the execution of the idea, not in the idea itself.

That we still live in an environment where business is obsessed with internecine competition and ignores the potential benefits that may stem from collaboration is sometimes exploited by consulting firms. Because clients do not talk to each other, consultants act as their intermediaries, taking ideas and solutions from one organisation to another. Consultants therefore play a crucial and valuable role in spreading new thinking. Imagine what the business world would be like if consultants were not there to facilitate this process of intellectual arbitrage: it would take longer for companies to adopt new technology or follow best practice elsewhere; lessons learned about what works would take far longer to filter through; more initiatives would fail; and organisations would be less willing to consider new ideas. The disadvantages are that consultants can become too powerful; they can be the sole arbiters of whether a new idea is worthwhile; and they can be motivated to sell a new idea to clients who do not need it.

This chapter looks at the mechanisms that drive the imperfect consulting market. Taking one of the big, new ideas of the moment – transformational outsourcing – it examines how a new management idea takes hold. There are two things clients can do to help them distinguish between genuinely valuable ideas and the vast array of irrelevant ones: examine the quality of thinking and research behind the idea; and check how effectively the idea has been executed in practice. This is not revolutionary, but it does require clients to break through decades of self-inflicted isolation where consulting is concerned and talk to each other.

High-concept consulting

Chapter 3 argued that new management ideas play an important role in driving demand for consulting services. Both clients and consultants should be cautious about adopting such ideas and should be clear about what value (if any) they will add to their organisations, tailoring them to suit their own needs rather than following a prescribed methodology too closely.

Blockbuster consulting is big business. Business process re-engineering (BPR) set the gold standard of what could be achieved. Between 1988 and 1995, Index (where James Champy, who founded the BPR movement with Michael Hammer, worked) increased revenues from $25m to $250m. Index was not the only firm to benefit – an entire market was born. Ironically, Hammer and Champy probably made even more money for Accenture than they did for Index.

Of the many management ideas that emerge each year, why do some grow into bona fide consulting markets? And what does this say about the way clients choose between them? Consulting companies can be a source of innovative thinking, but much that purports to be "thought-leading" could be better described as "thought-following". What matters is meaningful information, or the lack of it. In a world in which so much information is so readily available, it is ironic that clients are for the most part no better informed about consulting services than they were ten years ago.

It is easy to spot an emerging consulting market because there will be disagreement over what to call it. Each consulting firm will seek to "own" the way the market talks about a new idea until consensus emerges (usually in the form of a three-letter acronym). Indeed, it is tempting to think that business process re-engineering (BPR), enterprise resource planning (ERP) and customer relationship management (CRM) would all have continued to languish in consulting backwaters had they not acquired snappy titles. It helps, too, if one of the three words is particularly resonant: "re-engineering" suggested science and precision; "enterprise" touched a raw nerve among the many large corporations whose IT systems had grown up piecemeal; "relationships" appealed to those who had none.

"Transformation" is another such word. For ten years, consultants have wistfully talked of transforming corporations, making substantial changes rather than mere tweaks. More recently, the term has been coupled with another favourite to become "transformational outsourcing", and it will probably soon be known as business transformation outsourcing or BTO.

The next bandwagon?

"We no longer expect big corporations to be totally integrated," says Roger Camrass, director of business transformation at Fujitsu. "Look at an organisation like BP, which employs around 100,000 people. Given the scale of the company's operations, that figure should probably be five times higher, but much of what it does is done by third parties." Outsourcing, he argues, is not about IT, but about the ability of an organisation to adapt to changing markets.

The need to be flexible is changing the way organisations distinguish between core and non-core activities. IT was the obvious first candidate for outsourcing because it is a complex area requiring specialist skills. "It was comparatively easy for companies like Unilever (which outsourced its IT operations to EDS in 1982) to say, we are a detergent, not an IT, company," says Camrass. "But the game has moved well beyond IT, to procurement, legal services, human resources and finance." The debate about what is core and what is non-core to a business has also been fuelled by the recognition that some organisations are better at some things than others. This increases demand as organisations seek suppliers whose skills base complements their own. The first generation of companies to outsource was seeking to benefit from economies of scale, but companies now expect suppliers to provide specialist skills not available in-house.

The need for greater operational flexibility and specialist skills to be applied to core and non-core processes is forcing outsourcing to evolve. Rather than being a commoditised service cannibalising higher-end consulting, outsourcing is becoming more reliant on consulting. A new business model is emerging which brings the two sides together: transformational outsourcing.

"Transformational outsourcing originated with the big suppliers and they have two distinctive capabilities," says Mary Cockcroft, managing director of Pagoda Consulting, which specialises in IT consulting and programme management. "They deliver a service. By understanding more about how services are best delivered, typically in a back-office environment, they know how to organise them better. Because they work for many clients, they can also take expensive activities and spread the costs. But most of these suppliers now also have consulting expertise, the skills to change businesses – front and back office – in far more radical ways." This creates an opportunity to move away from the established approach to outsourcing, which has become a commodity service aimed purely at reducing costs. What most clients want is transformation at low cost, which generally means getting the right mix of basic services and smarter ones. Transformational outsourcing encompasses a wider range of services and is more complex than traditional outsourcing.

Using more consulting expertise provides a way around two of the most common problems that afflict conventional outsourcing contracts: lack of strategic clarity and failure to re-engineer processes before they are outsourced.

"You have to be sure what it is you are trying to achieve," says Cockcroft. "That will almost certainly involve both client and supplier doing a lot of work before the contract is signed. How, for example, will they recognise the benefits? It's all very well making broad promises, but what will they translate into, in practice?" It is a lesson, she believes, that ought to have sunk in from conventional outsourcing. "But it's still a problem because clients persist in having the attitude that they are offloading a problem and therefore don't want to invest any more time in it than they have to." Many conventional outsourcing clients also assume that improvements take place after the contract is signed. Too much attention is focused on supplier selection and contract negotiation, and not enough on preparing the ground. Transformational outsourcing is therefore predicated on the idea that the outsourcing client needs to be transformed as much as the process that is being outsourced.

Bringing consulting and outsourcing closer together is also something that Allan Leggetter believes will be crucial in the future. BAE Systems, where Leggetter is head of infrastructure, shared services, IT and e-business, is another highly experienced user of outsourcing services. "While focusing on reducing costs remains the right approach for some areas, one of the main areas for us in the future will be how we can use outsourcing to change our business. Too much attention has been paid to installing and running technology, and not enough to how we can change the way we work in order to take advantage of new systems."

Another problem with conventional outsourcing is that clients, and particularly suppliers, generally think in terms of transactions and contracts rather than relationships. "Suppliers have been good at putting big deals together," says Leggetter, "but they have not put so much effort into making the relationship, which should be a partnership, work in practice." Consulting offers a better model in which client–supplier interaction is based on trust and mutual respect, and this is increasingly what outsourcing suppliers aspire to provide.

Clients' search for operational flexibility is also challenging the ways in which they traditionally pay for both outsourcing and consulting projects. Conventional outsourcing contracts, once signed, can last for as long as ten years and clients have found themselves paying over the odds for unexpected changes. They have resented, too, the fact that suppliers' only motivation for reducing the costs of a given service has been self-interest. Open-book accounting, the bedrock of many conventional outsourcing contracts, is not the answer. "It's great for suppliers," points out Cockcroft. "They can effectively say look, it's costing us this much, this is what we'll charge you plus a 5% mark-up. There is no incentive to cut costs and the client bears all the risk."

The problem has been exacerbated by suppliers' success in cutting costs. "A typical IT outsourcing contract might involve the supplier in handing 30% of savings over the counter," says Fujitsu's Roger Camrass. "But most IT organisations are relatively inefficient: by stripping out waste and achieving economies of scale, suppliers can probably achieve a 40–50% saving. That creates a dilemma for clients – do you hand over the keys? Managers are looking for ways of getting out of the mortgage-like arrangements of most outsourcing contracts and, instead, want to establish a more open, transparent relationship. The idea of fixed capacity is obsolete. People want to move to an on-demand approach in which a continuous innovation cycle will prevent suppliers from becoming complacent."

For consulting projects, the problem has been twofold:

◪ Despite all the talk about working in partnership, consulting firms and their clients have found it difficult to break the habit of time and materials billing. Research shows that other, more innovative ways of structuring payment, such as payment by results, still account for only a tiny proportion of fee income. Consultants have found it difficult to identify projects where the outcome can be so unambiguously measured that fees can be made contingent on success. Clients have found it hard to contemplate giving consultants bonuses for success, even if they are willing to penalise them for failure.

☑ The cost of consulting usually comes off a company's bottom line. Unlike hardware and software expenditure, which can be amortised over the life of the equipment, consulting is assumed to have a one-off impact. As budgetary belts have tightened since the millennium, the fact that expenditure on consultants is charged to the profit-and-loss account, rather than the balance sheet, has made the business case for many new projects difficult to defend.

Outsourcing suppliers and consulting firms need to find ways in which payment terms more actively align their interests with those of clients, can be spread over time and can be scalable depending on the level of work undertaken. Options include variable pricing, setting no minimum price, upfront savings, a guaranteed return on investment, year-on-year service level agreement improvements, open-book pricing and risk/reward deals. Such deals depend on minimising the capital investment organisations have to make upfront and tying the consulting firm to delivering results.

However, shifting all of the risk and not much of the profit to suppliers is unrealistic and unworkable. All too often, clients see suppliers providing a poorer than expected service simply because service levels are set to meet a pricing model that is so low that the supplier cannot afford to invest and skimps on the service to ensure adequate margins are achieved.

What matters in the end is that the client gets results. Conventional outsourcing has a mixed track record. Given the benefits transformational outsourcing is intended to deliver, can it perform better?

Traditional outsourcing focuses on doing the same things in the same way but leveraging economies of scale and skills to reduce costs by 10–15%; transformational outsourcing is supposed to deliver more substantial improvements. In this respect, transformational outsourcing is not so much inheriting the mantle of BPR as overcoming its weaknesses. "Transformational outsourcing is a means by which organisations can deal with the complexity which business process engineering left

untouched," says Pagoda's Mary Cockcroft. Camrass agrees: "The pro-
ponents of BPR chickened out of dealing with the critical processes
because they were too difficult. They focused on softer, easier ones
instead – human resources and finance – where you could eradicate a lot
of traditional manual work. There is a greater expectation today that
suppliers will come to the table with genuine innovations."

Does this bandwagon have legs?
Four factors will determine whether transformational outsourcing – or
indeed any of the other new management ideas that appear – is worthy
of serious consideration:

- There has to be a genuine need for transformational outsourcing.
  It may not be the perfect solution, but it is attempting to address
  the dissatisfaction many organisations feel with conventional
  outsourcing.
- Alongside a pull from clients, there has to be a push from
  suppliers. No management idea will take off if it is not in the
  commercial self-interest of consulting firms, technology vendors
  and even outsourcing companies to promote it. For firms that
  have substantial feet in both camps, transformational outsourcing
  offers a means of overcoming the real cultural differences
  between high-margin consulting and low-margin outsourcing.
- There also has to be hard data. Transformational outsourcing will
  only be adopted by a broad range of clients if there is tangible
  proof that its benefits outweigh its considerable costs. Being able
  to demonstrate a positive return on investment has become
  something of a mantra among consulting firms, stung by criticism
  of past ideas which have yielded few benefits. It is also in danger
  of becoming something that clients pay lip-service to, a box they
  have to tick to get their business case approved, rather than a
  source of meaningful comparison.
- The service has to differ from suppliers' existing services in some
  way. It is tempting to say that there is nothing new under the sun
  and that management ideas, like old wine, frequently get poured
  into new bottles. But the consulting industry does see substantial
  changes in the way services are offered: offshoring is one, and
  transformational outsourcing, because it combines consulting and
  outsourcing, may be another. Clients are not stupid: the majority
  are able to distinguish between consultants claiming they have

something original to offer and those that actually do offer something original.

The first two factors (pull from the market, push from consulting firms) determine the potential appeal of a new idea; the last two determine whether it lives up to that potential. As they look at what their competitors are doing and at what the business media is telling them they should do, clients therefore need to consider:

◾ the quality of thinking and research behind the idea;
◾ how the idea will be executed in practice.

Innovation and the search for hard data

It is hard to find a more subjective term than thought leadership – what is innovative to one person is obvious to another – but this does not prevent it from appearing on the website of almost every consulting firm, large or small. Nor is quantity any guarantee of quality. Every year, thousands of books, articles and papers appear, but, as with brand-building, there is a tendency towards homogeneity. Almost half of everything published on thought leadership in the consulting industry between 2002 and 2004 has focused on perennial favourites: business processes and technology. Consulting firms are always nervous of being left behind in a burgeoning market and compensate for their insecurity by leaping on even the most rickety of bandwagons.

Chris Meyer is more aware than most of the structural challenges to innovation in the consulting industry. As the author of *Blur: The Speed of Change in the Connected Economy* and *Future Wealth,* he also ran Capgemini's Centre for Business Innovation until it was closed down in 2003. "New ideas are always emerging and maturing in business. There is a constant cycle of creation into best practice into consulting methodologies into software you can download. Consultants occupy a space in that life cycle, somewhere between the initial discovery and turning it into a methodology," he says. "Smart consulting firms know when to get out of a particular market and will know where they fit in the value chain." For the majority of consulting firms, it does not make sense to be too sharply positioned on the cutting edge. Innovation takes time and investment, and because you do not know where you will end up, it makes it harder to plan and allocate resources. It also requires a specific culture. "Exploration and exploitation are fundamentally different activities and have different economics – it is the difference between divergent and convergent thinking," says Meyer. "Exploration makes people who are accustomed to exploitation nervous because it challenges their organisation and structure. Capgemini is becoming more of an IT company and less of a consulting company, so innovation is less important as a source of competitive advantage."

Looking back at business process re-engineering, it is significant that both Michael Hammer and James Champy were principally involved in running a research service, rather than consulting. "We did not invent BPR," says Hammer, "we discovered it. When consulting firms talk about research, they are usually referring to a process where they set up a survey and collect answers to a specific question. But big ideas are far more serendipitous than this. We did not set out to solve a particular problem; we were just nosing about, talking to organisations that had been able to produce dramatic improvements, before we started to realise we were observing some consistent phenomena." "There was certainly a point when we said this is a big idea, let's write a book about it and create a new market, but it took us 2–3 years of looking at companies before we got to that point," adds Champy. "We kept going into companies which had invested heavily in IT without seeing much in the way of business improvement; they still had delays getting goods and services out of the door. We're both systems thinkers, so that's how we looked at the problem: what were the dysfunctions in the broader systems that underpinned these organisations? We realised that fragmentation and specialisation in work meant that organisations thought in terms of tasks rather than end-to-end processes, especially as they grew in scale. At the same time, we found some companies that had managed to buck that trend: an insurance company that had managed to collapse a 24-day lead time in sending out new policies to two hours; and a car manufacturer that had totally altered the way it worked." This depth of research paid tremendous dividends. "Re-engineering was, and still is, a very good idea," says Champy. "It really does enable organisations to change the nature of work at the most fundamental level."

"The timing was right, too," says Hammer. "We'd reached a point where many organisations felt stuck. If we'd launched the idea ten years earlier, organisations would not have been ready for it; ten years later, at the height of the dotcom boom, they would have been too busy to listen. The entertainer Eddie Fisher used to joke that it took him 20 years to become an overnight success, and that's how it felt with re-engineering. We first started talking about it in 1987, six years before the book came out, but we had already received such powerful, positive feedback that interest in the concept grew essentially by word of mouth, well ahead of the publication date."

One of the unfortunate side-effects of this apparently instant success was to encourage consulting firms to try to repeat it. "Lots of people said gosh, that's doing well, let's try to do that too," says Hammer. "In reality, it's very much a case of many being called but few being chosen. There aren't a large number of big ideas out there that consultancies can expect to articulate and capitalise on. The past decade has seen many big-idea books but few big ideas. Indeed, if you look at many of the substantial ideas that have emerged, before and after BPR, like those of Michael Porter or Clayton Christensen, they didn't come out of consulting firms in the first place. That's not a reflection on consultants' brainpower but on the environment of the consulting firm, which is designed less for reflection and more for problem-solving. To be successful in a major consulting firm requires real and rare skill, but it's not correlated with producing innovative ideas. The success we achieved with re-engineering is not necessarily replicable."

Champy is similarly scathing about the level of effort being put into research by today's consulting firms: "Consulting firms do not deliver a lot of value, certainly not the degree of business and process change clients deserve," he says. "They are stuck looking at the world through their own lens, developing ideas they think are important, based on work they have done, so what they come up with is incremental, not innovative. The hard news is that no single lens is sufficient to move performance."

Like Hammer, he is sceptical that the industry will ever come up with another blockbuster on the scale of re-engineering. Business schools are partly to blame because they create yet another lens that managers think they should look through. Boring and impenetrable business books do not help. Client cynicism cuts off the wellspring of new ideas at source. "A flow of ideas, most of which have not delivered business improvement, has given us a generation of disbelievers," he says. "They tried re-engineering, but their projects failed because they did not understand it. Now I tell my clients, if you want to undertake a change initiative, don't label it, because as soon as you do people stop taking it seriously." Ultimately, Champy is doubtful whether there are any big ideas waiting to be discovered. "It's not a question of how hard you think but how hard you look. Can we break through the way companies operate today? I still look and every once in a while I see a glimmer, but I don't think an idea on the scale of re-engineering is likely to be repeated in my lifetime."

For clients – and consultants – still brave enough to look, two lessons stand out.

Strength in numbers (1)

The first is that the ideas that genuinely change clients' lives for the better come from clients themselves, not from the think-tanks of consulting firms or business schools. Consultants cannot rely on one, two or even ten clients in the quest for new thinking. Hammer and Champy's work involved dozens of organisations before a clear pattern emerged. Looking at the business bestseller lists for the past few years shows that the books which have been almost endlessly researched – *Built to Last* by Jim Collins and Jerry Porras is a good example – are also the ones with the longest shelf lives. Where consultants (and academics) can play a valuable role is in seeing apparently isolated issues as part of an underlying system; clients see their own experience but not necessarily that of others.

"You only have to look at the quiet revolution in strategy consulting to see how important it is for consulting firms to develop their thinking alongside clients' thinking," suggests Meyer. "Strategy is a contingent question. In the 1920s, capital was tied up in plant and machinery, so strategy was about industrial planning because capital was the scarce resource to be allocated. By the time the Boston Consulting Group developed its experience curve, businesses were going through a stable time, so it made sense to talk about fighting for market share. In the 1980s, strategy was about quality management; today it is about the shift from competition to collaboration, becoming an adaptive organisation and finding the strategic tools to help manage this environment." At A.T. Kearney, Michael Tram agrees: "We have to be as close as we can to clients. For a firm like ours, innovation is essential; clients expect deep industry knowledge and creative approaches. It is completely implausible that we could put a group of consultants – however bright – in a room together by themselves and expect them to come up with the next big thing. We use our relationships with universities to challenge ourselves, but we have to get clients involved if we are to come up with approaches which will make a real difference, which are both innovative and pragmatic."

But the overwhelming majority of consulting firms have a scattergun strategy when it comes to thought leadership. If someone does a good piece of work for a client, they might be given the opportunity to convert their ideas into an approach that can be sold to other organisations.

Service or product-development budgets are given to business units or partners; sometimes something comes of it, but sometimes it does not. Many firms use research as post-justification: having had what they think is a good idea, they go and look for the facts to support it. All in all, a large part of the hundreds of millions of dollars spent by the consulting industry on developing new ideas every year is wasted.

So here is a trick question: which business consulting organisation has five Nobel laureates among its alumni? The answer is not one – but IBM's technology labs has.

IBM Business Consulting Services used to throw as much money at thought leadership as most of its leading-edge competitors, but in 2001 it decided to pull all such activities together under the auspices of the IBM Institute for Business Value. Based in a functional but grey business park on the outskirts of Amsterdam, it is a place where serious work is done. "Our aims are to enhance IBM's own understanding of business issues further, to demonstrate to the marketplace that we understand and develop them, and to educate our consultants in how to think about them," says Peter Korsten, who runs the institute in Europe, the Middle East and Africa. The institute is unusual in terms of the resources it controls (funding around 50–100 full-time consultants, typically seconded for two years) and the reputation it commands internally. "Coming here is seen to boost your career," says Korsten. "We attract the high-flyers, and we give them exposure to senior executives across the world they would not normally get."

The IBM Institute for Business Value is unusual in other respects, too. Like Hammer and Champy's, most of its research is done with clients. The research agenda is reviewed twice a year and is driven by initial analysis of issues facing clients. But although the research is based on clients' needs, it is not funded by them, nor is the output directly tied to sales targets. "We try to monitor what impact our research has in overall business value: media mentions, conference speaking engagements, client meetings, and so on," says Korsten. "But we are not looking at the financial return on a project-by-project basis. We have to be able to try things out. We never know where the gold nuggets are going to be, but we are more likely to find them if we apply a structured, systematic approach to a large number of issues."

Underpinning all this is the culture of a technology company – not a consulting company – that has been a long-term investor in research and development. Between 1993 and 2005, IBM generated more than 28,000 US patents, nearly triple the total of any US IT competitor during this time and surpassing the combined totals for Hewlett-Packard, Dell, Microsoft, Sun, Oracle, Intel, Apple, EMC, Accenture and EDS. In 2001 it became the first company to reach the milestone of receiving more than 3,000 patents in one year from the United States Patent and Trademark Office. It employs over 3,000 people in and spends $5 billion on technology research and development. Vacancies at its prestigious lab in Zurich (where those Nobel prizes were earned) regularly attract 300–1,000 applicants. In this context, the institute is probably only starting to scratch the surface of what IBM is capable of undertaking in business research. "For the largest clients with the most complex, global problems to solve, who else has the scale and resources to help?" asks Korsten. "Our aim is to set a new standard for research in the consulting industry."

Strength in numbers (2)
The second lesson is that consultants have to be able to demonstrate that, having understood the principles, they can apply solutions which work. "Thought leadership does not really carry much weight with us," said one client interviewed for this book. "Just because someone can write a paper, it doesn't mean they can do something in practice." "Thought leadership does have a bearing on whether we choose to work with that firm," said another, "but that's not always a good thing because it provides no guarantee of success. We have certainly had situations where we hired a company that had produced excellent material on paper on a particular subject, but the team we ended up with did not live up to the standards or expectations set."

"Ideas are only interesting if they lead to results. Clients should ask to see a dozen examples of what has been achieved before they 'buy' an idea," advises Hammer. "The main reason BPR succeeded is that it works. It was certainly an idea, but it was not just an idea. We can cite literally hundreds of cases where organisations have applied the ideas and got astonishing results. For instance, the sales process of a trucking company was taking 14 days to respond to queries. Now they can get back to customers in one day and their success rate in winning business has gone up by 70%. That's nothing to do with the abstract quality of the idea: it just works."

Bob Buday helped Hammer and Champy market their ideas in the early days of re-engineering and now runs his own firm helping consultants develop and market their thought leadership. "The use of the term 'thought leadership' has reached deafening proportions," he says. "What set re-engineering apart from the mass of consulting ideas we see on the market today was not just Hammer and Champy's novel diagnosis and prescriptions, but the indisputable and detailed examples they could point to of companies that had adopted the ideas at the heart of re-engineering and got results. One reason so many consulting ideas fall flat is that they're not backed up with enough – sometimes any – actual results. Business leaders are always on the lookout for new ideas. However, some consultancies that say they have expertise don't always have a strong ability to deliver that expertise with results."

How firms take an idea and turn it into a consulting service is crucial, Buday argues. "You have to be able to translate complex concepts into crystal-clear consulting frameworks," he says. "You need people who can be trained and who can train others. You need investment in method development and training and development. If you look at this as a pure marketing exercise – and many firms do – then you run the risk of creating demand for a compelling consulting idea that you really can't deliver. That's what happened with Index: despite having lots of talented consultants, the firm didn't devote enough resources to giving those consultants effective re-engineering methodology, training and development. Other consulting firms such as Accenture and Deloitte, which invest heavily in methodology and training and development, ran away with the business. The sense pervades the consulting industry today that you can float an idea and wait to see if clients are interested before you work out how to deliver it. I'd like to see equal attention paid to how to deliver the ideas, not just to market them."

Information is still power

No matter how brilliant a management idea is, in the hands of a cavalier consultant it can prove disastrous. Consulting firms have to attract the attention of clients ("share of mind"). An article in the *Harvard Business Review* (HBR) is generally reckoned to earn a consultant tens of thousands of dollars, and this is only the tip of the media iceberg. In a highly competitive market, they need to demonstrate their credentials faster and more loudly than their rivals. Even where genuine research is carried out, what internal control does a consulting firm's research team have over the way their marketing colleagues sell an idea? IBM virtually invented the term "e-business" in its marketing in the mid-1990s; it is now doing the same with the concept of "business on demand". The reputation of IBM's institute will inevitably be linked to the way in which IBM's marketing machine takes its ideas into the marketplace.

Champy recalls ferocious arguments with editors about the language he and Hammer used; indeed, their first publisher pulled out on the grounds that it ceased to believe the book would ever be finished. It is a point reinforced by Buday: "Marketing is still a relatively new discipline where consulting firms are concerned. Applying traditional promotional channels and tools – brochures, advertisements, or booths at trade conferences – simply does not work when it comes to thought leadership. You need educational marketing channels, such as books, HBR articles, white papers, conference presentations, and so on, which executives do not view as blatantly promotional. In addition, the ideas you then convey through those channels must be in clear terms: plain English not consulting jargon; accessible but not simplistic."

Clients need to know what is happening in terms of demand (Which other organisations have adopted this idea? What benefits have they obtained from it?) and supply (What do suppliers gain from promoting the idea? Why is it in their interest that clients buy it?). There is no shortage of potential sources. Business journals and consulting firms' websites bristle with case studies, but the former are more interested in creating newsworthy copy and the latter will naturally highlight only the positive examples. Moreover, for every success story, there is a failure: individual instances mean little either way. What clients need is a better, more informed idea of overall trends, and this is where business research companies come in. As there are few opportunities for clients to speak frankly to each other, they have to rely on intermediaries to do their due diligence for them.

Consulting firms take research companies seriously, too. Most large firms have teams of dedicated account managers whose role is to facilitate access to the organisation without overstepping the line in terms of marketing to them. They recognise the influence research companies have with clients, especially when it comes to selecting the right consultants for a particular piece of work.

Business research is big business, but is it good business? Companies researching the consulting industry rely on consulting firms' co-operation to gain access to the right people. If an analyst is especially negative about a firm, that firm could refuse access in the future. Research companies, too, are under pressure to produce results, to get reports on hot topics to the market as quickly as possible, and this can mean cutting corners in the research process. But the most serious questions are raised by the economic model underpinning most research firms.

"Research companies play a crucial role in determining the market value of public companies and the market perception of private ones," says Richard Granger at the UK National Health Service's National Programme for IT. "They charge clients for their research reports and consulting firms for internal advice. We paid £1.5m to one research company to help us assess potential suppliers, but the bill was the wrong way round. We taught them more about large-scale IT projects, pricing arrangements and negotiation than they taught us."

Off the record, many consulting firms say that their ratings by a research company rise in proportion to the amount of research they buy from them. "We were in the bottom 25%," said one managing partner. "When we bought $150,000 of research from them, we suddenly found ourselves bumped up the rankings, even though we hadn't done anything different." "We're seriously considering cancelling all our subscriptions and saying so publicly, because we're sure others will follow suit," said another. "At the moment, we'll keep paying because we're frightened we'll be singled out and downgraded."

A management concept is only as good as the results it produces. Clients need to ask more questions and talk to the organisations involved to see if what the consultants say is really true. But they also need to be pragmatic: they need to find out what goes wrong; they should not expect any management concept to work 100% of the time; and they need to carry out due diligence.

"Clients could also benefit from talking to each other," says Buday. "If I was a buyer, I'd want to go to all the events and talk to the people in the audience who had used a particular firm or tried a particular approach. I'd want to know how a firm implements a concept, the problems it encountered, and the ups and downs. Hearing about these things makes a concept more believable. Not enough kicking of tyres goes on." Even consultants agree: "Clients need to speak to more clients," says David Barrett at Corven. "For all the talk about clients being more sophisticated, they're not always as smart as they could be. They often take references late in the process when a decision has effectively been made and they're making sure there are no reasons why they shouldn't hire a chosen firm. They should make these checks earlier to inform the choice of firm and have a conversation on the lines of 'tell me how they worked, what their style is', and so on."

The trouble is that, apart from conferences, there are few forums where clients can get together and talk. Technology companies have user groups, but where are their equivalent in the consulting industry? "I don't see any role for a consultants' user group," says Dick Cavanagh, president and chief executive of The Conference Board. "Choosing consultants is a bit like picking a doctor or finding someone to do your taxes. Organisations have to decide this for themselves. However, we often get people at Conference Board meetings saying things like: have you used such and such a firm recently; do you know someone who's good at such and such a problem; what are firms charging for doing this? But there's a limit as to how far you can go. Every consulting assignment is different, and it's not easy to compare them in abstract."

"If I were an executive, I'd have three or four people out there who would think and read on my behalf," says Champy. "Busy executives should ask themselves: who are my agents, who are my sources of ideas? I listen to smart people. If I'm speaking at a seminar, and I can see there are some interesting people talking, I'll stick around to hear what they have to say. You should never rely on just one person, one consulting firm, because they'll never have the whole answer. Resolving complex issues requires more than one tool."

"I get very suspicious when people talk about the next wave," says Hans-Paul Buerkner of the Boston Consulting Group, a firm which, more than most, can lay claim to a heritage of genuine innovation. "The most important thing clients and consulting firms can do is exchange ideas and test and challenge their operational feasibility. If you have simplified an idea to the point where it is applicable to many clients, you have lost the opportunity to create competitive advantage. Past waves may have contributed to growth in the consulting industry, but they also gave a false sense of security. No one should jump to the conclusion that there is one big idea which will solve everything; the same idea may yield different results under different conditions. Truly great companies do many things right, not just one thing."

A missed opportunity

Many clients complain about lack of transparency among consultants, but before doing so they should examine their own attitudes, particularly their reluctance to exchange information. There are some consulting projects that should be treated as genuinely confidential, but the majority of them are not. Clients could gain so much valuable information if, when considering a new initiative and hiring a consulting firm to help them evaluate and/or implement it, they were to solicit feedback from organisations that were already evaluating and/or implementing it. Transparency starts at home.

12 Metamorphosis

The consulting industry and consulting firms

"THE CONSULTING INDUSTRY has all the principal features of a profession," says Lynton Barker, chairman of Hedra, a technology and business change consultancy and 2004 president of the Management Consultancies Association in London. "It is sufficiently large in scale to support a community of individuals who agree on what consulting is. It is global and recognised throughout the world. It consists of a core group of skills and entails professional activity such as the ability to organise and communicate, to recruit and train new individuals, and to promote its own knowledge. It has services that can be priced and for which there is sustained demand."

Unlike medicine, law, accountancy or architecture, however, there is no governing body to monitor standards or guarantee ethics, and no professional qualification by which individual consultants demonstrate their expertise to clients and employers. Consequently, consulting has to find other ways of demonstrating professionalism. The pressing need to demonstrate good practice to clients, and, more recently, the demands of increased collaboration with other consulting firms, are ushering in a new era of collective activity for the industry.

Hitherto, consulting firms have relied on their individual consultants to form and cement relationships with clients, to deliver on their promises and to act overall in an ethical manner. They have regarded the quality of their people as their most important source of competitive advantage, so they have been unwilling to cede this fundamental role to an independent arbiter. "Commercial success depends on the client relationship," argues Mike Bird, a partner at Kepner-Tregoe, "and clients will trust individual consultants at a personal level and through them the firm. One hurdle for greater aggregation of firms is that when you join with others, it's difficult not to dilute the intensity of the relationship with the client. Consultants also have egos. They believe they can solve any problem and that they don't need the support of other firms."

The previous chapter looked at how clients' ability to make effective use of consultants was diminished by their continuing reluctance to exchange information and act in greater accord. This chapter examines the ways in which consulting firms are beginning to work together and how they will need to in the future.

Collective activity in the consulting industry

The consulting industry does have its trade associations – the Association of Management Consulting Firms (AMCF) and the Management Consultancies Association (MCA) in the UK, equivalent national organisations in the rest of Europe such as the Bundesverbandes Deutscher Unternehmensberater (BDU) in Germany, and the pan-European organisation of trade associations, the European Federation of Management Consulting Associations (FEACO) – and increasing numbers of consulting firms are electing to belong to them. The MCA, for example, estimates that its members now account for 60% of the UK consulting market. However, the role of these associations remains fuzzy. Is their job to lobby on behalf of their members, to set standards, to facilitate lobbying and knowledge-sharing, or are they simply clubs for like-minded people? The main problem is that consulting firms have little idea of what they can achieve by acting in concert as opposed to independently. Most firms believe that they alone are best placed to promote and protect their interests. For some, accepting that collective action is necessary or useful would be an admission of weakness.

Nevertheless, direct and indirect collective activity is widespread and is focused on five areas:

- **Consortia and commercial consolidation.** Client demand for specialist skills, coupled with the operational need to achieve economies of scale, continually pushes consulting firms together. Small firms may merge with other small firms; large firms may acquire small ones; small and large firms may find themselves working together on projects.
- **Intellectual property and knowledge arbitrage.** The increasing complexity of consulting projects makes it harder for one consulting firm to have all the skills and experience required. Recognising this, more consulting firms are working together to develop new ideas and jointly taking them to clients. Commercial aggregation is also being seen through more standardised descriptions of the work consultants undertake, such as similar titles for services and descriptions of what people do, and more consistency in how people's roles are described.
- **Lobbying.** For most industries, lobbying focuses on policy-related

issues, principally on regulation that may affect the sector. For the consulting industry, much of this is oriented towards the federal government in the United States or towards Brussels on European Union issues. The scale of the public-sector market for consulting and the publicity surrounding it means that a good public image is something firms will collaborate to achieve.

- **Resource management.** Employment standards are converging. Salaries have become more uniform as have management practices, including the employment of freelance consultants. Employment data – for example on salaries – are increasingly shared among firms.

- **Codes of best practice and good ethics.** Working through trade associations, procurement departments and other client interest groups, many consulting firms have agreed to follow codes of practice aimed at making their client relationships more open and accountable and often drawn from the standards already adopted internally by firms. Even where such codes are voluntary, commercial interest provides an effective carrot to get consulting firms to sign up to client-specific codes, such as those in the public sector. The Sarbanes-Oxley Act in the United States has also imposed a greater need for scrutiny and consulting firms and associations are striving for a consistent approach to this.

Awareness is dawning that the principal issue for firms is not overcoming the competitive responses of other consulting firms, but working together to improve clients' understanding of what consulting can do for them. In other words, the real challenge is how to expand the market, not how to beat other firms. "Consulting differs from, say, auditing, because the employment of a consulting firm is discretionary," says Barker. "The sustainability of the industry depends on its ability to adapt to the needs of its clients."

Consequently, pressure on consulting firms to collaborate more is increasing. "The days of the generalist are numbered," says Mark Hatcher, director and head of public affairs at Cubbit Consulting. "They're now finding it hard to survive, and they need expertise through joint ventures to bid for and carry out projects." Clients are more sophisticated. "Buyers are more intelligent about their needs," continues Hatcher. "They have more experience of past projects and relationships and some are ex-consultants." Client scepticism has increased in proportion to their knowledge, making the collective behaviour of the consulting industry a more important issue. Bad news is good news from the media's point of view, and high-profile failures are highlighted while successes are not. With taxpayers' money financing large public-sector projects, a new dimension to the industry has opened up. "The consulting market has matured from a sales-led activity to a marketing-led activity, and there is a constant desire to widen the market. As a result, reputation has become even more important," says Bird.

Collaborate, or compete?

These pressures mean that the consulting industry must make some hard choices regarding collaboration between rival firms. Indeed, a metamorphosis is already under way on the important issues of standards and ethics, reputation and thought leadership. "As an industry, we need to demonstrate we are aware of clients' concerns by creating, and using, a common ethical framework," argues Bird. Standards need to be raised further in practice and in perception, and a better defence of the value consultants contribute and new thinking on management issues should be developed.

Standards and ethics

"Ethics should be important to a consulting firm, but they do not have to be," admits Peter Brown, vice-chairman of Kurt Salmon Associates and chairman of the AMCF. "Most sectors start out with elements of professionalism only to lose them over time. Professional values need constant renewal. Within Kurt Salmon, we talk about our values constantly; we hold up examples of where we followed them and of where we failed them. We regularly revisit them, and they are a core part of our training programmes because we believe everyone is responsible for applying and enforcing them."

The need for the industry to raise its game in setting standards is widely recognised among consulting firms. "Consultants must demonstrate high standards of ethics, and common expectations must be set for what they are. Clients have a reasonable expectation that consultants will comply with minimum standards," says Bird. Brown argues that greater openness is crucial: "Clients would like to see a consistent level of disclosure about business relationships that may influence specific recommendations. If a firm has a partnership with a particular hardware or software company, clients need to be aware that this could influence their suggestions. Undisclosed agreements do not serve the consulting industry well. Many firms already make such information available, but some do not, making it difficult for clients to compare like with like."

He also points out that current guidelines often focus on advisory work and take no account of systems implementation and outsourcing. "The ethical environment in which consultants operate is more challenging than it used to be, because the consulting industry is less homogeneous. Guidelines for advisory work are not always relevant to someone installing a new IT system. Today, half of all 'consulting' is done by companies whose main business is selling packaged solutions. They may have alliances with or equity stakes in particular vendors which may be of great benefit to clients so far as providing an integrated solution is concerned, but clients need to be aware of them and understand the implications. The logical place for such guidelines to be developed is in the consulting trade associations." Many associations are already on the case. "We have recently revised and updated our membership criteria," says Sarah Taylor, director of the MCA, "and we have a process by which we audit members' compliance with them."

But the perennial problem with standards and ethics is that they are a matter of choice, and unethical firms can freeload on the standards of others. "In regulated professions there are barriers to entry, but anyone can become a consultant," says Taylor. "A variety of firms have entered the consulting market, including auditors and actuarial firms, marketing, PR, advertising, IT services and property firms. Some big corporations have consulting arms that now offer services to external clients." "There isn't a cohesive industry," says Barker. "It's too complex for single, integrated visions." Moreover, as Betsy Kovacs, executive director of the AMCF, points out: "The public is savvy enough to know that professional codes do not always protect against incompetence or greed. The power of the market regulates – there is the retribution of the buyer in the long run."

Reputation management
Continuing commercial aggregation means that large firms need to uphold a reputation. They need to demand a high level of professionalism and ethical standards from their consultants, which in turn should lead to more transparent ethical standards. "One of the challenges for management consultancy associations and federations, such as the BDU or FEACO, is to become better known to clients by making their existing codes of conduct more visible," comments Rémi Redley, president of the

BDU and FEACO.

It is one thing to ensure ethical standards are adhered to, but quite another for clients to perceive this to be the case. Most consulting firms are acutely conscious of the reputational damage the industry has suffered in the last few years. On the no smoke without fire principle, they admit there is a degree of truth in the accusations typically levelled at them, but they would also argue that much of the public opprobrium stems from ignorance. "There is a question about how far management consultants demonstrate sensitivity to public interest. The trade associations are trying hard to advance understanding about management consulting, enabling the transmission of knowledge, comparison of skills, and so on, but it does not begin to compare with the learned professions," says Hatcher. At the MCA, Taylor agrees that although there has been a sea change in consulting firms' awareness of the industry's collective reputation in the past few years, more needs to be done: "The reputation and perception of consultants are hugely important. The future of the industry depends on changing perceptions of it. There's a lot of emotion around the use of consultants, particularly on big change-related programmes, and people can feel threatened. The media also have an anti-consultant and anti-business bias, and the work consultants do is often complex, confidential and difficult to talk about. The marketing and press-related activities of trade associations like the MCA can help raise awareness and change perceptions. We have best management practice awards, have developed a good relationship with the media and provide the users of consulting with advice. But we need to work more as an industry to demonstrate the value of consulting." "We need to move the perception of the industry to match clients' actual experiences," agrees Bruce Petter, Taylor's colleague and executive director of the MCA. "Its reputation has not kept pace with the reality of consulting and the value it adds to industry."

But why is it so difficult to prove that value? The problem stems primarily from the difficulties in linking consulting work with broader-based measurements of business performance. Clearly, a consulting company installing a new customer relationship management (CRM) system, for example, can be measured in terms of the speed and costs of delivery, and the finished system can be tested against the initial set of requirements. It may even be possible to benchmark users' attitudes: does the new system help them do their jobs better? A new system, which is faithful to the original design and satisfies end-users, will undoubtedly contribute to improved business performance, but it is not always easy to show a direct, causal link between the system and its ultimate goal of improving sales and/or profitability. Moreover, the benefits of that CRM system are quite different from those that may result from, say, a management training programme. Management capability is far more difficult to measure, but even if it could be quantified how would its value be compared with a new CRM system?

Measuring the cost of consultants is simpler than measuring the value, which is why clients generally focus on cost. However, consulting firms have recently woken up to the importance of thinking more carefully about the thorny issue of "benefits realisation". Effort is now being put into finding ways to articulate, if not always quantify, the value consultants bring, but there is still no consistent way of doing this. It is not possible to point to a simple figure and say this is what consultants have contributed to the economy.

Thought leadership

Consulting is a high-intellect activity, and demonstrating its thought leadership and innovation should be crucial in representing its professionalism and forging new markets. "The essence of a profession is that it is 'research-based'," argues Hatcher. "It advances knowledge and understanding, for which a body of people is responsible; extending the frontiers of knowledge and sharing and communicating knowledge are what they do. As such, there is a lot more scope for thought leadership in the industry than at present."

Thought leadership may be one of the defining features of a profession, but the sheer variety of consulting work once again creates a unique challenge. "The sustainability of the consulting industry is not based on the requirement for people to use the thought leadership it generates, but instead depends on adapting that thinking to the needs of a specific business," says Barker.

Most of the activity that purports to be "thought leadership" is superficial, based on a limited amount of data and field testing. Firms increasingly see it as marketing and as a central means of differentiating themselves. True advances in business solutions are in a different category and are more closely guarded by the firms responsible for them.

The point that the entire consulting industry benefits from innovation and thought leadership that expands the market for consulting services seems to have been missed. When will the consulting industry recognise the need to air and test business innovations, and to collaborate and publish tried and tested methodology? This will be an important means of accelerating the knowledge arbitrage that the industry contributes to economic progress, and is an essential step if consultants are to help bring about business change.

The threat of regulation

Where does this leave regulation? "To provide innovative solutions and help companies to be competitive, the profession is constantly moving into new areas," says Redley. "To develop and impose a legal framework would be inappropriate as it would be contrary to the role of management consultants." Others agree. "You don't want regulation of an intellectually sophisticated discipline. One argument for the current arrangement is that it's too broad to identify what regulation would be," says Hatcher. "There isn't a cohesive industry," argues Barker. "It's too complex for a single, integrated set of rules. Consultants respond to needs; they don't follow a standard process."

Law-based regulation would be unlikely to achieve any desired outcomes and would not engage professionals in the aims and ethics of their own industry. In short, it would undermine, not reinforce, the professionalism of the consulting sector. As Bird says, "You can regulate by law but this tends to be bad; you simply get compliance with the letter of the law and not its spirit. Self-regulation is far better because it sets out what you aspire to."

But self-regulation also raises questions. Most important is who should regulate and what should be regulated. "There is a hierarchy in ethics: individual ethics should be higher than those of the firm, and those of the firm higher than those of industry. For example, there could be a situation where consultants could be pressured to compromise their principles to meet the demands of their firm. Being able to appeal to an external ethical framework could enable them to resist such pressure," suggests Bird. "Ultimately, any regulatory environment needs to cover both firm and individual behaviour."

"In self-regulation," says Hatcher, "the challenge will be how far the public perception of management consultants is the same as consultants' own perception of their standards. There's a need to communicate value to the end-user as well as the client." "There's always more that can be done as a collective," concludes Kovacs. "We've come a long way in terms of setting standards, providing opportunities to exchange ideas and representing the industry to external audiences. But we still need to do more to help clients understand the value of consulting."

Metamorphosis now

"Enron produced a lot of scepticism about professional advisers," says the Boston Consulting Group's Hans-Paul Buerkner, "but these memories will pass – if professional firms don't provide further examples of bad advice. Every firm tries hard to avoid this. We all think far more carefully now about whether we can actually do what the client is asking us to do. But the pressures are enormous. We can't possibly guarantee that every individual team will always do everything right."

Change – metamorphosis, no less – is already under way in the consulting industry. It began with a wave of consolidation and mergers and the end of a long run of "next big things" which fuelled consulting demand in the 1990s. Activity now focuses on rebuilding the reputation and behaviour of the consulting industry and on self-regulation. In parallel, firms are learning from each other through collaborating on client work and changing internally as a result. Understanding clients better has become a priority. What form the collective conscience of the consulting industry will eventually take is by no means clear. However, the pressure for collective action and change at all levels is undeniable. Somewhere, deep inside its secretive cocoon, the consulting industry is maturing.

13 Relationship

Clients and consulting firms

"**T**RUST IS A BIG ISSUE," says Mary Cockcroft of Pagoda Consulting. "Trust was the basis on which relationships were built. Trust has gone out of the relationship, and anyone who can inject an element of trust via their value proposition will have a significant advantage. The days when consultants could win work simply by promising a 30% reduction in costs have passed, to be replaced by a much more rigid scope and a focus on the delivery of benefits."

The model for the client–consultant relationship has traditionally been one-to-one: an organisation would have a contract with one consulting firm covering one piece of work. Clients used different consulting firms in different areas but, by and large, these areas did not overlap and each could be treated as a discrete unit. As the term implies, it was as much a relationship between two people as a contract between two organisations.

Although most clients and consultants still think and talk in terms of "relationships", the interaction between the two sides is more complex:

- On the client side, more people have become involved in the procurement process, partly because of the increased scale and scope of some consulting topics, and partly because of growing oversight from corporate procurement departments.
- On the consulting side, the traditional means by which consultants have built relationships – marketing, selling and delivering their services – are being superseded in a world in which several consulting firms are involved in a given project. It has become harder to say where one consulting project starts and another finishes, so the success of one consulting firm may well depend on the work of other consultants.

This chapter will explore the interaction between clients and consultants at an organisational level. Rather than focusing on personal relationships, it will look at how, as the role of consultants has moved from being purely advisory to involving execution and even financing, clients have sought to retain control by establishing new contractual arrangements and governance structures.

The professionalisation of procurement

When the dotcom bubble burst in spring 2001, it left an army of underfunded consulting clients and overpaid consultants. Dotcoms went bust and larger corporations cut their budgets, abandoning some projects and deferring many more indefinitely. The hero of the hour became the procurement department, which was promoted from relative obscurity by the overriding need to reduce costs. Its remit was enlarged to include a new and substantial budget item: professional service fees. Faced with around 25% surplus capacity, consulting firms were not in a position to complain.

As a result, almost all consulting firms have found themselves facing more formal processes for winning work, longer sales cycles and higher business development costs, even for comparatively small-scale projects. Most believe that procurement teams focus too much on price. At the Management Consulting Group, Kevin Parry, the chief executive, believes that procurement processes are increasingly a waste of time. "There are some professional procurement departments staffed by sophisticated people who know what they want to get out of using consultants, but the majority are more accustomed to buying paper clips. They ask for endless information which we suspect they never read." One consultant tells the story of turning up for a meeting about some follow-on work with a long-standing client, a major corporation. Expecting to see the person he normally reported to on the client side, he was instead seated in a corridor next to his competitors and had to make his pitch to a group of people he had never met before. "They wanted us to lose our nerve and offer substantial discounts. It was like the dog being asked to beg for the bone."

But it is not just price that bugs consultants. From their point of view, professional procurement departments also get in the way of relationship building. The people with whom the consultant works most closely, and therefore gets to know best, are no longer the people with the purse strings.

It would be tempting to view such client behaviour as a temporary phenomenon, likely to diminish as demand for consulting starts to grow more quickly than supply. However, few people think this will be the case. Steve Cardell, chief executive of Axon, a middle-sized consulting firm specialising in enterprise resource planning implementation, says:

"When I entered the industry 12 years ago, consulting was a trust-based relationship. It is quite different today as clients are prepared to play consulting firms off against each other. There are many more shared risk/benefits deals, and clients are more aggressive about saying that if we won't work to their terms, we won't get the work. Aggressive procurement techniques, applied at an early stage in the sales cycle, might be appropriate if you are negotiating a contract for an IT project, but they are difficult to apply to areas like change management. Clients are reacting by cutting out intangible activities. It is not the economy that is driving this, but an attitude of mind."

The end of the amateur

Leading the change has been public-sector procurement departments. Professional services have become an increasingly important cog in the government machine: as public-sector institutions have shed people in pursuit of ever lower costs, consultants are increasingly used to plug the knowledge gap. Beau Grant has 20 years' experience in procurement at federal and state levels; he is also a spokesperson for the National Institute of Government Procurement (NIPG) in the United States. "Consultants are often brought in for a specific purpose but end up staying longer than regular employees," he says. "But I'm not sure we manage these consultants effectively." Grant sees several problems with the conventional way in which consulting work is bought and sold: woolly thinking about why consultants are being brought in; a lack of performance standards that can be tied to quantifiable deliverables; and inadequate attention to measuring a consultant's suitability for a piece of work. "We allow consultants to come in and tell us what we need to do without giving any preliminary thought to what we think we need. We hand over a vague brief to someone who is not well versed in the project but who is supposed to negotiate the contract for a price that is usually exceeded. We end up not knowing what we've got and paying for something we're not sure we needed, and are left picking up the pieces when it doesn't work." It might be tempting to point an accusing finger at consultants for selling over-aggressively in a shrinking market, but Grant is clear where the fault – and therefore the remedy – lies. "It's *caveat emptor*. If a client's willing to pay a consultant by the hour, there's no way the consultant is going to stand back and try not to sell more work."

The underlying problem, he believes, is that many of the people who initiate the process of hiring consultants do not have appropriate training. "The only way to fix this is to develop specialist skills in buying consulting services: in writing specifications, for example. The attitude at the moment, that anyone is capable of doing this, is a legacy of an era in which managers were not expected to have in-depth expertise."

Does hiring former consultants provide a way round this? More than anyone else, they should be familiar with the tricks of the trade. Grant is not convinced. "The problem with bringing people in from the private sector is that they have little real understanding of how government works."

Instead, Grant – and the NIPG – would like to see people being certified in procurement. "We need to train those requesting consulting support to define their requirements precisely, but we also need procurement officers whose job is to take those requirements and translate them into a formal statement, taking the business's objectives and redefining them as deliverables to which costs can be attached." He would also like procurement officers to take an independent role, scrutinising decisions to hire consultants and making sure that those selected win the work because of their specialist skills rather than their political connections. "Their role should be to ensure a fair and equitable process by developing briefs, soliciting and evaluating proposals, and establishing how success will be measured." The focus must be on outcomes, not outputs. "Consultants can make a career out of open-ended contracts," says Grant, "and government has not been very good at getting beyond this because it has not historically focused on outputs. Many projects go awry because of this alone."

The situation is, however, complicated by clients – the federal government in particular, says Grant – which are bad at defining the baseline they are starting from. "There's been so much upheaval that a lot of corporate knowledge has been lost and this hampers organisations' ability to measure what they do." Even finding out how much they are spending on consultants at a given moment can be a tough assignment, and most are not accustomed to sharing this kind of information among different functions and business units. More effective monitoring by centralised procurement teams will help, but with the intense pressure on costs, there is often little money left to invest in managing contracts once they have been signed.

High-level information, not low-level prices

This has certainly been the experience at AstraZeneca, a pharmaceuticals giant. The company uses consultants in a number of ways: as managers for large-scale projects involving substantial change to the business or as systems integration experts undertaking the implementation of a new enterprise resource planning system. But there has been a gradual shift away from handing over projects to teams of consultants. Instead, AstraZeneca is likely to make more use of its own staff, confining external input to where it is really needed. Discrete tasks are now being given to freelance contractors or offshore service providers. "We want both sides to be able to walk away from a completed project with the satisfaction of a job done well," says Janice Smethurst, who is responsible for overseeing AstraZeneca's overall use of consultants. "We were concerned that we didn't have sufficient control of the largest projects because of the number of people involved. When you're caught up in a project and you're up against a tight deadline, if a problem comes up and a consultant says I've got someone I can bring in, it's not easy to challenge that. Responsibility lies with the client to make sure consultants are being effectively and efficiently used."

In 2002, AstraZeneca developed a company-wide policy for engaging external advisers which ensured that all contracts over a certain limit went out to tender. It is a two-pronged initiative. Larger projects have the input of someone from the central procurement team who advises on supplier selection and management. At the same time, business units have to submit information on how they are using consultants so that the company can build up a comprehensive picture of where its money is going and reduce the duplication of effort likely in any large, global organisation.

"We've also built an infrastructure around this," says Smethurst, who oversees the process. "We've got a standard approach across all business units and we've installed a system which allows us to carry out more of the process online. We can issue a 'request for proposals' (RFP) electronically and bidders can post questions to a noticeboard; these can be public (all the other suppliers will see the question and our response) or private (they remain confidential because they're relevant to only one supplier)."

In the future, online tools may fundamentally change the procurement process. Some organisations are already experimenting with reverse auctions, where consulting firms put in open bids for work, are allowed to see the lowest bid and can reduce their bid if they choose. But these will never, Smethurst believes, become the sole basis of selection. "There's definitely a drive to do this in professional services," she says, "but winning work will still be dependent on having credibility, on being the best firm for the job, whether that means the best able to demonstrate an innovative approach, the longest track record, or the greatest expertise. Lowest rarely comes into the equation. The main thing is that you find the right consulting firm and make sure their charges reflect reasonable market rates."

The picture is similar at Barclays. Antony Ray, Smethurst's equivalent there, says that the company's overall use of consultants has decreased in recent years as the level of in-house skills has grown. "As a procurement team, our responsibility is to put together a preferred-supplier list through a combination of market research and competitive tendering. We begin by issuing 'requests for information' to find out what these firms do in more detail and to identify which suppliers have the skills we are likely to require in the short and medium term. At the end of the sourcing process, we end up with a detailed matrix of who does what and what they are good at, which is a vast improvement on the high-level information we used to work from. When an assignment comes up this may be given directly to a preferred supplier when below a pre-agreed value, with the larger assignments being bid for competitively among selected preferred suppliers." Ray's responsibilities do not stop when the contract is signed. "We have to ensure that milestones are met; we have regular review meetings with suppliers to check things are on track. We want to avoid the situation where the consultants have de facto control."

Suppliers, he says, are stoical about this, and most, if not always happily, are prepared to work within the new frameworks. Business managers, the end-users of consultants, have also had to learn that they need to go through a rigorous selection process. "It's good for a consulting firm to have contacts within Barclays. It means they're more familiar with the organisation, who to talk to, how to get things done. But the choice of consultants has to be a logical decision; the personal side should not come into it too much. Consulting firms overplay the 'trusted adviser' card. It's perfectly possible to have a good working relationship with someone you've not necessarily known for a number of years."

Here to stay?
The role of central procurement functions has undoubtedly been boosted by increased cost-consciousness among clients in recent years and an oversupply of consultants, but will their importance continue to grow as the market picks up?

Although few organisations will admit to it publicly, there is already frustration among the internal customers of procurement departments, particularly among senior executives who are accustomed to having their own way. For some people, procurement policies are bureaucratic overkill, and as the restrictions on consulting budgets are relaxed, they will seek to circumvent the rules, rather than play by them. But although such mavericks may be able to buck the trend, they are unlikely to reverse it completely. In the first place, it will be hard to disentangle the policies and procedures that procurement departments have put in place. As every organisation knows, the difficulties of embedding processes are nothing compared with those of trying to remove them. Moreover, there is no economic incentive for clients to retreat. One of the benefits of centralised procurement is that it provides an overview of expenditure on consultants, which most organisations have not had in the past and many still lack. This information will prove far more effective in reducing expenditure on consultants than having procurement professionals involved, however effective they are at negotiation. It reduces the possibility of two business units hiring two consulting firms to work on the same issue; it may also help clients distribute more work among a smaller number of consulting firms, thus reducing the length of time the latter spend learning about the client at the start of a new project.

What is likely to change, however, is the threshold at which the procurement function becomes involved. A slight relaxation in spending limits combined with a backlash from senior executives will mean that more projects – particularly small-scale, primarily strategic and advisory work – will evade the procurement radar. Those involved in procurement may complain, but they will find it hard to stem the flow altogether.

Standing on each other's shoulders: the move to multi-sourcing

For some time clients have been pushing consulting firms in contradictory directions. They want access to specialised skills. If they are going to pay hundreds, perhaps thousands, of dollars a day for a consultant, they want to be sure that he or she is an experienced, exceptionally well-qualified, preferably world-class expert. Anything less and they will ask themselves why they bother. But at the same time, they want to tie consulting firms to results, often by involving them in the execution of any recommendations they may make. The demand for specialist input puts consulting firms under pressure to fragment: consultants are more likely to form spin-off boutiques if their specific skills are in particular demand. However, the need for follow-through pulls them together, as more people with a greater range of skills are involved.

These conflicting trends have been evident since the early 1990s. The first response of the consulting industry was the "one-stop shop", the notion that all a client's professional service needs could be fulfilled by a single firm offering accounting, tax, corporate finance and legal help as well as broadly based consulting and IT services. Although it has not entirely disappeared, this model has foundered on clients' unwillingness to believe that a single firm could offer the world-class skills they sought across the board. A jack of all trades, the one-stop shop was inevitably perceived as the master of none. The collapse of Enron increased clients' suspicion that the model was designed to cross-sell services rather than add value to them. Indeed, there is little evidence that the one-stop shop was effective. Even within a broad-based IT and consulting practice, there was little synergy between purchasers, and consulting firms were still pigeon-holed into one or other role.

As an alternative, some consulting firms have adopted the role of a prime contractor. Rather than assume they had to supply a client's entire needs from their own staff, they subcontracted specialist work to smaller firms or to sole contractors while guaranteeing the project's overall budget, timetable and results. Economic uncertainty bolstered this approach as it enabled consulting firms to convert fixed labour costs (consultants on their payroll) into variable ones (consultants on someone else's payroll). Once again, clients have begged to differ. Although prime contracting may satisfy their dual need for specialist skills and follow-through, it concentrates a great deal of power in the hands of the lead supplier. Clients have little choice about which specialists are brought in; if their relationship with the prime contractor breaks down, the rest of the supply chain may collapse as well; and they may end up paying premium rates to an organisation which is little more than a shop window. As with so much else, the lessons clients have learned in dealing with technology are now being applied to consulting – do not rely too much on a single supplier; do not lock yourself into one platform.

The buzzword now is multi-sourcing. Rather than ceding responsibility to one supplier, some clients are encouraging consortia of firms to work together on a more equitable basis, with their own staff taking on the central co-ordination. "The problem with the single supplier model is that it's the consulting equivalent of the relationship between a major debtor and a bank: the larger the debt, the less the bank can risk a default," says Richard Granger of the UK National Health Service. "The debtor ends up being able to set its own timetable for making payments. Where a client depends on just one supplier, the balance of power can shift substantially in the supplier's favour."

But Granger says the consulting industry is changing. "Ten years ago you couldn't get people from different firms to work together; there was too much personal animosity. That has improved, but there is still some way to go, when you compare practices with other industries, such as the oil industry, where multi-sourcing has been standard practice for many years. We have to balance the carrot and the stick, offering the top-performing suppliers the chance to earn extra fees at the expense of the worst-performing ones. In a sense, it's an ecosystem where the suppliers at the front are picking up work from those at the back."

"Working on the Olympics is something to tell your grandchildren about," says Patrick Adiba, and he should know. Atos Origin, where he works, is responsible for the world's largest sports IT contract, acting as the International Olympic Committee's worldwide information technology partner in Salt Lake City in 2002 (operated by Schlumberger-Sema), Athens in 2004, Turin in 2006 and Beijing in 2008. Maintaining high standards in the face of widely varying local infrastructures and bringing together a mass of specialist technology firms that have to co-operate, the Olympics puts the firm under unique pressure. "The expectation is that the IT will be flawless, and people do not necessarily appreciate the effort, expense and complexity behind the scenes. We are responsible for the integrated solution including sending data to press," says Adiba. "Not capturing the results is not an option."

The Athens 2004 Olympics were watched by 4 billion people worldwide. More than 10,500 computers were installed, as well as 900 servers and 4,000 printers. Moreover, Atos Origin, while in charge of bringing all this together, had little control over the choice of other technology suppliers. "We're like the keystone," says Adiba. "If your partners have been chosen for you, you have to work harder at the relationship. And we're all highly dependent on each other. If one bit – say printing – fails, then everything fails."

What makes the relationship between so many suppliers work? The high profile of the Olympics helps, as no one wants to be seen to fail. There is also a clear sense in which everyone feels as though they are working for a common goal: the greater good. Having the right kind of processes in place helps as does regular communication, making sure that information goes to the people who need it. But the crucial elements are less tangible. "There's no blame culture," says Adiba, "more an emphasis on sorting out problems together. Some clients would be quick to run back to the contract and point to the small print, but that would be pretty pointless here because it wouldn't fix the problem." Trust, he believes, is also crucial. "It tends to happen instinctively. If you're sitting down with senior people from other organisations, having an open and frank debate about an issue, things cease to be problems."

Inforte is a Chicago-based consulting firm which helps clients develop and implement customer relationship and business intelligence programmes. Founded in 1993, it employs just over 300 people. Dave Sutton is the company's president and chief operating officer. "We're encountering more and more multi-sourcing deals, especially since we've increased the amount of work we do in the federal sector," he says. "Clients want the best people and no one firm has a monopoly on them. It's the difference between getting a general contractor to build a new house and hiring the best architect, the best designer, the best electrician and so on yourself." Inforte has worked closely with Bearing-Point on some contracts. "In the federal sector, BearingPoint has specialist skills in systems integration and contract management but Inforte has more experience on the marketing strategy and communications side. Put the two together and you create something much more powerful. BearingPoint may have a level of scale and federal-sector experience we lack, but we've got other valuable expertise, so why shouldn't we be able to collaborate?"

The challenge for clients, he believes, is to find the right type of firm to work with, as many consultants find it hard to work in the collaborative environment envisaged by multi-sourcing. "There has to be a genuine desire among the suppliers to work together. Clients rightly focus on the outcome they want to achieve and are not interested in people who quibble over whose methodology is used. They should look for suppliers that have demonstrated expertise in a particular field, but without developing too great an ego. Most major firms have spent the past 20 years trying to be good at everything when they're actually collections of specialist knowledge." Sorting the thought leaders from the thought followers is crucial. "This is not just a question of whether someone's written a 'white paper' on a particular subject. You have to look at the level of investment a firm is making in its intellectual property, whether it has recognised spokespeople capable of setting the agenda in that field rather than just responding to it."

Celerant Consulting is an operational consulting firm and an affiliate of Novell, an infrastructure software and services company. Dwight Gertz, Celerant's head of executive education, argues that the trend towards multi-sourcing will intensify. "It's happening across all sectors," he says, "but it's more a function of client sophistication than the result of a specific corporate agenda. Under pressure to perform, corporations are starting to appreciate that the one-stop shop involves an implicit compromise on quality."

But endemic dissatisfaction with generic consulting is only one of the drivers, he believes. The distinction between clients and consultants has been eroded by a combination of wider business school education and the movement of people out of consulting into industry, which was accelerated by the downturn in the consulting market in 2001–03. "The pressure on consultants will, if anything, grow," says Gertz. "Clients have been to the same business schools as their consultants and are equipped with the tools and techniques that used to be the preserve of consultants; many are ex-consultants. They are more discerning and demanding, and better able to recognise quality when they see it." Former consultants, experienced in the management of complex projects, are more likely to take the prime contractor role themselves. They also know how consulting firms work and understand their commercial priorities, and are able to use this information to pull together individuals or small teams from different organisations without ceding control to anyone.

There are also drivers on the supply side. Many of the public-sector contracts let under multi-sourcing arrangements would have been too large, too complex or too risky for any one supplier to fulfil in isolation. Contracts like the State of California Child Support System, signed in April 2004 and worth around $800m, split the work between several suppliers (in this case, IBM, Accenture and a host of smaller firms).

"It's healthy," says Gertz. "It forces firms to be clear about what they're capable of, and restricts the temptation to enlarge the scope of their work." It will force, he believes, greater differentiation and a more intelligent division of labour in an industry dogged by homogeneity and unnecessary competition. "If we do it properly, the constant exposure to other things that clients buy ought to help our understanding about what we do and what we do best," he says. "Consulting firms should learn from each other."

But there is also a risk that the client will not be able to pull together the disparate parts of the project and that the deal will collapse under the weight of its own complexity. "Clients have to realise that this isn't an easy option," counsels Gertz. "It's hugely demanding in terms of time and effort. If they don't get the structure and incentives right in the first place, they'll face continual jockeying for position among suppliers. Also, it's one thing for clients to accept the theory of collaboration but quite another for them to feel comfortable that the different consulting firms will all be acting for the collective good. Clients get suspicious when consultants congregate."

The new relationship model

Whether a consulting team is made up of consultants from one firm or many, making sure it adds value depends on the basis of consultants' incentives and the framework within which their work is monitored and evaluated.

In the golden days of the professional adviser, a handshake and an invoice based on the amount of time spent on a project were enough to ensure that consultants delivered fair value for money. But a consulting project today – perhaps negotiated through a central, neutral procurement function, perhaps involving several consulting firms – cannot be built on trust alone. If you are relying on a consulting firm to deliver work worth millions of dollars, you need to be able to do more than believe its promises. Moreover, it is clear to clients, even if it is not always clear to consulting firms, that the increasing emphasis on business development goals which accompanied the rapid growth of the consulting industry in the 1990s has engendered behaviour that is often inimical to clients' best interests. Consultants remunerated and promoted on the basis of how much business they bring in will inevitably focus on that, even if it involves selling clients work that they do not need. And the behaviour of some consultants tarnishes the reputation of all: clients now believe that even the most junior of associates has sales targets.

However, in trying to override the corporate agenda of a consulting firm, clients have gone from one extreme to another. The traditional mode of paying for consulting services – fees based on time and materials – has been replaced by a performance-related approach, where fees are contingent on success and poor performance is penalised. "We've gone from a carrot-and-stick approach to a stick-and-stick one," argues Alan Russell of LogicaCMG. "Everyone recognises that time and materials billing, even where there were penalties for late or poor-quality delivery, was too open to abuse. It accommodated indifferent work and is one of the main reasons why clients don't see consultants adding value." But the new wave of risk-based consulting, in which consulting firms have to guarantee results, brings its own problems. "Such contracts are often highly adversarial," says Russell, "with endless negotiation over even minor infractions. They're too heavy-handed and don't ultimately improve the quality of work. What we need is the carrot-and-carrot approach, in which both sides come together in partnership recognising the commercial realities of each other." "The best deals are those where everyone leaves the table happy," agrees John Condon of BearingPoint. "If one party does not, then sooner or later there'll be a problem."

This is easy to say but difficult to achieve. Two ways of doing it are emerging in the marketplace.

Measuring outcomes

The first is to shift the focus of a project away from inputs and even outputs, and to look instead at outcomes. This is what the Vehicle and Operator Services Agency (VOSA), a UK government executive agency responsible for ensuring roadworthiness and carrying out roadside checks on vehicles, has done. Ten years ago, when its IT systems were first outsourced, EDS won the contract. "Like everyone else at the time, we were looking for the lowest possible costs against predefined service levels," says Nigel Shenton, head of ICT and partnership manager at VOSA. "But that wasn't the kind of contractual structure that would serve us well in a world where we had to be more flexible." Shenton and his team wanted to find a supplier which would be prepared to be measured on the achievement of broader business goals. "So we looked for metrics that were more closely linked to our ability to do our job: how effective we were at detecting offences at the roadside, for example." Shenton remembers with amusement that when he told a group of potential suppliers what the value of the winning bid would be, they initially thought he had let the information slip out by accident. "We hadn't. We said we wanted to pay this much, but here's our shopping list of all the things we want to get for our money." Rather than compete on price, suppliers found themselves offering to do more and more for the same money. "We concentrated on value, not price," says Shenton.

In a new deal, signed with Atos Origin, a proportion of Atos's profit margin is retained unless VOSA's performance in metrics such as these improves. "Half our measures are conventional ones relating to service levels," says Shenton, "but the others are associated with business drivers. Atos may be a preferred supplier, but we're not contractually bound to go to them for all our IT needs. They have to keep delivering value if they want to win work." The contract itself is also different. "It is not a 300-page document," says Shenton. "It focuses on the outcomes we jointly agree to achieve and the principles of behaviour we want. The biggest challenge for us has been getting a supplier like Atos to deliver a genuinely joined-up, fully managed service which stretches across the traditional organisational and cultural divisions between its consulting and systems development teams. The contract was essential in ensuring we got this."

According to Simon Albutt, consulting director, transport at Atos Origin, "From the consultant's point of view there are also great benefits from working in this way. Although the contractual arrangement is non-exclusive, being a preferred supplier in a long-term contract makes it easy to identify new opportunities and have an open debate about the possible options. Risk-and-reward contractual arrangements are becoming more common in transformational outsourcing programmes and having a structure that encourages pragmatism and flexibility rather than lengthy contractual negotiations every time a change to the project is envisaged benefits both client and supplier. Professionally also there is great satisfaction in seeing real business change come about from changes made to processes, tools and equipment – and all the better for being a jointly run initiative."

Pay-as-you-go consulting
As is so often the case, trends established in the hardware and software industries eventually make their presence felt in the consulting industry. Clients accustomed to leasing their hardware from suppliers are increasingly asking software vendors to find ways of spreading purchase costs over time, rather than paying a single, upfront licence fee. Crucially, they would like to pay only for what they use, not for a given number of users. This can be difficult for vendors to countenance, especially when they are publicly listed companies whose share price is based on meeting short-term revenue targets. This model has also been an integral part of outsourcing since the mid-1990s; indeed, it is an important reason for the outsourcing sector's rapid growth since then.

This thinking is now spreading to consulting clients and is the natural corollary of getting consultants to focus on outcomes, not outputs. Why, they ask themselves, do we have to pay for consultants when we use them? Why not pay as we benefit from them? It may seem a small shift, but the implications are huge for both parties. Payment arrangements may vary from fees determined by use (the software model) to circumstances in which the consulting firm effectively leases its consultants by funding the initial years of a long-term project (the hardware model). Either way, only the largest, most cash-rich firms will be able to do this. It also gives IT and outsourcing-based firms an immediate advantage as they have more experience of structuring such deals.

Gary Miglicco at BearingPoint is responsible for one of the most unusual payment arrangements in the consulting industry. His project dates back to 1999, when the Texas government issued a request for proposals for a self-funding internet portal. "The initial thinking was very vague," says Miglicco. "Portals were a relatively new concept back then, and we had to work closely with the state, its agencies, partners, and so on, in order to come up with a way of making it a proposition from which everyone gained." One option would have been to fund the portal out of general state revenue, but market research indicated that most citizens would prefer it to be self-funding, paid for by those using it. The resulting financial model had to accommodate two opposing needs: the state of Texas had to be able to put additional services on the portal as cheaply as possible; and BearingPoint needed to make a profit. Thus the state gets 10% of gross revenue and 50% of any profits once BearingPoint's costs are taken into account, giving the state an incentive to look for new opportunities and BearingPoint an incentive to provide the mixture of paid and free services which would attract users. "We had to earn the right to make a profit," is how Miglicco sums it up. "There was nothing in the contract that forced agencies to use the portal, so we recruited a marketing and outreach team to promote the services."

Texas Online has been live for over four years. It now offers more than 400 services, and is on track to increase this to more than 600 by June 2005. It generated around $28m in revenue in 2004. Some 1.4m citizens a month access the site, one in three of whom are new users, carrying out 1m financial transactions a month; $1.3 billion in state revenue is collected this way. BearingPoint has since signed up to provide the cities of Houston and Dallas with a similar service. "This could well set a precedent for other, similar work," Miglicco concludes.

But at the end of the day …

Smart procurement, the involvement of multiple suppliers and finding new ways to charge for consulting services reflect ways in which clients and consultants are actively trying to find new ways to restructure their relationship. They are a challenge and an opportunity. But equitable relationships cannot be founded on money alone. They depend on having more open, regular debates at the highest possible level between the organisations involved. People still matter; personal relationships still matter. They may no longer be decisive in winning new consulting business, but they might earn you a "second look" when a competitor may be about to win a piece of work with an existing client. They may no longer be the channel through which problems are resolved, but they may help strengthen your commitment to solving the problems. And people always prefer to work with people they like and respect.

14 Portfolio

Clients and projects

SOMETIMES THE EASIEST QUESTIONS to ask are the hardest to answer. You would think that every organisation would know how much money it spends on consultants, but that has rarely been the case. With managers in different functions and business units commissioning consulting projects independently, it has been hard to come up with a total sum. As organisations have introduced central procurement departments (see Chapter 13), they are now able to collect information about their expenditure on consultants in its entirety, and to see how apparently discrete consulting projects may complement one another or overlap.

Clients operate in the present while preparing for the future. A crucial part of their activity focuses not on making money but on spending it to secure the future through programmes designed to change their business. How much activity this constitutes will depend on the nature of their business, the dynamism of their operating environment and the broader economic business cycle. The faster the pace of change, the more activity will be devoted to change, and the more important it will be to get its development and deployment right. Organisational change, whatever it affects and whatever form it takes, is often implemented through consulting projects, and where this is the case the approach to these determines how well a company is likely to meet the challenges confronting it.

Taking an integrated approach is important where:

- a large number of projects are happening simultaneously;
- there is a large degree of overlap and interaction among projects;
- there is a fast-moving environment;
- there is a history of projects being cancelled late in the day;
- there are barriers making it difficult to start or finish projects;
- there are scarce funds or resources.

Most organisations exhibit some or all of these characteristics. In these cases the actual, as distinct from the theoretical, direction of the organisation's strategy is the direction in which all the projects are taking it. Without looking at change projects as a whole, how can you be sure this really matches the business strategy?

This chapter describes how the competing demands of new and existing projects are balanced, and how a client can make sure that the change programmes proposed make sense strategically as a whole.

Looking at project work in aggregation

One reason organisations hit problems with change projects proposed by consultants or internally is that they do not integrate or embed them in their broader strategy. Often one project will be in conflict with another, and it is common for there to be no overall, shared view of the activities that are the most critical to long-term success, despite the obvious point that a portfolio approach is essential if the evolving direction of the organisation is to be managed. This is usually because the management mechanisms for planning and acting for the future are markedly different from those required for day-to-day operation.

What is a portfolio approach to managing change? Put simply, it recognises that the numerous projects most organisations undertake are linked, at the very least through competition for resources. They may also be connected because they are mutually supportive, or because some cannot be implemented without others. It is ironic that even when this is the case, they are often evaluated and managed in isolation.

If projects are not integrated, it is more likely that they will not contribute to the overall strategic goals of the organisation. By adopting a joined-up portfolio approach, you will be in a much better position to decide what you should and should not be doing; how your projects contribute to overall strategy; and often which things should be cancelled because they run counter to the overall strategy or because they are simply too long term. Some throwaway projects with short-term benefits will also be identified. Moreover, portfolio analysis enables clients to map overlapping elements and eliminate them.

Nigel Bell probably has more experience than most people in portfolio management, having worked first in the pharmaceuticals industry (credited with pioneering this approach) and as chief executive of the NHS Information Authority (where complexity and resource constraint made it a necessity). "Portfolio management means different things to different people," says Bell. "Some use the phrase to describe either managing projects as if they were investments, using purely financial measurements, or doing more than one thing at once, as with large, complex programmes, so that risks, gaps and overlaps can be identified. Fundamentally, I see it as a management philosophy and framework which allows organisations to invest in trialling new ideas – essential for innovation – while minimising the risk that they'll end up committing valuable resources to something that's not worthwhile in the end. The pharmaceutical industry has a dynamic and evolutionary approach to drug development. It's not easy to develop a traditional business case here: the initial investment is enormous; the project management challenges can be horrendous; and there's a massive attrition rate. If you're going to fail, the key is to fail early. Once beyond the earliest phase, there are a series of tests to do and hoops to jump through. At each point, the company needs to check the fit between the portfolio of projects and its overall strategy. Is the drug novel? Does it represent a technical advance? Is the market for it still an attractive one? In the pharmaceutical sector it's acceptable, even honourable, to halt a project when appropriate; it's seen as stopping wasting money, as freeing up valuable resources, not as a failure." According to Bell, portfolio management also helps companies take risks, precisely because there is a clear acceptance that not every project will be completed: "The drugs development model makes it acceptable to start a project in order to learn what you don't know. You can't always think your way to something new, you have to get on and do it. But there's still a macho belief in many organisations that if you start something, you have to finish it; to do anything else would be to admit you got your initial assessment wrong. This is ridiculous of course; the decision may well have been correct given your knowledge at the time. In pilots, prototypes and the sort of phased approach most of us take for granted, there's an implicit recognition that we'll know more after each than we did beforehand; it's called learning, and there should be nothing embarrassing in that."

There are five steps to the process:

- ◪ Identify objectives in ways you can measure projects. Think in terms of scenarios so that projects can adapt to changes in circumstances as they progress.
- ◪ Make sure that different projects are taking the organisation in the same desired overall direction. Each project may deliver particular outcomes but the general direction (revenue generation, cost reduction) needs to be clear across the portfolio. The benefits of each project must be clear, with a clear link to the portfolio overall.

- Seek alignment between projects so that they are not contradictory. Overlaps and duplication must be identified. With each new project ask "is there another project we can now cancel?".
- Check progress and priorities at regular intervals against changes in the business environment to see what benefits of different projects will (or can) be delivered earlier (or later) than originally envisaged.
- Manage projects carefully with all activity defined and organised.

Note, however, that portfolio management is not appropriate for some types of consulting project:

- Small, one-off projects, which have a clear and well-defined purpose. The thrust of the approach will be to move as quickly as possible and implement it.
- Very large programmes, fundamental to the firm's strategy and the importance of which is well established. If the programme is large enough, it usually forms a core around which other projects must fit. In essence, it constitutes a portfolio itself into which other projects should be drawn and evaluated according to their compatibility with the programme.
- Quick-hit projects, which are often a reaction to some kind of external shock: typically a regulatory one, but perhaps a critical challenge to a firm's core activity from market shifts or a competitor's activity. Such projects should be focused on in isolation, prioritised, given sufficient resources and implemented quickly, after which they can be reintegrated in the organisation's broader portfolio of projects.
- Portfolios of portfolios. For many firms, particularly large or diverse firms or multinationals operating across different, perhaps quite separate markets, the logic of the portfolio view may be relevant within a sector or region or type of operation but not beyond that.

The portfolio approach is a continuous process of evaluation, co-ordination and modification of projects, not a one-off activity. It requires an organisational mechanism, such as a permanent or temporary secretariat, to work well. Without this, the individual project managers have no means of assessing projects against overall strategy, or of being able to judge whether the benefits of their project will be undermined or overwhelmed by other activities.

Applying portfolio management principles to consulting projects

"Portfolio management is the vehicle by which a company can move from strategy into action by rearticulating aspects of strategy as a series of investments that need to be made to deliver against the main objectives of the business," summarises John O'Rourke at Catalise, a consulting firm specialising in this area. "It's a way to map your resources against your objectives. Chief executives are often frustrated because they cannot mobilise their organisation behind their strategy, and portfolio management provides them with a systematic process for prioritising their investments and enables the effective syndication of these priorities across the business."

He is in no doubt that portfolio management is the way forward when it comes to seeing how consulting projects fit together: whether they complement or negate either each other or internal projects, and the extent to which they represent a good use of money. Organisations, O'Rourke believes, should bring all discretionary investment projects together so that they compete for funding from a common investment fund. "Projects should not be viewed in isolation," he says. "There is no such thing as an 'IT project' or a 'consulting project'." Instead of managing projects, organisations should manage investments; the role of the line manager should be to maximise the return on the investment, not get to the end point of a project. "Once they understand how to make best use of their funds, managers will be in a better position to decide about the use of consultants. They will also be better able to decide what kinds of teams are most appropriate – the choice does not have to be between keeping something in-house and farming out the entire process. It allows for a more modular approach to execution and teaming and allows organisations to leverage best of breed skills from external suppliers."

What are the crucial factors in taking a portfolio approach to consulting projects?

Leadership
Businesses generally view consulting projects in relative isolation, partly because there is often no leadership with authority to:

◪ aggregate all project activity, especially that involving consultants,

and check it is, and is seen to be, consistent with the direction of
the firm's strategy;
- provide overriding authority in terms of the direction of the
portfolio, irrespective of internal politics;
- monitor and manage the portfolio in a similar way to the rest of
the business.

All these things can be difficult to do. But if they are not done the
chances of money being wasted on consulting projects must be greater
and there must also be a greater chance that a consulting project will
produce damaging results that are counter to the organisation's overall
strategic aims.

Value

With portfolio management, consulting projects will be assessed for
their value in aggregate as well as in isolation. This helps an organisation
focus better on the way it uses consultants and on which kinds of consulting projects produce value and which do not.

To value consulting projects, begin with high-level benefits such as
increased market share, reduced overheads and better research and
development. Then look through the portfolio to see which elements
contribute to these objectives. This will reveal gaps and overlaps in
achieving strategic aims. The portfolio can then be reshaped around
value, and the ability of each consulting project to contribute to the strategy of the firm.

Approach

An organisation will often answer the question "Why are you doing this
project?" with "To implement system X, or process Y". This indicates
that its consulting projects are not embedded in its strategy. The answer
to "why" for any project should always focus on outcome, not on the
steps to get there; for example: "to add Z million to the bottom line", "to
expand market share", and so on.

Risks

Projects have risks. Within any portfolio, it is certain that some of these
risks will materialise. Managing risk at the portfolio level is always
better than on a project by project basis because risks are often linked
and have an impact on more than one project. Identifying risks, especially on consulting projects, is not simple. Most people assume that

things will go well and are reluctant to concede that they may not, and plan and budget accordingly. Portfolio and project risks can, however, be identified by brainstorming, past experience of similar work and, importantly, through a rigorous cross-examination of the consultants and their experiences on similar projects. This is an area where consultants can be extremely valuable, yet it is one clients are reluctant to explore for fear of appearing negative. Nevertheless, it is important for clients to recognise that some consultants may see this as an opportunity to expand their role in a project and earn more money. This is yet another risk to take into account.

Once risks are listed, analysis proceeds with an assessment of the likely probability of occurrence and the likely impact of each risk. The easiest way to do this is to prepare a probability–impact matrix and to focus on the high-impact, high-probability risks. It is often useful to separate linked risks (where if one risk occurs the other linked risks are likely to materialise as well) and independent risks (which may occur individually irrespective of what happens in the other risk areas).

For portfolio risk planning, a separate project is created focusing solely on the ways in which the risks can be mitigated. It is given its own budget, even though these activities will occur in the individual projects in the strategic portfolio. In other words, the risk budget is held centrally and not attributed to individual projects. This may not be popular with those running individual programmes, but it is necessary to make sure that the risk funds are properly allocated. The management of risks then becomes transparent, and projects call on the central contingency budget to deal with risks that arise during implementation. This is a rational process that is easy in theory, but difficult in practice.

Resources

The management of resources is perhaps the most complex area. For many clients, managing the resources – from people to infrastructure – of a range of consulting projects can be an unfamiliar activity. For consultants it is all in a day's work, so many clients seek assistance from them, or at least they ought to. Without focused attention as the portfolio evolves, resource crises are inevitable, as are constant extensions to the consultants' briefs.

It is possible, but rarely advisable, to produce and manage aggregate resource plans for the whole portfolio. It is more useful to focus on critical resources, especially in areas where it is difficult to find additional skilled resources at short notice.

Skills and culture

The essence of capability development is to seek to create an environment in which the client organisation learns from its project experiences with consultants, allowing them to do much of the work for which they would otherwise have hired consultants. The mindset and culture of the project environment is rightly quite different from that of the traditional organisation structured around business functions. It requires an entrepreneurial culture that can rise to the challenges of rapid change. This presents a challenge for the consultants too, although it is one they frequently shirk. Clients should set consultants specific targets for cultural change during the conduct of projects so that permanent change occurs within their organisations.

Agility, flexibility and the ability to adapt rapidly to new circumstances are the hallmarks of organisations that have successfully learned from their consulting projects. These characteristics are more enduring than the technical skills learned from consultants, although they are more difficult to absorb.

Communication

So many consulting projects fail through lack of acceptance, or outright rejection by those who are affected by them, that the importance of effective communication cannot be overemphasised. For successful communication to occur, all stakeholder groups must be identified as well as the most appropriate channel of communication. Consulting projects succeed better and bring more benefit when the organisation is aligned with them. Communication probably brings more benefits relative to effort expended than any other activity. Nevertheless, because it so frequently crosses the boundary between clients and consultants it is usually neglected. Communication should focus on activities that will lead to success for the projects and on those individuals most affected by change.

The deciding factor: management responsibility

It is puzzling that so few clients view their consulting projects as a portfolio. One reason has been lack of information: with individual business units and managers commissioning their own consulting projects, it has been hard for people at the centre to picture their overall consulting expenditure. But John O'Rourke also argues that accountability for most projects is inappropriately located: "Some people will always be guilty of building up baronies which are notoriously difficult to break down. Chief financial officers and chief executives like portfolio management because it gives them an objective basis on which to prise investment management responsibility out of the hands of divisional heads who should probably not have had it in the first place. But this requires a big act of corporate citizenry by these heads and it is therefore crucial to explain why they should give up control and have investment funding centralised. This is where strong stakeholder management comes in."

In today's rapidly changing organisations, the apparent reluctance of senior executives to take overall responsibility for their expenditure on consultants and to include it with other forms of investment is a significant failing. That organisational politics frequently make it impossible for an insider to take control of the entire portfolio should not be an excuse.

15 Career

Consulting firms and consultants

AS FAR AS MOST CLIENTS ARE CONCERNED, consultants come in two flavours:

- ◪ experienced industry people who may be doing a spell in consulting for career advancement before returning to industry, and who treat consulting like an accelerated MBA programme;
- ◪ inexperienced younger consultants (often new graduates) who join for the excitement and kudos.

Clients like the former and tolerate the latter – sometimes.

Jeremy Raymond was at Coopers & Lybrand (subsequently part of PricewaterhouseCoopers) and worked with IBM when those organisations were building up their consulting practices. He is now an independent consultant who specialises in working with professional services organisations, usually on development and human resources issues. "The career paths open to consultants essentially remain variants of the traditional up-or-out approach," he comments. "The greater involvement of consulting firms in implementation, rather than pure advisory work, and now outsourcing have meant that consultants are more likely to stay with a firm longer than they might have done ten years ago. There is less burn-out when your consulting firms can offer careers that are more like line management. Offset against this are the larger numbers of senior people now switching to the client's side, sometimes to become buyers of consulting. Having an alumni network you can sell to has always been a feature of the strategy houses, but other firms are now actively pursuing this approach, for example encouraging interim management opportunities. As always, there continue to be people who want to break away and work on their own."

At the same time, Raymond believes that lay-offs in 2001–03 have created a more discriminating market for professional skills, with firms choosing to use more short-term labour rather than recruit full-time staff only to have to make them redundant when the market turns down again. "Clients are also becoming more choosy and this affects the attractiveness of the consulting industry, which has always struggled to strike the balance between what work is available and what work highly competent people are attracted to do. As client organisations hire more people who are ex-consultants, they will have many of the capabilities they had previously sought from consulting firms. They will be less susceptible to management fads and more likely to farm out only smaller, specialist pieces of large projects – business modelling or market analysis – where the objectivity and speed of the consultants cannot easily be matched. In the past, a new consultant going into a strategy firm might have expected a rich diet of challenging, high-level work; now they may be disappointed by the smaller scale, repetitious nature of much of the work. An attractive culture and working environment is becoming a more important ingredient of the mix that retains people."

In the relationship between a consulting firm and its consultants (and through them its clients), the "leverage model" has been an important factor. Leverage maintains a balance within a firm of consultants who have varying degrees of experience, in which the more senior consultants bid for and lead a project and the younger ones do most of the leg work to earn highly sought-after promotions. Firms made good money from this model, but as the industry matured they became greedier, increasing the ratio of junior to senior staff, with the result that clients complained that experienced consultants did the selling but left the work to be done by junior staff. As consultants moved from major consulting firms back into jobs with clients, clients became better educated in the use of consultants. The leverage model began to crumble as clients insisted on their work being undertaken by experienced staff with demonstrable skills.

Outsourcing and longer-term implementation projects (in which consultants are assigned to a client for long periods) have also changed the firm–employee relationship. A more stable working structure – more of a nine-to-five environment – complemented the more dynamic and unpredictable ways of working that typically characterised the industry. The leverage model also faces strong competition from offshore companies with cheaper resources. Last but not least, firms are finding it more expensive to recruit and train consultants and have therefore become much more focused on retaining them.

The relationship between firms and individual consultants is central to the success and development of each. Because of the dynamic tension of the relationship, it is important that each knows where the other stands, and understands the motives for the other's decisions. Individual consultants may be employees of a firm or associates (undertaking short-term and/or part-time work for a firm on a regular basis), or they may be working freelance for a firm on an ad hoc basis or directly with clients.

Consultants as employees

To a large degree the dynamics of the relationship between consultants and their firms are no different from those of any employee–employer relationship. But all firms have their special characteristics, and among those who work in consulting there is a marked individualism and mobility. The client–consultant relationship also shapes that between employer and employee (firm and consultant). When consultants move clients can go with them, and firms should always be aware of their consultants' concerns and ambitions.

How to deploy consultants efficiently is a crucial skill for any successful firm; similarly, how individuals are deployed will largely determine how their careers develop. The allocation of consultants and their time is at the heart of the success of any consulting firm. The aim is for high "utilisation": endeavouring to make sure that some 70% of a consultant's time is chargeable. But to balance this with the needs of individuals they must assign the right people to the right work. Often the same small group will be used to sell many projects, reducing the opportunities for others to gain experience and for the firm to broaden its capabilities. By contrast, the career aspirations of consultants mean they all will jockey for the best projects, the ones that will allow them to acquire experience across a range of activities and industries to suit their longer-term ambitions. For the firm, reconciling today's projects and current client concerns with those of current employees and the consulting firm's future human resources needs is a difficult balancing act that determines, to a large degree, who is assigned to what.

The leverage model has been viewed as the main weapon in a firm's armoury for balancing its aims of making money and maintaining itself as a sustainable entity. It has some basic structural qualities – new consultants have to cut their teeth somewhere – and it reflects the demographic profile of the labour market. But the notion that good leverage automatically yields good profits is a myth: younger recruits can lose the company money, as their remuneration is high relative to their charge-out rates to clients. Leverage does improve a firm's competitiveness, as it lowers the average fee rate across the pool of consultants, but this does not mean that all the profit is made at the base of the pyramid. A firm is more likely to make most of its money from experienced consultants who have not yet progressed into management roles. This is often the case in larger firms whose generational balance is easier to maintain. With smaller and particularly niche firms their positioning requires a greater level of specific expertise and leaves less room for a generalist to fit in easily. For them leverage is less significant.

Another concern of firms is measuring their consultants' output. Well-known for its anti-social working patterns, the industry has been marked by what is now called "presenteeism", with people reluctant to be seen leaving the office early, regardless of the effect on output. At one level, only inputs can be measured. New graduates, for example, have no way of judging their own outputs. Inputs, in the form of hours worked, is the only way they can measure what they have achieved, even if they have actually achieved little.

Central to all the decisions throughout the career path of a consultant (and by extension a firm) is the equilibrium between life and career. For the individual, this may be what guides decisions on moving between firms, taking opportunities within a firm, turning to a more associative form of employment or leaving the industry altogether. With the arrival of family responsibilities, time, location and working structure may be different from what individuals planned or foresaw, or certainly experienced, at the beginning of their career.

A consulting firm must balance its consultants' needs with its own and create a sustainable line of succession in an environment where the market changes rapidly and its skills mix must respond accordingly. For a consultant, mapping a career path, developing technical disciplines, defining a relationship with the firm and still leading a balanced life can seem impossible.

A consulting career has five distinct phases, each having discrete types of interaction between the individual and the firm.

Beginning in consulting

Individuals choose to go into consulting because they are attracted by the intellectual challenges, the opportunities, the lifestyle and the remuneration of the business. What matters most is to establish where they can get valued experience and personal development that will help in the future.

Consulting firms recruit for many purposes: to replace skills that have departed; to build additional skills in a field that offer growth opportunities; or simply to get some clever young people on board and develop their potential.

Many firms stick to one or two recruitment channels. One is referral programmes, where staff are rewarded for introducing new people to the firm, which have been shown to save significant sums in finding good people. "There is a strong networking ethos in consulting," comments Christine Dyke, formerly organisation development and training consultant at PricewaterhouseCoopers and now a director of Partners in Development, a niche business specialising in consultancy skills. "Firms do pretty well at keeping in touch, and this is helped by the fact that people move around. Mergers accentuate this natural movement and add to the process of quite diverse networking."

Gaining credibility and skills

Once employed, a consultant will focus on gaining as much experience and as many skills as possible, as quickly as possible. This means doing a variety of work. "Consultants coming into the organisations do want loyalty and to be cared for and for the company to demonstrate good stewardship. But they also want flexibility. In the past this was usually the opportunity to take a career break, but increasingly they want to give something back to society, which is why Accenture has developed a relationship with vso [Voluntary Service Overseas] and founded its own charitable organisation: Accenture Development Partnerships," says Sue Rice of Accenture.

The nature of the industry can make the role of the firm all the more important at this stage. "It is important to make sure consultants get attention. They spend a lot of time with their clients and can end up identifying more with the client than with their firm. They have to be kept connected to the firm – these are 'softer' issues, like keeping in touch, mentoring arrangements and career planning. Consulting firms have not traditionally been good at this," argues Dyke. How much consultants get out of their firm may depend on how pushy they are. Jeremy Franks of Deloitte notes that new consultants usually respond in two ways: "A lot of people, the majority, will take ownership of their training and development, but a few expect to be spoon-fed."

If a firm genuinely regards its people as its greatest asset (and there is a big difference between the lip-service typically paid to this and the actions of firms that truly believe it), it will recognise that the improvement of the individual underpins the improvement of the firm and will provide high-quality training programmes.

Variety of work and training are important when consultants are deciding about their future. "After about four years, many consultants realise this type of work is not for them and go on to other careers," says Jules Beck of CSC. "Working for a company like CSC allows individuals to change their careers without leaving the firm. We focus a great deal of energy on finding an avenue for their skills to avoid this potential talent drain. With a variety of career paths, you have a greater opportunity to retain people in whom you have invested a lot of money."

Midstream career

Having benefited from good training and the experience of working on a number of projects with clients, consultants have a markedly different relationship with their employers. They are charged out at high rates and spend most of their time on client work. They are more likely to "own" client relationships, and if they leave they take their clients with them. Consultants are aware of this and can shift the relationship with the firm accordingly. "Consultancies want a healthy turnover but when business is good, better people want something else. At this point, the power is with the consultant," says Dyke.

For a firm, the question now is whether a consultant can sell and develop business. An accomplished consultant can keep and gain clients, and is someone in whom a firm has already invested a lot and is looking for a return. In an ideal world, a firm would want to build itself around as many midstream consultants as it can. But "at midstream people often ask 'is it still for me', and they need help at this juncture to see the way forward," says Dyke. Building and then sustaining a firm which has unusual strength in experienced and midstream consultants is near impossible. Moreover, there has recently been a reduction in the number of graduates entering the industry, decreasing the supply of midstream consultants. This and the growing importance of expertise as clients become more savvy means that firms are finding it difficult to get the experienced midstream staff they want.

Although the midstream is often the high-point of a consulting career, and the most productive stage of someone's career for a firm, the interaction between firm and consultant at this stage can be disappointingly limited. A consultant focuses on doing great work and a firm's attention is on those below and above: newer consultants and managers.

It is important that firms give consultants enough room for movement, and that consultants make sure that they have enough freedom to achieve their aims. If firms get this right, they will find that consultants will contribute more to the intellectual capital of a firm, with ideas and technical innovations, and bring in clients.

Management roles

In the next stage of development, a consultant turns to an inward-facing role: management. The skills gained are directed to the firm and the development of the team. For the individual, the challenge is how to make the transition to managing part of the practice. The skills required are persuasion and people management in a relationship that is quite different from that of client and consultant. It is a higher form of consulting: essentially consulting for other consultants, to help develop their skills to gain new business and conduct existing relationships.

This phase raises important questions for a consultant and causes the most problems for a firm. How can it accommodate more senior consultants in inward-facing roles and maintain the value creation of the midstream? Often the only way out is growth: if a firm grows, it will need more managers to oversee the bigger business. This acts as a spur to growth.

A consultant moving into a managerial role is leaving the dynamism and variety of consulting projects for a more "grown-up" and in some senses more mundane role. It is dangerous territory because some client work will remain an important part of the job, and it can be a challenge to keep your skills and knowledge up to date without the constant stream of project work a manager has previously been exposed to.

Return to "reality"

People leave consulting for various reasons: the nature of the work, or interests or opportunities elsewhere; because a firm no longer needs particular skills or needs to reduce its headcount; or a shift in demand for types of consulting, which may be unappealing. Moving on is always in the mind of a consultant, even though it may not happen. Building up a network of contacts and colleagues will always help you move in another direction, and networks are essential if you want to set up your own business.

Alternatives to the firm–employee relationship

Not all those who go into consulting will work in a stable relationship with a firm (or several firms consecutively). At some point, often quite early on in a career, they may choose to work in a less structured relationship. The concept of the "free agent" would have been alien in the consulting industry a decade ago, when freelance consultants tended to be people who had been made redundant or taken early retirement, or who were finding it difficult to get a job. Today, however, being a freelance consultant often reflects a conscious choice of very able people – a fact that clients realise. Consultants may have young families and want to stay closer to home with fewer career pressures. They may see a particular opportunity for their skills and resent a consulting firm taking such a large proportion of the fees they are capable of earning. They may simply want to balance work with other interests or travel. The dynamics of the world of consulting are particularly amenable to other ways of working. Affiliation and association are possibilities, particularly where an individual has specific skills that a firm may not want to use all the time but are invaluable for particular projects.

It can be tough for firms to balance their human resources needs, particularly in a volatile market. Firms want to avoid having too many consultants on the payroll, yet they need to be able to take on clients quickly. Accenture is typical of many firms – large and small – now juggling full-time and "associate" consultants. "We have more contractors than in the past, although they are still only a very small proportion compared with our full-time employees," explains Sue Rice. "We have to look at whether it's right to build skills in-house if we are likely to need them for only a short period. We can also make use of other organisations' skills via alliances and relationships with other companies. There are also other mechanisms of balancing demand and supply which we can explore with employees, such as mutually agreeing leaves of absence."

It is not easy to get the balance right. "We're cautious. We do have an associate network and we do use it, but it has to be selective. It can be difficult to find the right person. Our primary focus is building strategic relationships with a small number of organisations that complement our skills," says Beck. Lack of loyalty and quality control are issues. In the short term consulting firms also make more money from full-time employees, so there is an incentive to minimise fees paid to freelances. A consulting firm has no incentive to train freelance consultants; even full-time employees typically have to work for a firm for three or four years before it sees a return on its training investment in them.

Why have consulting firms?
From a client's point of view, the use of freelance consultants can be attractive, though usually only for small-scale projects or specialist input into larger ones. Why pay premium rates to a consulting firm when you already know the person you want and have worked with them before?

What is there that a consulting firm can do that a group of freelance consultants cannot?

The answer comes down principally to knowledge, but it also involves breadth of expertise and perspective, and the ability of different consultants to work together. Freelance consultants may well find themselves cut off from their original source of technical expertise. They may have less access to the kind of leading-edge consulting work that keeps their skills up-to-date; they may miss out on the informal exchange of information and experience with colleagues; or they may not be able to afford licences for research databases.

The development of knowledge constitutes one of the principal components of consultants' and their clients' assessments of a return on their investment. A consultant's technical skills have to be under constant development, so an aptitude for learning is important in itself. But just as important is the development of a "consulting perspective", which enables the constant learning of new skills in a dynamic market environment. Arguably the most important skills that may be acquired through a consultancy career are the enduring skills that enable development up the career path. These include interpersonal and communication skills and an ability to inspire trust. At a more practical level, consultants will add to the expertise of a firm through a constant development of case studies and best practice, learning from their work and enabling the firm to develop solutions from experience. Databases of best practice are common. Crucially, a firm will expect a return through contributions to its intellectual property and thought leadership.

A firm will want to benefit from the creativity and knowledge of a consultant, but any consultant knows that their personal knowledge will be crucial to future opportunities, including those with other firms. Early on, both consultant and firm will want to profit from their relationship and invest time and resources in it. The investment that each makes in the other can be seen as developing a two-way score card, representing a balance of exchange over the period of a career. There is a sort of educational "contract", where the development of the consultant is a win-win for both individual and firm. As there is an exchange of knowledge and development between consultant and firm, so there is a more direct monetary trade-off between them. Firms want, above all, productivity – to utilise their human resources to the fullest possible extent. Within the context of career development, as well as routine remuneration consultants need motivation, monetary and developmental, as a trade-off for achieving this for the firm.

This balance between knowledge, investment and money is what makes consulting firms valuable for their staff and the clients on which they ultimately depend for their existence. The firms that are most profitable are usually those that have sought and found the right answers for their relationships with their consultants. They are also those that recognise that much of the value created by consultants comes from teams of clients and consultants working together.

16 Life cycle

Client projects and consulting teams

As director of strategy at Kingfisher, a European retail group, Ken Whitton dealt with everyone from big-name consulting firms to niche players focused on specific issues. "We were lucky enough to be able to afford the brightest and the best," he says. "We never had to worry about the basic technical skills of the teams we hired."

But alongside the appreciation of the value consultants could add was a niggling worry about the extent to which their ideas were adopted. "I suppose it was the black-box aspect," speculates Whitton. "If you create any kind of project team, separate them from the mainstream business and ask them to focus on one issue for a period of weeks, the project inevitably takes on a life of its own. Assumptions and hunches get made early on, most of which are not made explicit. The consultants believe they are following an unimpeachable chain of logic based on hard facts from their research and analysis. Maybe they are. But if, as often happens, the first output a company's managers see is a beautifully presented 20-slide PowerPoint presentation, there is the reaction: 'Where did that conclusion come from? Have they really understood?' Of course, this is more likely to happen the more innovative the consultants' approach and the more radical their recommendations, which is why you bring in consultants in the first place."

This problem remained even when Kingfisher staff were seconded to the project team and made joint presentations to the company's senior management. "The real problem was not that we had outside consultants telling us things we didn't accept. Having our own guys on the team helped us past the 'do they understand us?' issue. But even if the analysis is accepted, there's always a big difference between intellectual understanding and achieving the emotional commitment that is essential if real action is to be initiated. That can usually be achieved only when managers themselves live with a problem over time and are fully involved in investigating the issue and formulating a response to it. It does not happen from hearing one presentation, no matter how brilliant. Therefore the result of many projects is that managers may be impressed with the consultants' analysis, but they do not act on their recommendations."

"The same is true of any kind of project, whether it involves consultants or not: barriers emerge between the project team and the rest of the organisation which make it difficult for their findings to be assimilated," says Whitton.

With the monthly run-rate (the amount billed for a typical team of consultants) averaging $150,000, he sometimes finds himself asking why so little consulting seems to stick. "Consultants bring science; they can analyse anything and come up with an answer. But, particularly with strategy consultants, it is invariably big-picture stuff. Most managers are craftsmen, not scientists; they deal with the day-to-day issues of getting the 'machine' to work. They are dealing with the same issues as the strategists but from a vastly different perspective. It's like Einstein talking to a NASA engineer: both know a lot about space travel and would share a passion for the same objective of getting the rocket to fly to the moon, but would they be able to understand each other and work together constructively? And if not, who should make the move to understand the other?"

Why do consulting projects go wrong?

The only real value-added activities in consulting are doing work for clients and delivering results. The rest of the business consulting system can be seen as an artifice enabling this production to occur effectively.

Imagine the scene: the consulting contract is awarded, the client project is approved and work is about to start. The first day dawns, and bright and eager client managers and consultants set about their preparations. But during the morning a few difficulties arise. It transpires that there are some important changes to be made to the contract and some even more important changes to be made to the project. It is not clear where the project team will be based, and they have had to accept temporary accommodation until a better home can be found. It turns out that several members of the client's team are unavailable or reluctant to be involved. They have found themselves indispensable roles elsewhere which will keep them fully occupied for the duration of the project. Likewise, the consulting firm proposes changes to its team. Important team members have been overcommitted and are not now as available as was promised. Meanwhile, the software developers (a third party) have offered their own ideas about participating in the project and are lobbying for its structure to be altered. They threaten to defer promised delivery dates on important software unless they can be sure of a central place in the project team. As if this was not enough, since agreeing to the project brief, the client project sponsor (the champion) has been promoted and a new sponsor has yet to be found, as most potential replacements are reluctant to take on responsibility for this risky programme.

This may be a caricature, but it is close to the truth in the case of many consulting projects.

At this point the behaviour of a client team is determined, and its composition, ways of working and objectives are set. Career objectives and the desire to increase personal marketability and knowledge play a part alongside the usual desire to perform, and to be seen to perform well, in their role on the project. The behaviour of a consulting team's members is driven by the rules of engagement their firm dictates, which are usually many. They are motivated by their professionalism in wanting to deliver quality and timely work, as well as by the metrics through which their firm measures and rewards performance, such as chargeability, level of responsibility and the ability to meet deadlines. Third parties such as technology vendors have their own rules and viewpoints.

The interactions between these groups of people and the impact they have on the outcome depend crucially on one thing: the project life cycle. There are few fixed, repeated interactions on consulting projects and little opportunity to learn and modify behaviours for the next time around. The life cycle of a consulting project has three distinct features:

- a dynamic environment where daily change is normal, and indeed demanded;
- a division of activity into phases with significant shifts in skills and effort across the phases;
- a shift of focus from quality to cost to time and back to quality as the life cycle unfolds, although throughout the cycle all three are subject to balancing acts.

These factors complicate the relationship between client, consultant and other parties and failures can often be attributed to the fact that consultants live in the project world and manage life cycles intuitively, whereas many client staff, especially line managers and those who report to them, do not.

The way to deal with this is to identify the shifts of emphasis that occur at different points of a project and switch focus as the stages evolve. Questions to ask and answer are, for example:

- What happens in the start-up phase, and what expectations and trends are set?
- What occurs during mainstream project delivery?
- What happens at the project close?

Start-up

The sales process creates expectations on both sides, and the first mistake often made is not sharing them. The consultant is wary of appearing ignorant; and the client is wary of giving away a position at an early stage. As soon as the consultants are chosen, the relationship and level of communication between client and consultant, which may have been at arm's length during the sales process, change dramatically. At one end of the scale there are formal meetings, plans, communication and so on; at the other there are the more human interactions. How will team members get on? Where will the balance of power lie?

Resource allocation

The project team must be chosen carefully and the right technology put in place. Rudimentary matters such as the location of meetings need to be decided on, but the minutiae should not get in the way. Nevertheless, where the consultants work is a critical factor. Should the client insist that they are based on site? Should the client's staff be in the consultants' office? Or should they work in some third location? Whatever the pros and cons of these options, the most common choice is for the consultants to work within the client organisation. But project work does not always fit in with the day-to-day running of the client organisation. Often this means that the project is allocated unsatisfactory, out-of-the-way office space, without any thought about the impact this might have on the work. Many clients get their priorities wrong in providing the tools and environment for their consulting teams. Consultants are expensive and it is counterproductive to cut minor costs in supporting them. Clients often do not think carefully about the staff they assign to the consultants, simply finding people who can be easily spared from normal work. Nor do they always consider the support consultants may require in terms of space, technology and people.

Contractual interactions

In the time between the specification and the start of a consulting project changes often occur. Procurement can be a generic process and may not always reflect a client's unique requirements. This is the time to be clear about the purpose of the contract. Is this a programme with a laser-like focus on results, where the spirit of the contact is more important than the letter? Or is it process-based, where the work plan and activities are set in stone? Consultants prefer the former, yet many client staff join the project team anticipating the latter. Either works, as long as both sides understand the underlying intent of the business arrangement.

Working with third parties

Most significant consulting projects involve not only the client and the consultant but also a third party, such as a technology vendor, a specialist consulting firm, or perhaps even customers of the client. These parties may have contractual relationships that are integral to the project; or they may be part of a larger contractual relationship with the client, such as an outsourcer. The importance of these connections on larger programmes, and the propensity for them to go wrong, cannot be underestimated. Turf wars break out; pecking orders are challenged; and a blame culture may take over.

The most common cause of unworkable relationships is money. It may be that third parties think they can undertake some of the activity at cheaper rates. Their cost structures are often different and they have the ability to perform routine consulting tasks at much cheaper rates. Clients should be sensitive to consultants' concerns and the impact changes to the project may have on their consulting firm's margins. The key to resolving this is to recognise that economy (use of the cheapest resources) is only part of the value picture and to give due weight to effectiveness (doing the right thing).

Midstream

Once the formal stages of starting a project have been completed, the informalities of working together soon take over. Whatever the project organisational chart says, people typically adjust their roles to a point where they feel comfortable. This can be a good thing – the kind of roll-up-your-sleeves mentality which clients applaud – but it can also result in problems surfacing and going unnoticed. Client–consultant relationships cannot be left to chance.

Clearly, successful completion of the project should be the principal aim of the team. Getting the work done is the dominant driver of everyone's behaviour.

Building the client-consultant team

Experience shows that teamwork is crucial to delivery, and the relationship between a client's staff and consultants can be tricky. Clients may resent the image of consultants, conveniently forgetting the anti-social hours and disruption to personal lives that are consequences of the consulting lifestyle. Consultants can be arrogant and undervalue the contribution that insiders can make to solving project problems.

Much is made in consulting of the "seamless team", but this is a myth. The key to building a team and working within it is to understand the individual perspectives that are brought to it, not to paper over them. Mutual respect for what each side brings works best. It is essential to build and run the team in such a way that people's individual talents and variety of perspectives add to the performance of the team as a whole rather than cause conflict which detracts from the team's results.

It is important, too, to understand and make allowances for people's differing motivations, personal as well as corporate. If consultants seem arrogant, clients should ask why this is so: what are they getting out of the project and do they feel comfortable asking questions and challenging the client? Or is apparent arrogance a sign that they feel unable to communicate freely? If it is, the team is not working.

Interpersonal relationships

It is often the softer issues that make or break a consulting project, and these must be managed as well. They will define how the team and individuals within it react when things go wrong. Do people in the frontline feel they have control? Can they challenge technically senior people if they feel the project is not on track?

A central question is how to amalgamate groups of people from the two organisations and promote collaboration. Good relationships are not merely friendly relations. They are founded on respect for each other's expertise and contributions. Simple things such as different working hours, dress codes and ground rules for basic things like expenses can have a disproportionately large impact. Good relationships are often founded on joint achievements and a broader recognition of everyone's contribution to progress.

Knowledge transfer and skills development

A fast-moving project may not seem the right place to think about developing people's skills, but in reality it is a testing environment where new challenges and working with new people offer many opportunities for learning. Even if consulting firms think about this in relation to their own staff, they are often guilty of ignoring the issue in respect of clients' staff, although the latter have just as much right to expect personal development. However, for various reasons such as internal politics, isolation from the mainstream and a lack of understanding of the work, this is not usually the case. Internal politics can overwhelm rationality as team members seek to manipulate the project to suit their career objectives and get the recognition for their work that they deserve. Such influences need to be acknowledged and dealt with openly.

Knowledge transfer – the training and educating of client staff – is crucial for the successful implementation of a project. It needs a different approach at different stages of the project cycle, yet there is often an expectation of a single interactive transfer process. This explains why effective knowledge transfer is rare.

Of course, knowledge can take many forms: documentation, technical data, a specific skill, or simply an attitude of mind. For example:

- **Knowledge repositories.** These can be documentation libraries, handbooks and "lessons learned" documents, as well as specific items such as user manuals and project plans. These are arguably the most tangible forms of knowledge, although people often make the mistake of regarding them as the only important elements, and frequently contractual documents place too much emphasis on project documentation, most of which is never referred to. With today's technology, these materials are best stored electronically for ease of access.
- **Methodologies.** Methodology is the term frequently used by consultants to describe everything underlying their approach. From a client's standpoint, the critical issue is what is necessary with regard to the methodology employed to enable a given project or programme to be replicated without consultants. A decade or so ago, methodologies were guarded like state secrets. Since then it has become clear that consulting work of lasting value must almost always incorporate the transfer of significant intellectual property to the client. This usually involves the methodology of the particular consulting project.
- **Trained staff.** The most significant element of knowledge transfer is training and developing client staff and providing effective succession plans for transferring important knowledge to those responsible for carrying on the work.

■ **Consulting mindset.** Although this may seem a strange category of knowledge management, many consulting tools and approaches simply do not work if they are not applied with the right mindset. Some of a client's staff should be coached in the way in which consultants think and approach problems so they can act effectively on project activities and in the future when the consulting team has left. The important features of the consulting mindset are independence and objectivity, a good appreciation of and perhaps a bolder attitude to risk, and an understanding of the temporal nature of project work, where new activities and new challenges are the norm.

Balancing long-term and short-term objectives

In a static world, the completion of a series of pre-planned, short-term objectives will deliver long-term benefits. However, few consulting projects take place in such a world. A team that concentrates on short-term objectives may achieve good midstream results in a project that, when complete, is likely to disappoint. This comes as a surprise to many project team members who see diligent execution of a project plan as a rationale for their work. Regular reflection on whether the original objective is still worthwhile, repeated challenges to the project and its results, and external review are necessary and desirable to achieve a worthwhile outcome relevant to the environment as it has developed. That this may be uncomfortable for the client and project staff is a reality that needs to be managed.

Project management

The daily formalities of managing a project require a balance between the necessary details of organisation and the bigger picture. The management focus has to be on the future. Looking back at failure, aside from lessons learned, is not productive. Tracking and reporting progress are elementary, and necessary, parts of project management, as are many aspects of routine management. But attention to the minutiae of the project should not be allowed to overwhelm a sense of the big picture. The forward-looking approach should seek to predict and discuss problems and provide potential solutions, so that the team can react quickly to anything that goes wrong and move on.

Change control

The execution of changes is perhaps the most important interaction between clients and consultants. Neither side likes to destabilise the status quo. Consultants cannot be seen to use changes to extend their role or increase their revenue; and clients would be seen as frivolous if they continually altered the mandate and details of the programme. Changes must be handled constructively and the contractual arrangements are central to this. Both sides must have a clear understanding of the intent of the contractual arrangements, of the business consequences of any changes to both parties and of the culture of each party. The critical factors are clarity and trust.

Closing down

Project closure is frequently the least visible and most sensitive activity. This is the stage where costs escalate, skeletons are disclosed and the best staff depart early for the next exciting project.

Follow-up

Large programmes are often messy and difficult to close down effectively. Administrative matters drag on and costs drift upwards. The best way to handle this is to create a subproject, or a project within a project, to make sure the close-down process is re-energised, treating it as a new project to be executed with enthusiasm and completed quickly and effectively. Curiously, it is often helpful to introduce new people to do some of this work, to overcome the battle fatigue that will be evident in the original team.

Results measurement

Value for money, tangible results and business value: these are laudable objectives, very much in vogue. But how can a project demonstrate that it has delivered? In a changing world, it is difficult to compare a project's outcome with what might have been achieved without it. Changed circumstances can devalue or enhance the results. The only credible mechanism for post-project results measurement is to define a base case for what would have happened without the project and a scenario (often the project business case) for what would happen with the project, and to compare these with what actually occurred. Although technically correct, this is frequently a pointless exercise. Circumstances will have altered too much since the old project documents were written.

A more practical approach is to establish at the close of the project the answers to the following questions:

- What new capabilities has this work brought to us?
- What business value do these capabilities have?
- What new potential for future business advantage do they bring and how can we exploit this?
- If we had to do this again with the full knowledge of this outcome, would we have pursued this course?

The brave might (privately) ask three more questions:

- What did we get wrong?
- How might it now be fixed?
- Is it worth fixing?

Long-term operational staffing

Projects are not operations; they are culturally different. The issues in transferring project activity from the consultants and client team to the eventual users of the project outputs are similar to the difficulties of managing third parties in the programme. It is therefore useful to look at the user group as a distinct entity, with its own concerns and defined interactions with the project. There will be many anxieties and differences of opinion and a lot of politics involved.

The way to achieve a smooth transition is to define effective performance measures for the individuals concerned. This calls for a significant shift at a late stage in the project life cycle. Delivery objectives, so dear to the hearts of the project team, should be replaced by transitional objectives. The routine day-to-day objectives of the users or operational staff should be replaced for a while with learning and developmental objectives, to encourage them to absorb the project and achieve an effective operational transition.

Hiring from the other side

It is common for clients to seek to hire individual consultants whose performance they have admired during project work. Likewise, consulting firms seek talented industry specialists, often from their client base. A lesson from the past decade is that this practice should be encouraged. New career alternatives provide good motivation for the conduct of project work on both the client and the consultant side, and a cross-flow of staff is a natural part of a good team relationship.

Maintaining a long-term relationship

The relationship between client and consultant is the keystone of the consulting project. Throughout the project life cycle, how they begin the project, organise themselves, balance objectives, communicate and make provision for its long-term implementation are critical to the project outcome. Bernard Edwards is chief executive of Salamander, a consulting firm specialising in business transformation. He is clear about the impact of good relationships throughout the life cycle: "It is transform and be transformed. It is not something you are untouched by only to return to the day job. The relationship should be a pinnacle of your client or consulting career. You should be able to say, we went to a new place, a place we could not see or did not know existed, a place outside our world. We did new things, things we know now that we could not have done before or even dreamed of. We changed, and we will never be the same again."

5
ROUTES TO SUCCESS

"Working together effectively requires a degree of honesty on both sides."

17 The successful client

MOST PEOPLE JUDGE THE SUCCESS of consulting projects in personal terms and use consultants to make them look good. But consulting projects seldom turn out as expected. When the dust has settled, clients will often rewrite history – either as a great success or as a great disaster – depending on how well they as individuals have done. Not surprisingly, things rarely turn out just "OK".

Barry Glassberg, director of e-services at the UK's Inland Revenue, is responsible for a several million dollar consultancy spend. Under pressure to reduce costs by 2.5% every year, he believes strongly that external help is essential for reforming an immense tax bureaucracy: "I have made regular use of consultants in various jobs over the past decade, and I can say, without any doubt, that most of the projects I have been involved in would not have been delivered without them."

Glassberg's views suggest that success or failure depends on four decisions:

- ◪ When should you use consultants? Question whether you really need outside help. If you do, be open about it. Know why and say why you need it. Above all, set out where you want to go – the results you are looking for in your business and in your career. These factors drive motivation.
- ◪ How should you choose between consultants? Challenge them to challenge you. Look at the structure of the project and of the candidate firms. Test yourself on the balance of content, people and process you need. Mix these elements well.
- ◪ How should you manage your consultants? Set out how you want to work: your position on risk transfer, working style, tangible results versus intangibles, and what can and cannot be done. Define your project in detail and go to work.
- ◪ How should you evaluate the success of the results? Continually define and redefine what success is, not just the process that achieves success. Establish what is in this deal for your consultant. Use this as the foundation for the relationship. Good consultants are looking for more than just fees. Find out what it is for each potential candidate.

One reason the nature of business consulting has begun to change is that organisations have become more thoughtful about when they should use consultants. With less money to spend on outside help during the economic slowdown, they spend more time and effort distinguishing essential consulting from fashion items or the merely nice-to-have. Once a decision to use consultants has been made, you will find that the procedure has become more complicated than it used to be. Should you hire individual consultants or a package of consulting services? How do you get the best out of teams that may be drawn from several consulting or technology firms, combined with your own staff? With more participants, how do you know which are and are not delivering value and getting you the results you need?

When to use consultants

Use consultants only when you will get better results than you can by doing the task internally, or by choosing another route such as outsourcing, or by not doing the task at all. In well-chosen, well-executed consulting projects, the cost of using consultants should be related to the tangible business benefits, with consultants being remunerated on the basis of results, not just time spent. If a consulting project will yield only intangible benefits, think twice about undertaking it. Intangible benefits can be hugely important (improvements in customer or employee satisfaction, for instance), and they often feature in consulting projects that exceed client expectations, but they remain hard to quantify and to defend internally.

The right style

Consultants like to think of consulting in "styles" such as resource consulting (usually known as body-shopping), advisory work (writing reports), implementation (taking responsibility for the delivery of the end result) and outsourcing (taking over running certain functions for a business). This is because their consulting business lines are usually set up in different ways in these four areas.

When hiring a consultant, focus on who does what, making the best of your expertise in the problem, your internal resources and your knowledge of your business. Decide on the importance of speed and on which skills you want to absorb for the long term so as to get lasting improvements. Also be concerned about control, and how you will keep an eye on the project as it evolves.

Making the best of your expertise, resources and approach to control is not the focus of consultants, largely because they do not know or understand your capabilities as well as you do and cannot assess them. Some consultants no doubt take the view that it is not in their short-term interests to encourage you to make the best of your expertise, but the best consultants recognise that by building on their clients' strengths and capabilities they will provide a better service, which will help them build better long-term relationships.

Using your resources

Given sufficient time and money, you could probably do everything you hire consultants to do. You could employ staff with the background you are looking for, or train a team of people in the skills you need. That clients do not do this is sometimes a sign of internal politics or simply of laziness. Managers, faced with a problem, often jump to the conclusion that they need outside help. The rush to consultants may also be a sign of lack of confidence or ignorance: how do you find the right people or methods? More positively, it may stem from the recognition that consulting firms offer economies of knowledge.

Economy and consulting are words you seldom see together. This is, after all, the industry that famously borrows your watch to tell you the time, and then bills you for it. Yet it remains true that a consulting firm, when it hires an experienced and expensive individual, spreads the cost across several clients. When you are trying to resolve a one-off problem, it makes sense to use such individuals for a limited period of time. You pay only a part of their employment costs, and you benefit from the knowledge they accumulate as they move from client to client.

There has been a wave of deregulation and privatisation of utilities in Europe over the past decade or so, leading to a feeding frenzy for what limited consulting expertise existed in utility regulation. In the United States, California led demand for a similar wave of activity. Consulting staff transferred from already deregulated countries (such as the UK) to meet demand elsewhere; smart clients (mostly in Germany, France and Italy) cherry-picked the most experienced international consultants for short but critical inputs. The understanding they gained of utilities elsewhere fostered a trail of acquisitions throughout the world.

People, content and process

In Chapter 4 it was argued that there are three positive reasons for using consultants: people, thinking and process. The mix depends on your needs and, interestingly, the state of the economic cycle. In an upturn there is investment cash to develop and test new services, and the content dimension is dominant. In a flat economy, services have been commoditised and process is dominant. In a downturn, the right people are usually most important. For longer-term projects this can turn out to be more critical than it first appears. It also means that lessons from a different part of the economic cycle (for example, Glassberg's views described in Chapter 17) need to be adapted for current and future conditions.

Faced with a new challenge, you should establish, over the lifetime of a project, what mix of people, content and process you need. You should look for these inside your organisation before seeking outside help. Consulting projects are almost always described in terms of their objectives and activities, so you need to specify the mix of the main elements. "We hired company A because it had implemented the software package we had selected for many other organisations and could guarantee it would be up and running before our year end" provides a more accurate picture of why the consultants are being used and where they can help than "we hired company A to put in our new computer system".

Consulting should not be a knee-jerk management response to problems. It should be a cheaper, better and faster way to obtain the people, thinking and process you need, over and above what is already available in your organisation. Consulting should never replace or marginalise your own staff; it should complement them.

Choosing consultants

In the old world of client–consultant relationships choosing was simple: you defined the roles, made a shortlist, selected and proceeded. Now it is harder to draw clear boundaries round a "consulting" project; projects have sharply polarised towards the very large and the very small; and procurement processes have become more formal.

Project structure

New project structures abound: offshoring, self-financed projects, payment by results and partnership/outsourcing deals (described elsewhere in this book). In this new world, the decision that consultants are needed has a major impact on the structure of the project.

Instead of giving one consulting firm a broad remit, it is sensible to break down projects into clearly defined tasks, each of which may require different skills and, potentially, different combinations of client and consulting staff.

A consulting firm may have the right experience for working in one area but not in others, so you are more likely to pick and choose a variety of firms rather than rely on a single firm for the skills needed (multi-sourcing, in consulting parlance). Inevitably, managing consultants from different firms on the same project at the same time requires more work. For example, you have to negotiate terms with each firm and make sure that erstwhile competitors co-operate. For many clients, the extra effort is an acceptable trade-off for the increased control you can exert. Consulting ceases to be the black art that clients have so often complained about in the past, when it was often something "done to" client firms.

Polarisation

Clients often end up juggling too many projects, and the scale, scope and complexity of the undertaking make them unwilling or unable to take responsibility for overall co-ordination. From choice or necessity, they hand over control to one of the larger consulting firms, which is good at managing projects of this nature and may be prepared to bear some of the risk. So polarisation occurs and large and small consulting assignments become the norm, with little in between.

The co-ordinating consulting firm may choose to do most of the work involved itself, but it may also subcontract elements of it to smaller, more specialised firms. Consulting work is thus increasingly split between:

- small-scale projects (under $250,000) in specific areas where in-house expertise is scarce and a consultant has detailed knowledge and specialist experience. Independence is important – clients need to be sure that the consultant has no self-interest in promoting a particular solution – as is innovative thinking;
- large-scale change projects (over $5m) where momentum needs to be created and sustained. Specific expertise is less important than a firm's record of successful delivery, and innovation is less important than being able to deploy tried-and-tested methods to guarantee results.

Clients believe consultants are capable of delivering value in both modes, although many say their preference is for the small-scale option as this allows them to retain control. Large-scale change or "business transformation" projects are more likely to be given to consultants because clients simply cannot handle the work themselves, but even then the client usually pursues this strategy reluctantly.

The most sophisticated corporations buy carefully, in smaller projects, and prefer to turn the flow of consulting on and off when business conditions demand. They undertake larger programmes only when they are essential, such as to comply with government regulation or to implement large-scale technology changes. Projects in between are rare.

The dissatisfaction so often expressed by clients arises when a client thinks it is buying small-scale specialist teams but a consulting firm thinks it is selling transformation. Typical complaints are that:

- projects are staffed with inexperienced people who are unfamiliar with the business and may be learning on the job;
- consulting firms profess to bring expertise and leading-edge thinking, but deliver only "warm bodies";
- consultants apply a standard solution to what the client perceives to be a unique problem;
- consulting firms try to sell clients services they do not need.

This problem can be exacerbated by the signals clients send out during the procurement process.

Procurement

A recurrent mantra in consulting is that clients have become savvier. Although consultants have been saying this for 40 years, there is now some justification, as many consultants have moved into management roles and become clients themselves. Poachers turned gamekeepers, these individuals use their knowledge of the way consultants work to exert more effective control and negotiate better terms. While resenting the downward pressure on fee rates, most consultants would say that this plays an important role in improving the effectiveness with which clients use consultants, and that this practice ultimately expands the consulting market.

At the opposite end of the spectrum, there has been the inexorable rise of the procurement department. Accustomed to buying things rather than professional services, these departments exist to establish and police procurement processes and to drive down prices. This trend has come from the public sector where there are rules on competitive tendering. Private firms are adopting similar approaches, although there is little evidence from the public sector that elaborate procurement processes are efficient or cost-effective.

For small-scale specialist projects a less formal buying process works better. A firm should spend time discussing with prospective consultants the structure of the project, the nature of work and the objectives before the contract is signed. In the process it is worth asking consultants to suggest how they could make the programme smaller (for you and for them) and get the same results; this will help you identify what is really important. Look at all the elements of the consulting arrangement; for example, good cash flow is worth a lot in discounted fees to most consultants, so upfront payments and other devices may get you further than you think.

You should keep in focus the business results you want and be flexible enough to accommodate procurement changes that enhance those results. Be smart, look at all the options and give consultants a chance to propose different routes to the same or better results.

Use the selection process first to deal with project structure, fragmentation of resources and polarisation of services. Then focus on the rigour of procurement to get a better outcome, not just a better consultant. Think through the interdependencies of the new business consulting world. Be demanding but not unreasonable, and concentrate on things that will lead to success, not just to a comfortable life.

Managing consultants

The new consulting environment demands new thinking when managing consultants. There is more interdependence among the different parts of a project, and there should be a more equal, interactive relationship between all those involved. Although trust is important, making sure that the consultants you use share your objectives and have a common incentive to achieve them is fundamental.

Historically, consultants often managed consulting work poorly. Deadlines were allowed to slip, deliverables were badly defined, the scope of the work often changed, costs soared and the business suffered. Firms believe that the most important lesson from this experience and from recent corporate scandals involving consulting firms is that they have to be in the driving seat. As one former consultant saw it: "Managing consultants takes more time than most clients expect, or are prepared to admit. Perhaps counter-intuitively, if consultants see that their client is focused and determined to deliver a successful project, they will be more motivated to raise their game and deliver real value. Left to their own devices, the internal processes of their firms will drive consultants to broaden the scope of the project and maximise their revenue, rather than your business value."

The new rules

There are ten useful rules for firms to bear in mind when hiring and managing consultants:

1 Keep up with the experts. "You can outsource many things, but Enron has shown just how dangerous it is to have blind faith in an outside expert." The less clients know, the more time they are likely to waste with consultants and the more dependent they are on their opinions. Inferior knowledge leads to inferior consulting.

2 Leave nothing to chance. "We have learnt we have to define our problems, needs, expectations and the potential risks. Failing to scope the work is unfortunately construed as writing an open cheque, such is the reputation of consultants." Scoping the project should include a definition of business results, what needs to be done, exclusions and assumptions, the specification of individual tasks and acceptance criteria for the whole solution. It is also important to break down the work into controllable phases and to have a clear, up-to-date exit strategy. "You always need a Plan B."

3 Specify clearly who is responsible for what. "You need to see the résumés of the majority of the consulting team, to know how much time each member of the team will commit, and to agree the extent and means by which the consulting team will interact with your staff. If the scope is clear, agreeing this will be simple, but if the project is likely to involve changes within your organisation, these issues need to be thought through prior to employing consultants." Small cracks in a project structure become fissures under stress. You cannot rely on consulting firms stepping in to take responsibility for a problem that has been overlooked. Contracts are usually designed to encourage consultants to do their own job well, not the client's job.

4 Choose the right people, not the right firm. "People have become fed up with 25-year-old newcomers delivering packaged presentations on the basis of no industry knowledge whatsoever. So much success depends on the personal qualities of the consultant. Inspired and inspiring people are very valuable. Average consultants are not." This complaint, although as old as the consulting industry itself, has become more strident since 1995. At that time many consulting firms adopted a pyramid structure in which profitability depended on how effectively they could leverage the knowledge of a small number of senior partners across a large number of less experienced consultants. Although a firm's brand may be an important factor in getting it on the shortlist for a particular piece of work, the collapse of Arthur Andersen taught clients to make their final selection based on the individuals they meet. Choosing between shortlisted firms is now as likely to be based on one-to-one interviews as it is on the traditional "beauty contest" presentations.

5 Respect your consultants, and ask them to respect you. "Make consultants aware that they are facing equals. Be open about what you expect from them." Consultants can be like plumbers: looking at your leaking pipes, they shake their heads over the workmanship of their predecessors. There are few things more frustrating than being forced to repair something you already thought had been fixed. So it is not surprising that clients complain bitterly about consultants who, invited to work on something, question how the client has arrived at this point. Clients find this condescending and irritating, and evidence of consultants' unwillingness to acknowledge the constraints of the real world. But in asking consultants to respect your circumstances you must reciprocate, taking consultants' commercial imperatives into account.

6 Be open. "Working together effectively requires a degree of honesty on both sides. Many clients pretend that what they want is help when they really want the consultants to do everything. In other instances, clients do want consultants to do everything, but then interfere and try to fix the answer." For many clients, hardened by poor-quality consulting in the past, openness is anathema. Nevertheless, trustworthy communication is crucial to success.

7 Acquire long-term skills from consultants, not just an immediate "fix". "Skills transfer is one of the most important benefits of using consultants, because it gives us greater capability in the future." If they are poorly managed, consultants can strip away more value than they bring and promote dependency on consulting. Nevertheless, that most consultants are poor at knowledge transfer is not simply evidence of a conspiracy to increase fees, but proof of the obstacles to transferring skills between organisations. Most clients – and consulting firms – pay lip-service to an ideal but make little effort to achieving it. It needs to be built into your plan, and it costs money to achieve.

8 Demand that consultants make a difference. "Consultants should be encouraged to be creative, to make a real difference. There needs to be greater recognition by consultants that they have responsibility for the ultimate outcome, rather than just for advice that may lead to an outcome." Clients complain that consultants leave no "footprint" behind them, that the client organisation continues just as it did before the consultants intervened. Making an impact depends on more than consultants taking a broader view of an issue or bringing in new skills. Clients need to change too, and recognise that consultants will not take risks on "making a difference" as long as they believe they will be the scapegoats for failure. They must have a failure-tolerant environment, and if they are to avoid mistakes, they need to be coached intensively. Making a big difference usually means taking big risks, and there is often an implied shift from adviser to implementer. This needs to be recognised by both sides.

9 Share risks and rewards. "Consulting is often accused of breaking the link between risk and reward. In the old days, the risks were negligible, and yet the rewards were still high. Where consultants have been forced to share the risks with the client, the job is invariably done better, and both clients and consultants work well together." Both sides should benefit when a project goes well and suffer when it goes badly. Lower pricing by consultants and greater recognition by clients of the benefits of performance-based contracts are producing a slow but substantial sea change. An unambiguous pricing structure remains essential – you have to be clear on pricing – but most clients who go down the traditional "time and expenses" route subsequently regret the opportunities they have missed by not sharing the downside risk and upside benefits.

10 Do not rely on the contract. "Unfortunately, with all the requirements and safeguards written into a contract, if it begins to go bad, there is often no way to stop the downhill spiral. All the insurance and licensing in the world will not prevent the project capsizing." Clients are now wary of relying too much on the contract. As consulting contracts become larger and more complex, the probability that important issues get overlooked or ignored increases. Experience, especially from litigious America, is clear: where consulting projects succeed, it is not because they had the right contract in place.

These rules do not require genius to discern or appreciate. Indeed, it is depressing that clients continue to make the same old complaints, even while being lauded for increasing sophistication in their dealings with consultants. It must be because companies find it harder to practise than to preach. Why? Because they reflect the fluid boundaries of the new consulting world, rather than the them-and-us approach that has characterised consulting in the past two decades. Confrontational consulting may have become the norm, but it rarely delivers success.

Measuring consultants

To achieve consulting results consistently and reliably you have to measure, monitor and manage the successes being achieved at all stages of the process. You also need to create milestones at which some elements of business success become tangible.

The challenge

In a perfect world, every consulting project would have measurable outputs which would allow the contribution of a consulting firm to be compared not just with the client's expectations in that one instance, but with other work done by the same firm and even work done by other firms. Think how different the consulting industry might be if clients could rate the productivity of a consulting firm in the same way it might rate that, say, of an office cleaning company. Of course, part of the mystique of consulting is maintained precisely because it cannot be evaluated in the same way as office cleaning, so it has not been in the interests of consulting companies to resolve the issue.

Today, however, most consulting firms are aware that if they are to defend their fee rates, they need to be able to demonstrate value, not simply promise it. The problem is how best to do this. There cannot be a single solution that compares, say, strategy projects with outsourcing on a similar basis. A single standard reducing the output of consulting to the point where most consulting projects can be compared will also blur the different ways in which value is created. This means that the first step has to be to subdivide projects and examine the concept of value for each element, so that more meaningful comparisons can be made.

Value

Clients see consultants as generating three different types of value:

- **Effectiveness.** The inputs into a project are uncertain but output can be measured. This means that while it is possible to identify a clear goal for the consulting project, it is hard to identify a clear set of causal relationships between that goal being achieved and what the consultants actually do. Clients have to trust that the consultants they have hired have contributed to achieving the goal, but neither side can prove it. In this situation, you need to establish clear goals at the outset and make them the combined objective of everyone involved in the project, both consultants and internal staff. Everyone has to be given an incentive to do whatever it takes to meet the objectives.

- **Efficiency.** The output of a project remains uncertain (it is not possible to ascribe a clear set of goals with which everyone in an organisation agrees), but the work carried out by a consulting firm can be measured. An example would be a complex change-management project. The overall objective of the project might be hard to define (how can you measure whether an organisation has changed?), but consulting firms involved in the project might be playing clearly defined roles, such as designing and delivering an internal communications strategy. In such situations, the discussion of what constitutes value should focus on the input the consulting firm makes.

- **Economy.** A consulting firm, perhaps through the use of offshore resources, can undertake routine technical tasks more cheaply. This new phenomenon arises from the growth of consulting in India, China and eastern Europe. These regions have marketed their high skills and low costs and western consulting firms often subcontract work there. Some of these firms have also built low-cost offshore practices so as to reduce average prices through their own staff. Clients have responded. General Motors, for example, will not now contemplate major technology programmes that do not include significant offshore resources.

Using these guidelines for value and the guidance on interactions elsewhere in this book, you should seek to set out a mix of targets – some tangible, some intangible – and the means to measure them. For intangibles, measurement will be through opinion surveys and feedback, independent reviews, and so on. Make this process transparent and be flexible in changing targets as the project unfolds.

The pharmaceuticals industry has a perennial problem with the costs and effectiveness of research and development (R&D). Research is "blue sky", and product development has a phenomenal failure rate, with only one in 10,000 or more compounds proving valuable and safe enough to make it to market, years after their initial discovery. Precious few of these are the blockbusters that drive profits. In this sector, consulting is a black art and tracking value is almost impossible. Smart clients never hire consultants in tightly defined areas without specific links to the bottom line. One client engaged consultants to improve management of its R&D programme with the stated objective of reducing headcount costs by 30%, but with value measured by the likely increase in the output of marketable compounds going into clinical testing. The consultant suggested a host of other intangible success measures designed to concentrate the minds of R&D staff on how they used their time. The result? The consultant made one huge difference: R&D began to focus more on commercial results and less on pure science. Two years later, R&D efficiency by the output measure had increased by 300% with 30% fewer staff, and with demonstrably better science.

The rules are simple:

- The criteria set for success are shared by as many organisational stakeholders as possible.
- The medium-term, practical impact of a project is what matters, not its short-term "wow" factor.

The fundamental anchor, nevertheless, is getting results. If these can be demonstrated, particularly if this can be done in stages as the project evolves, the evaluation process is easier and produces more convincing results for all.

Learning lessons

Some of the greatest inefficiencies and failures in consulting stem from clients who did not learn from past experience. Indeed, some of the worst consulting arises when clients who were dissatisfied with the work of a consulting firm in one area hire the same firm again to do something else.

There are four secrets to sustainable success:

- **Get the internal politics right.** In the frenzy to complete important work, communication and internal marketing of the benefits is often forgotten. Selling projects internally is also important; without acceptance little is gained.
- **Be a role model for your industry.** Do not be overly concerned

that competitive secrets will leak out. Most business achievements can be duplicated in time and your consultants will undoubtedly talk about what has been achieved. So do the opposite. Trumpet success and the results you have achieved, particularly with other clients and with analysts. Their own experiences, which they will then share with you, will help you achieve even greater success in the future.

- **Give credit to your consultants.** If they have done a good job, make sure everyone knows it. A good client who is willing to provide references is worth having and can give you a greater prominence in the consultant's client portfolio, along with cheaper prices next time.

- **Take care of your team.** This means more than celebration parties. Succession planning for internal people who take project roles is often poor. Staff seconded to projects usually find it difficult to go back to their normal job. Look for those who have demonstrated leadership, ability to absorb new knowledge and good risk management qualities, and build career paths for them. Besides being advocates for what has been achieved, they are often best placed to take your organisation forward.

And three don'ts:

- Don't overhype the success (let the results speak for themselves).
- Don't issue "lessons learned" documents (no one likes them).
- Don't overallocate blame for the mistakes (these happen even in the course of the best work).

Put simply, focus on the concrete business impact of what has been achieved, not on the fantastic process that got you there. If the results were great, you can be sure everyone will ask how you achieved them.

18 The successful consulting firm

THE CONSULTING FIRM – the corporate entity – is under attack: not a full-scale assault perhaps, but a war of attrition.

Clients are questioning the value a firm adds. When they can choose from an extensive market of independent consultants, many of whom earned their spurs in well-known, established firms, and all of whom are prepared to work at rates way below corporate charge-out levels, clients are inevitably asking why they should pay a premium for involving a firm. A firm is an intermediary, putting them in touch with the people they want to work with; at worst, it is an overhead. Increasingly, clients are voting with their feet. Rather than assuming that one firm has world-class skills in every area, clients prefer to multi-source or create virtual consulting teams with individual experts drawn from a range of different firms.

Employees, too, are questioning the role of the firm. In an industry which, on some estimates, laid off one-fifth of its workforce between 2001 and 2003, the image of the paternalistic employer whose people are its greatest assets rings somewhat false. For people wanting to travel, work more flexibly and start their own businesses, the constantly-on-call working life of a consultant appears increasingly unattractive. Even the money is not what it used to be.

Priorities for success

If the consulting firm is to survive, its role must be reinvented to suit a changing market. Managers of consulting firms should ask themselves what value the corporate entity can add to clients and employees who now have a range of options to consider. What can a consulting firm do that individual consultants cannot do by themselves? What will successful consulting firms do better than others? Other parts of this book have focused on the challenges and opportunities facing consulting firms in the environment in which they operate; this chapter looks at the attitudes and capabilities required internally if the consulting firm is to capitalise on its existence.

Integrity

Corporate scandals and a plethora of failed consulting projects reported in the media have cast a pall over the reputation and ethics of the consulting industry. Clients have reacted by establishing more complex procurement processes and drawing up more draconian contracts. Such processes and contracts have their place (and will continue to do so for the foreseeable future) but are by no means watertight.

Successful consulting firms recognise that their culture and values play the most important role in driving the behaviour of their consultants. When a project runs into difficulties, resorting to the fine print in the contract only exacerbates the problem, but having people who are predisposed to "doing the right thing" as opposed to "doing the thing right" makes all the difference. Consulting firms have been extraordinarily successful at attracting bright people who genuinely care about making a difference to their clients; they have also been equally extraordinarily cavalier in assuming that those values will survive the pressure of a corporate machine that wants them to work ever harder and sell ever more work. "We recruit eagles and train them to be turkeys," is how one senior partner put it. Successful consulting firms appreciate that those values need to be protected. They link client feedback and satisfaction directly into their appraisal systems and will not allow people to be promoted who cannot show they put clients first. They will not reward people simply for selling more work.

The test of success is whether firms make a positive difference to their clients. Successful consulting firms invest time and effort in clients in order to understand the incremental value they can add, as external consultants, over and above the resources already available to a client internally. They walk away from work where that value is not clear. They also know that integrity cannot be manufactured. Processes and procedures may drive compliance, but they do not instil the values on which integrity depends.

Honesty
The image of consulting as a black management art has faded, but many clients still find it hard to understand what consultants do and be optimistic about what consultants can achieve. Consulting firms have made many efforts to improve transparency, but they often lack the confidence to open their entire working process to clients' scrutiny. They are usually prepared to discuss only successful projects, not the lessons learned from failed ones. It has therefore become hard for clients and consultants to talk about the issues that really matter and to acknowledge that many of the issues consultants are expected to resolve are intractable, without any easy or obvious solution. The problem is

endemic. While clients continue to look for an easy way out, there will always be consulting firms that do not challenge their expectations; and those that do will always lose business to them.

Successful firms recognise the seriousness of this dilemma. They put enormous effort into trying to change clients' perceptions, making them see the problems rather than glossing over them. They run seminars for clients to help them better understand the consulting process and hire outside experts, at their own expense, to provide objective feedback to both sides.

Quality

The firm has always been the backbone of quality assurance and credibility in the consulting industry. Unlike medicine, law or accountancy, there is no qualification that consultants must have in order to practise. Instead, consulting firms, because of the way they recruit and train their employees, have played a critical role in reassuring clients that their money is being well spent. But where is quality management on the corporate agenda of the consulting firm today? With memories of total quality management initiatives a decade ago and the bureaucracy in which some firms mired themselves in trying to apply quality standards originally developed for the manufacturing sector, consulting firms are reluctant to talk about quality.

Successful consulting firms recognise that they have an important role to play in giving clients confidence that they will be getting a thoroughly professional service. They set the bar high and communicate to their consultants what the expected standard is in unambiguous terms. They will not tolerate work that does not match the desired performance, and consultants who repeatedly fail to meet it will be asked to leave.

Alongside other like-minded firms, successful firms work to develop a means of measuring, in an intelligent fashion, the quality of the contribution consultants make while also recognising that consulting projects vary widely and that no one system can measure every instance meaningfully.

Research

Independent consultants find it hard to stay at the leading edge. Without the collegiate environment and sophisticated knowledge databases found in the best consulting firms, their ideas quickly lose currency. One of the major advantages a consulting firm has is its ability to bring together up-to-date information about trends in different sectors. It is far better positioned than most business schools to know what is happening where. But this is an advantage that has been largely squandered. Although most consulting firms produce articles, "white papers" and reports, little of the output can be said to be innovative, and most is poorly researched.

This scattergun approach to establishing thought leadership is rejected by successful consulting firms, which invest more money in a smaller number of better thought out projects, designed to identify genuine insights. They recognise that the most valuable research takes time and do not demand instant gratification. They will involve other consulting firms, business schools and, above all, clients.

Value proposition

Every consulting firm likes to believe its services are unique, but clients rarely find the differences between firms so clear-cut. Competitors, too, get confused and end up seeing all consulting firms as potential rivals rather than possible collaborators. Successful consulting firms invest substantial time in identifying their areas of competence, pinpointing what value proposition each of these areas offers their clients and making sure that the focus of the entire firm is on delivering that value on a consistent and repeatable basis. The proposition is defined from the client's perspective, not the consulting firm's. Successful firms understand the role they play in their clients' lives.

They also develop a clear understanding of where their services fit in the broader value chain. Where do they sit in the revenue/delivery matrix? Is their expertise in relationships, products, brokering, diversification, transactions or transformation? They are not proud or insecure, and they do not waste time building expertise internally when they could bring in greater expertise from other firms. They build international structures when it meets their clients' needs, not to fulfil their own ambitions.

Successful firms do not acquire or merge with consulting, outsourcing and technology firms solely to achieve internal economies of scale. Although adding value to clients is usually the official justification for such moves, it is difficult to cite examples of firms that can demonstrate they have achieved this. Instead, clients complain that the firms involved take their eye off the market, become more concerned with internal processes than service delivery and make it harder for clients to find the specialist skills they require.

Results

Independent consultants find it difficult to charge for anything other than the hours worked. The sizes of the projects they work on, their economic circumstances and their usually limited role make it hard for them to be able to make their payments contingent on success or failure. A consulting firm is in a much better position to negotiate fee arrangements which explicitly demonstrate its commitment to its clients' success. Successful firms use their clearly articulated value proposition to defend the value they add and will not negotiate on fees. They will, however, abandon traditional time and materials billing in favour of contracts where their fees are calculated on the achievement of objectives (a result, not a report). Successful firms today see the work they are engaged in as a financially stable portfolio ranging from low-risk/low-return projects to high-risk/high-return ones and maintain a much stronger balance sheet than would have been typical of consulting firms in the past.

The trusted team

Success rarely comes from one person. Even a consultant working alone at a remote client's site needs back-up. Part of this back-up is logistical: there are people who will be responsible for developing consultants' technical and consulting skills, experts to give specific input, role models to follow. But a large part is emotional. Successful consulting firms do not leave their consultants to fend for themselves, only to blame them at the first sign of difficulties. They equip their consultants to do their jobs properly and then they trust them to do so, supporting them when the going gets tough. Such firms never assume that a project is easy. By respecting their consultants as employees they encourage them to respect their clients. Standards they set for clients are the standards they apply internally.

Consulting firms sometimes fall into the trap of treating their consultants as though they are interchangeable parts in the machine. The standard "part" is an individual whose deployment is determined as much by availability as by skills. Successful firms think more in terms of teams with complementary consulting styles and compensating strengths and weaknesses. They enable and encourage these teams to keep working together.

Almost all consulting firms are guilty of treating their support (non-chargeable) staff badly. The cultural chasm between fee-earners and non-fee-earners remains huge in many firms, and has left the consulting side undersupported and the support side demoralised. Successful consulting firms, however, invest time in educating non-chargeable staff in the issues clients face and the impact these have on the consultants who work with them. They rotate individual support staff among client-facing teams, sometimes sending them to a client's site to work with the consultants. They make sure that both chargeable and non-chargeable staff clearly understand the impact their functions have on client service.

The most important way to make sure a project does not just meet but exceeds expectations is to become part of a client's team. This means respecting the contribution a client's own people have to make, recognising that they know more about the business than an external consultant ever will, and appreciating that no client lives in a perfect world but has constraints that need to be acknowledged, not dismissed. It means having contracts and fee structures that motivate consultants to achieve the business outcome the client seeks, not just to write the report or implement the system and walk away. It means sharing the highs and lows of a project as well as offices.

Where collaboration adds value to their clients, successful consulting firms are prepared to work with other consulting firms. They are not frightened to share their intellectual capital with others, because they are confident in their ability to develop even better ideas and they know that management tools are only valuable when they are sensibly used. Where firms are prime contractors using subcontractors for some aspects of specialist delivery, they have the confidence to give their subcontractors credit when it is due. They know that the value they add as prime contractors – overall responsibility, co-ordination, and so on – makes their position secure.

As players in the consulting industry, successful firms work with other firms to educate clients in making more effective use of consultants and in rebuilding the reputation of the consulting industry as a whole. As partners in a consortium, successful firms do not try to muscle in on others' responsibilities. At a personal level, their consultants accept that they live in a strange world in which the individuals they collaborate with on one day will be the same people they compete against on the next. They have the professionalism and desire to get the best solution for their client, and do not waste time trying to score points off competitors.

Leadership

How many leaders of consulting firms can you name? Even among the present generation of leaders, few people are well known outside their own firm. Indeed, it is necessary to go back to Marvin Bower at McKinsey to find someone of a stature comparable to that of, for example, Jack Welch or Andy Grove. Management gurus may be two-a-penny, but consultants with genuine leadership skills are scarce.

There are lots of reasons consulting firms have not been good at growing leaders: for example, a consultant is supposed to be the modern equivalent of the power behind the throne, not the person on it; the collegiate atmosphere and consensus-based decision-making process of many firms mitigate against individualism. But there are bad reasons, too: for example, the fear of standing up for a course of action that proves to be wrong, of being held accountable.

But the consulting industry needs leaders. Clients want the people who advise them to believe in their advice, to argue the case with sceptics and to be prepared to deliver difficult messages when the occasion demands. Clients want people who can lead large, complex projects to a successful conclusion. Consultants want people they can admire and emulate. They want to be inspired by people whose values they share.

Successful consulting firms have leaders – people who have learnt how to lead by looking at the Jack Welches of this world, who are visible, supportive, charismatic and challenging. Unsuccessful firms have bureaucrats.

Redefining success in consulting

Success in consulting should not be synonymous with top-line growth. Consulting firms obsessed with seeing where they stand in the pecking order of global revenues are far more likely to sell work to clients who do not need it and to waste time on futile mergers or acquisitions in the race to gain market share.

A successful firm is a profitable firm. It:

- enjoys high levels of repeat business and a low cost of sales (because its clients knows it adds value);
- can charge higher-than-average fee rates (because its specialist skills command a premium and because it competes in terms of value rather than price);
- knows what its competitive advantage is (because it has invested

time, money and energy in working out what its clients want and finding innovative ways of delivering it to them).

Such a firm will attract and motivate excellent people because it offers challenging work and job satisfaction, not implausible stock options or sales-related bonuses.

19 The successful business consultant

CONSULTING CREATES AND IS CREATED BY CHANGE. The growth in the numbers of consultants from the 1950s to today, to perhaps 500,000 globally, is evidence of the extent of change in the modern economy. As change increases, the number of consultants, aside from cyclical factors, is likely to increase further still.

Consulting careers can go wrong in four ways:

- Lack of work is the most obvious cause of a downturn in a consultant's career. Proven ability together with good relationships with both their firm and clients will not only guard against this but will also help consultants revive a career that has reached a flat point.
- A merger may be unexpected but should be prepared for, as consolidation in the industry will continue. Again, a good track record and definable skills will help a consultant survive this periodic occurrence.
- Making a technical error or other mistake on a project can be decisive. The best a good consultant can do is to be as honest as possible and work hard to resolve the problem. If the mistake is of sufficient scale, resignation may be the only option.
- A loss of career momentum is perhaps the most difficult to cope with. Consultants may find themselves on a long-term project which offers little in the way of new challenges or opportunity for promotion. Having become expert in a particular field, they may start to think there is nothing new to do or say. Consulting careers have flat spots: good consultants know this and will remain positive when it happens. They will not make impetuous decisions, but will use this "limbo" period as a chance to plan their next career move.

Consultants should be prepared for the unexpected and should react positively to the challenges they find themselves facing. In general, no one is better equipped than a good consultant to deal with unexpected change. It is one of the qualities that underpins the consulting mindset.

This chapter focuses on the attributes of high-flying consultants:

- ◪ Foundations. These are the basics that are essential for all consultants aiming to improve their clients' business.
- ◪ Ramparts and buttresses. Foundations alone are not enough. Successful consultants also need a variety of client-handling, project-management and commercial skills to create sustainable results, firms and careers.
- ◪ Pinnacles. At the core of this book is the argument that the principal components of the consulting world are interrelated and mutually dependent. Therefore, to be and to remain successful, consultants need to be constantly aware and able to develop new skills, and to adapt to a changing environment.

Laying the foundations

Successful business consulting has three foundations:

- ◪ technical knowledge, skills or experience;
- ◪ vision;
- ◪ skills specific to consulting.

The first varies enormously from individual to individual, while the other two are common to all successful consultants, distinguishing them from mere technical experts.

Technical knowledge, skills and experience

As a consultant's career grows, specialist skills develop reflecting the nature of his consulting firm, the work it undertakes and the sectors its clients are drawn from. This skill set will form the basis of a consultant's marketability. But successful consultants recognise that it is a mistake to assume that the principal source of value lies in technical skills alone. They expect that as their career evolves, their technical skills base will evolve and change in line with changes in their market. They expect to be doing something new from the technical perspective every few years.

Vision and values

Successful consultants have a simple vision:

- ◪ A passion for serving their clients and the success of consulting projects, as measured by delivery of the promised benefits. In essence, consultants make their clients better. They add to the sum of knowledge about business, management and processes and implement positive change in practical environments.

- To be creative and innovative as they and their careers develop and change, and as the consulting market evolves. Consulting involves liquidity of knowledge: the development of ideas and innovation in business solutions that can be transferred from one organisation to another across industry and geographic boundaries, thus accelerating the pace of economic change. Consultants help connect global business and make firms and those that run them less isolated from ways other businesses do things. Without this exchange of knowledge, the take-up of business innovations would be slower, and there would be fewer opportunities for organisations to reduce their non-core activities and focus on their areas of expertise. Businesses would be limited by their internal capacity to innovate and adapt without the extra vision and knowledge that consultants can bring.
- A basic integrity underpinned by an appreciation of the ethics underlying what they do, and sensitivity to the commercial and social impact of their work. Good consultants have firm ethical and professional standards and do not find it difficult to balance commercial and professional objectives that not-so-good consultants might perceive as being in conflict.

Such vision and values are critical for long-term success in consulting. It is difficult to find influential consultants, well respected by clients, who do not share them.

Skills specific to consulting

So which personal qualities relate particularly to successful consulting as opposed to, say, successful line management? You need to understand and have empathy with the nature and dynamics of consulting as a way of working and a way of life. Technical knowledge alone will not be enough to enable you to become a successful senior consultant or to sustain a long-term career in this discipline.

Good consultants need:

- an open-minded approach to problem-solving and an ability to think laterally, disaggregating and reconstructing problems that have proved intractable to experienced client managers;

- an appreciation of what they can (and cannot) deliver, and what it takes to really make a difference;
- the ability to get the best out of people, and to develop and grow consulting staff;
- to recognise that there is a discrete set of consulting skills, separate from both business knowledge or expertise and technical skills.

These qualities will determine the intangible value you bring to your clients and the type of relationship you have with them. Is the relationship sufficiently open for you to draw attention to problems you think need to be fixed, or is it too strained to allow a frank discussion? What about you: do you mind having your feathers ruffled? Successful consultants are confident, but should not be arrogant enough to believe that they are always right.

Building the ramparts and buttresses
To be successful, consultants have to translate these abstract fundamentals into practical, profitable reality.

1 *Market influence*
Focus on your public relations, such as speeches and articles published under your name. Good consultants have an intuitive grasp of what it takes to make a name in consulting. They achieve market influence through either industry specialisation (having an excellent network in a focused industry and a firm view about the future business direction of the industry) or service specialisation (having focused technical expertise in a particular service or product discipline). They are bold and not afraid to forecast how things will be in future. They recognise that their clients look to them to open their eyes to the possibilities that lie ahead as much as to deliver tangible work today.

2 *Clients*
Focus on winning new business on your record. Good consultants keep their clients, with relationships based on more than friendship once a project is completed. They have the confidence to keep in touch, knowing that the benefits they have produced for the client will be valued more and more as time goes on. They see their client base, their client network and their achievements as their principal assets.

3 Delivery

Consultants have to keep their promises. Good consultants are likely to be more at home with the delivery stage than the sale. Rather than expecting to make no mistakes, they focus their delivery efforts on measured risk. Nor do they seek to exert complete control – if you are in complete control in consulting, you are not going fast enough. They recognise that when things go wrong, it is crucial that the immediate focus should be on fixing them rather than getting distrusted by attributing blame. This demands openness and the personal confidence to fix things.

4 Repeatability versus innovation

There is a balance between reliable, repeatable consulting work and thought leadership that advances business thinking through creativity or innovation. Good consultants manage to do both. They make advances in thinking, codify them, coach and counsel others to develop and carry on their ideas, and then return to yet more advances in thinking. They never get stuck in their career by being recognised as a permanent expert in any one thing.

5 Influence in the firm

Any influence a consultant has is based on respect, engendered through behaviour that bolsters the firm (good, consistent consulting sales and delivery), good profits and well-recognised achievements. Good consultants recognise that good networking is critical to gaining influence, and that the mutual respect of colleagues and the admiration of rank and file consultants are essential to progression. They also know that it helps to be famous for something – something simple that enables others to place their success in a category and that is preferably something to do with their client base.

6 Career

Good consultants recognise the need to adapt to market changes, and to develop new or stronger skills accordingly, preferably ahead of others in the industry. They understand that it is crucial to balance their personal career priorities with what is good for their firm. They are also aware that they need to be a team player, while also demonstrating that they are talented individuals – which is best done by managing teams in a way that individual talent (including your own) flourishes and is apparent.

Pinnacles in consulting

Nine things are especially important in today's complex, interdependent consulting industry.

1 *Project logistics*

It is essential to start a project positively. Failure to get the right consulting staff in place, to get the client to fulfil the commitments it has made and to position the project firmly within the client's organisation, for example, will set the tone for the failure of the entire project. Successful consultants stand their ground at the outset, knowing that success in the longer term depends on the first few steps. They get what they need on logistical matters by convincing their clients that it is crucial to success.

2 *Teambuilding and teamwork*

Understanding team dynamics – the forming and development of teams, and how to get them up to full performance rapidly – is a hallmark of a good consultant. A good team manager, who engenders mutual respect and understanding on both the client's and the consultant's side of the fence, is crucial to the success of a project. Clarity about each other's position will enable both sides to view the project in a coherent and unified way.

3 *Interpersonal relationships*

Constantly developing new relationships, apart from those within a consultant's own firm, is an important feature of the role. Good consultants gain rapport at an early stage, have considerable gravitas, are instantly convincing and inspire trust. It is hard to exhibit these particular consulting qualities without having a clear vision of what consulting means to you personally.

4 *Knowledge transfer*

Specialist knowledge has a shelf life. The days are gone when consultants could trade on some deep, secret knowledge pool, to be imparted one spoon at a time. Today, quite rightly, clients expect knowledge, special expertise and intellectual property to be transferred at every stage. Successful consultants not only transfer technical knowledge to clients but also seek to develop the way a client's staff think and behave in order to help them use the technical knowledge to best advantage now and in the future. This may sound like a strange objective, but smart consultants seek to make themselves redundant in their current consulting role, so that they can move on to more sophisticated and innovative work, leaving today's activities in the hands of clients and focusing on tomorrow's as yet unsolved challenges.

5 Project management
Successful consultants are good at project management, which should be focused on the future and the pre-emption of potential problems. Initial scenario planning to identify what may go wrong and how you will avoid it or deal with it is far more productive than a trial-and-error approach. Things will go wrong and lessons must be learned from mistakes made, but this should not be the *modus operandi*.

6 Results measurement
From the first conversations between consultant and client through to the completion of a project, the central focus must be on results. Good consultants identify quantifiable benefits and adroitly make people aware of other intangible benefits of what they are going to do. They focus everyone's effort on the result, not simply on the process of getting there.

7 Recruitment and transition
Good consultants recognise that the training and development of the next generation of consultants is their responsibility – and this is not just to sustain their consulting business, but also to develop their own ability through constant challenges from younger people who look at things with a fresh eye and have an enthusiasm for questioning old approaches.

8 Mutual investment and the development of knowledge
Thought leadership is regarded as a mutual investment between individual and firm by both successful consultants and successful firms. On one hand, a firm and its clients gain from the development of new ideas; on the other, consultants' marketability improves if they have a reputation for innovation. Successful consultants also appreciate that knowledge and skills are ephemeral. Today's expertise rapidly becomes tomorrow's commoditised knowledge, and innovation should be a way of life rather than something talented people do in think-tanks.

9 Productivity, motivation and the allocation of resources
Commercial objectives and profitability are of overriding importance in

a consulting firm. High profits enable firms to attract and retain high-quality consultants. Profits are also necessary to underpin research into new thinking and development of new ideas. Successful consultants recognise that not every project is a fantastic, leading-edge new opportunity. Some routine work is inevitable, and being realistic about allocation of time and resources is a hallmark of a consultant who understands the commercial reality of the consulting business.

Pride in being a consultant

You cannot be truly successful at anything unless you believe in its value. It is sad, but true, that many consultants today take little pride in their work. They do not argue when they are told that their special skill is to borrow someone else's watch to tell them the time. Indeed, some believe that is all they do. Successful consultants do far more than that; moreover, they know they do and they preach it. They understand what the industry stands for and what it has achieved. Successful business consultants are proud to say: "I can and I do change client organisations permanently for the better."

6
A BLUEPRINT FOR THE FUTURE

"Answering the big question – who are we? – is the biggest challenge facing the consulting industry today."

20 The likely evolution of business consulting

"WHAT IS THE MAIN LESSON we have learned about working with consultants?" asked one client. "The power of working together."

A theme of this book is that neither clients nor consultants benefit from seeking to promote their own interests exclusively. It is clear that the aims of each side need to be closely matched. Each party needs an incentive to behave and contribute in a way that supports collective effort, not self-interest. At an individual level, people simply have to get along. A close working relationship, mutual respect and openness among the people involved will carry a project through the bad times as well as the good far more effectively than a contract. Clients and consultants will succeed together, or fail separately.

So what about the future? How will the new rules of the game be played out over the next decade? In the short term, the barriers to greater co-operation between consulting firms and between consulting clients appear insurmountable. The competitive state of mind is hard to change, at least at the upper levels of the business consulting ecosystem. At the lower levels, however, there is already far more flexibility as:

- clients use several firms where in the past they might have relied on a single supplier;
- the relationship between consultants and the firms they work for becomes one of choice rather than dependency;
- managers view consulting projects as part of a portfolio of internal and external initiatives;
- clients and consultants recognise the need to adapt their style of working during the course of consulting projects.

There remains the possibility that powerful third parties, such as software vendors, outsourcers and offshore players, will put an end to the current system of consulting, but that possibility has become less likely. Instead, the consulting industry has adapted, moving its point of economic advantage from knowledge (moving expertise around the economy, or advisory consulting) to resources (moving skills, or implementation consulting), then into processes (moving business processes, or outsourcing) and more recently into geography (moving work between countries, or offshoring). Outsourcing and offshoring have thus become part of business consulting, not vice versa.

This bodes well for the future of the consulting ecosystem described in this book. Nevertheless, there will be considerable evolution within the components of the ecosystem and the seven interactions between them. Here are some predictions of what will or may occur.

Components
The client market
The barriers to sharing information will break down as collaboration across markets accelerates. It will be easier for, say, telecommunications clients to learn from and share with retail or utilities clients than to share with their immediate competitors, thus ending the isolation of clients and fostering a broader understanding of consulting. With the exception of the public sector, sharing will not happen within sectors for some time. Across regions, multinational corporations and globalisation will promote consistency in the role of consultants and the degree to which they are used, although cultural barriers will prevent overall standardisation. The issues consultants tackle and consultants' perceived place in the local economy will, however, standardise in most places. There will be more convergence in prices, and offshoring will accelerate this as low-price players seek to raise their prices to western levels, and western firms find ways to decrease their prices to remain competitive globally.

Client organisations
Clients will become more rational about and consistent in the use of consulting, focusing on proven linkages to results. They will then form more partnerships with consulting firms as the consulting industry matures, and this will resolve the dissatisfaction with procurement processes. The recognition that a formulaic procurement process can only ever result in formulaic consulting will become widespread.

Projects
Failure rates will slowly drop. The adoption of better project and programme management will help, as will the reduction in project size and length. Organisations will start to realise that large, long projects often fail because things change. The e-business era revealed that speed was

possible, so projects will shorten, with more focus on short-term results as complex work is done in stages. Slow acceptance of the portfolio approach to business change will continue to hinder progress in many areas.

The consulting industry
However, the opportunity to recognise co-dependency, reduce competitiveness and collaborate on issues of common interest will be taken up only slowly by the consulting industry. Clients will continue to mistrust an industry that does not always demonstrate that it trusts itself. As a result, overall market growth will remain constrained by issues such as reputation and ethical standards. National associations will collaborate more as their largest and most influential consulting firm members press them to deliver value in ways that they cannot when acting alone.

Consulting firms
Firms will polarise far more firmly around the six segments described by the revenue–delivery model. Differences in this new landscape will sharpen, driven by client needs and demands, differences in ownership structure (private or public), varying degrees of globalisation and in the case of some players the constraints of the Sarbanes-Oxley Act in the United States and other regulatory influences.

Consultants
Human resources dilemmas will become more acute as firms continue to try to make the leverage model (in which the time and expense of a small number of senior, experienced consultants is spread across a larger number of junior ones) work at a time when clients demand more experienced staff. This model will be further undermined by experienced offshore resources offered at a fraction of the cost of new onshore graduates. As a result, consultants' careers will come under scrutiny as the fundamentals of some firms' business models come under pressure, with consequent change in income expectations and employment models.

Interactions
Reputation: industry to market – the good name of consulting
The theme is tipping points: how close is the consulting industry to encountering a scandal on the scale of the one that destroyed Arthur Andersen and threatened the entire accounting profession? Such a scandal would not necessarily be of consultants' own making. To end

life as consultants know it, many factors would have to be in place. Some apply now (a consistent list of things clients would like to see changed); and some do not (the equivalent of Senators Sarbanes and Oxley, willing to push an agenda of change through the regulatory machine). Some are increasing (the scale and ambition of the largest consulting projects); and some are decreasing (an improved economic outlook makes people less likely to dwell on corporate failures).

The reputation of the consulting industry rests on a knife-edge. The more responsible consulting firms will increasingly recognise that the industry has a collective reputation and that this needs defending just as much as individual firms need differentiating.

Isolation: market to clients – correcting an imperfect market
Information is both the engine of and the brake on a management bandwagon. Genuine thought leadership will be the summing up of dozens of real-life examples, backed by quantifiable results from practical implementation.

None of the intermediaries aiming to help clients find their way through the mass of material which purports to be new ideas are particularly satisfactory:

- Marketing brochures produced by consulting firms can reduce the most rigorous research into simplistic straplines.
- Commercial research companies can fall victim to an economic model that makes them dependent on the organisations about which they are supposed to be objective. Like all intermediaries, they survive because they control information that is scarce – and charge premium prices for doing so.

Disintermediation is one possibility. The term "collaborative consulting" has been around for some time and there is a compelling case for getting consultants from different firms to work together to solve problems. No one firm has a monopoly of the skills, ideas or experience required to solve the complex issues facing corporations. So why not use the best people, irrespective of where they work? And what about "collaborative clienting"? Many businesses face similar issues, even though they are dealt with differently from company to company. For areas that offer no potential source of competitive advantage, clients will benefit from working together, sharing the results of their work with consultants and learning from each other's successes and failures.

Another possibility is reintermediation. Consulting firms that help clients choose between consultants already exist, although many clients are understandably wary of being seen to be solipsistic enough to pay for consultants to advise on hiring consultants. However, there will certainly be more consulting firms specialising in the due diligence of short-listed consulting firms and auditing such firms' work-in-progress. This is another market ripe for the intervention of online companies, such as those offering analysis and ratings of business consultancies (not just IT consultancies and other technology suppliers) for a flat-rate subscription (thus precluding the temptation to be more charitable to those who pay more). In the longer term, one research company may begin to dominate the market by developing a methodology for comparing consulting projects and client satisfaction levels by consulting firm in much the same way that, for example, InterBrand has been able to set the benchmark for valuing brands. Both consulting firms and clients should try to pre-empt this by starting to work together on how they think consulting projects can be best assessed and compared. If they do not, they run the risk of ending up with a methodology which neither side likes but which both are forced to use.

Metamorphosis: industry and consulting firms – industrialise or die

Given the possibility of regulation, why not jump rather than wait to be pushed? A consulting firm that is seen to live by a higher standard of ethics and conduct than its peers, and can show that this has a positive and measurable effect on the effectiveness of its work, stands to gain far more than if it had invented re-engineering, e-business and customer relationship management combined. This would represent a new age in consulting services and the quality control of them.

Clients, rightly and understandably, want to have some guarantee for what they are buying. The problem is that this guarantee has been interpreted in terms of being a rigid process: "Z will happen because we will go through stages A–Y with you." However, the more prescriptive a process becomes, the less scope there is to take into account a client's unique set of circumstances and the benefits realised shrink. Overly rigid methodologies have destroyed the value they were intended to protect.

Collaboration on individual projects will, ironically, strengthen the divisions between consulting firms at a corporate level. That so much work is being done by consultants from different firms working together will threaten participants' sense of identity. If anything, they will try harder to make themselves appear separate and different. The spectre of government regulation will trigger further conflict as firms look for ways of insulating their image and status.

At some point, an organisation committed to fighting for better consulting will step into this disarray. It might be a group of users: public-sector clients, because of their non-competitive nature, would be best positioned to do this. It might be one of the existing trade associations of consulting firms or institutes of individual management consultants. It might be a new entrant, such as a leading business school, spotting a commercial opportunity as much as an altruistic endeavour. Seeking to side-step inter-firm conflict and increased regulation, this body will focus on doing two things:

- Creating a "learned society" to which consultants will aspire to belong in much the same way as, for example, engineers might want to join the Institution of Civil Engineers or the Institution of Mechanical Engineers.
- Linking this society with the highest possible standards of consulting. What will make it a compelling proposition for consultants and a source of genuine differentiation for clients is that members will have to demonstrate that they are better, more effective consultants than non-members.

Relationship: client organisations and consulting firms – collaboration not competition

Today the consulting industry resembles the film industry in the 1930s. There are a few big players who dominate the entire value chain, much as the big Hollywood studios owned film rights, sets, equipment and even stars. The film industry is now much more fragmented. A shift in power to film stars, the unbundling of the distribution chain and the increasing level of specialist skills required have combined to create an industry in which studios own the intellectual rights to a book or script but outsource almost every other part of the process to a producer, a director, individual stars and a host of smaller companies that focus on just one area (set location, make-up, casting, costume, security, and so on). Tomorrow's consulting industry might look the same, with clients owning the "rights" to an idea and using internal and external specialists to design, develop and implement it. Consultants will come together for a project (a film), and for its duration their loyalty will be to the project not to their employers, assuming they have employers.

Consulting firms will nevertheless exist. Mergers and acquisitions and large-scale technology projects will create sufficient demand to sustain a small number of large firms offering a complete, seamless process from strategy through to continuing management and support. Strategy firms will become the directors and/or producers, drawing up the overall roadmap and making sure that the destination is reached on time and within budget. Almost every other function will be done by smaller groups of consultants (some from big companies, some from small and some independent), and each consultant will be world class in their particular field.

Will this produce better consulting, any more than fragmentation of the value chain in the film industry has produced better films? It will certainly produce more sophisticated, intelligent and creative consulting, as different people bring different perspectives to a problem. It will certainly reduce the amount of time, money and emotional energy wasted on the fruitless competition that has marked the consulting industry in recent years, none of which has really added value to clients. But the short answer to the question is "no". Project-by-project collaboration will not generate better consulting by itself, but it is likely to create the environment in which clients and consultants can work more effectively together. This is what will get better results, and this is where the future lies.

Portfolio: clients and their projects – the future of business change

You can divide the activities of any organisation into two categories: those that keep things going on a daily basis, and those that are concerned with change. An increasing proportion of activities undertaken by organisations fall into the latter category as managers try to respond to market pressures. The bulk of consulting work falls, or should fall, into that category too. How an organisation manages its portfolio of consulting work will therefore be an increasingly important measure of how well it manages its future. Getting the portfolio right – balancing the long-term against the short-term, the high-risk against the low-risk, and the easy against the difficult – will be critical to success.

This shift will change clients' attitudes on many levels:

- The boundaries between clients and suppliers (consulting firms, outsourcers, and so on) will blur and, in some circumstances, become irrelevant.
- The portfolio of change-related work will become an

organisation's source of innovation and creativity. Here, by contrast, the distinction between day-to-day and future activities will be clearer and harder to circumnavigate.

- ◪ The relationships between all those involved will be more fluid. Integral to the idea of a portfolio is that every time a new project is suggested the entire portfolio is reviewed, and some existing work is dropped as new work is taken on. It will therefore become the norm for long-term consulting and outsourcing to be redefined, perhaps even cancelled, before completion. This will cause more problems in an already polarised industry. Only large-scale consulting firms will be able to absorb such abrupt changes of course. Smaller firms will choose to manage their risk by focusing on discrete, specialised areas, limiting the extent to which they are tied into long-term delivery.

- ◪ The rules of engagement will therefore be different. The focus will be on business outcomes, not conventional inputs and outputs. Consulting firms will provide financing as well as resources. Instead of being viewed by clients' staff as career backwaters, consulting projects will be sought after by ambitious managers keen to hone their skills in creating and delivering their organisation's future.

Career: consulting firms and consultants – more flexible working

Consulting is now an insecure career. When demand fell dramatically in the early 2000s, it became clear that the only way most consulting firms would survive would be by cutting the numbers of consultants. The industry's image as a "people business" was shattered as roughly one-fifth of consulting firms' staff were laid off; neither it nor they are likely to be restored. With recovery has come recruitment, although the majority of firms are reluctant to do too much too quickly, worrying that they may end up with the high level of fixed resources they had before. They will therefore continue to try out different employment models: associates, temporary subcontractors and alliances.

From the individual consultant's perspective, this will trigger a shift in loyalty from the consulting firm to clients' projects. Consultants will be more likely to spend periods of time either in consulting firms or working for clients, either as employees or as freelance consultants, essentially following existing projects rather than running after new sales. Indeed, the cultural divisions between those that deliver and those that sell consulting will become even more marked than they are at present. The most successful consulting firms will understand and exploit this trend, giving consultants more latitude in terms of their relationship with the firm but more accountability in delivery.

Life cycle: projects and consultants – the evolution of projects

The long-term success of the consulting industry will not be determined by the actions of governments (which, when they regulate, are likely to regulate the wrong things), or by the actions of consulting firms at a strategic level (which are unlikely to overcome the internecine mindset of recent years), but by the actions taken by clients and consultants when they work together on projects. If both sides (and it needs to be both) focus on creating value in their immediate work, the crisis of reputation facing the industry will disappear.

Two keys to success will be knowledge transfer between the parties and cultural changes through absorbing the project-based approach. These processes vary greatly across different stages in the life cycle of a project, but this is largely forgotten as attempts are made to plan even the longest projects in minuscule detail before they have started. Clients and consulting firms will in future recognise this and invest far more – and become more sophisticated as a result – in these two areas. So far, they have only scratched the surface of what might be achieved.

Knowledge transfer will also be the back door by which online open-access consulting becomes a reality. Many firms have experimented with offering internet-based services, but they typically overestimate the value clients attach to abstract methodologies and high-level case studies and underestimate how helpful it is for clients to be involved in developing approaches rather than being served them on a plate.

Consultants also offer clients a different culture. As they live on project work, they are more focused on completing something and less likely to be put off when something goes wrong or changes. Indeed, clients already say that one of the main reasons they use consultants is to create momentum. As clients redefine more of their work as project-based, they will adopt a more consulting-like culture. This trend, and related shifts in the way clients' corporate portfolio of change-related projects is managed, will blur the distinction between individual clients and consultants.

Perhaps this cultural fusion, when it occurs some time in the future, will mark the true coming of age of business consulting.

Shaping the future of business consulting

Here are three closing thoughts for clients and consultants:

- **Have high expectations.** Insist on these and work to exceed them. People will rise or fall to the level of your expectations. The best consulting can and does deliver extraordinary results. You should be satisfied with nothing less, whichever side of the table you find yourself on.
- **Stand for something.** As a consultant, redefine your ethical and professional view of your work. Focus on innovation, collaboration and commercial viability. As a client, insist on business results and only go forward when you are sure of your ground. At that point leave behind internal concerns and standard practices and take the risk. Step forward boldly and with confidence.
- **Work for a better consulting and business future.** Insist on mutual respect between consultant and client. Give credit where credit is due. Always focus on results.

APPENDICES

1 Leading consulting firms

Accenture
1345 Avenue of the Americas
New York, NY 10105
US
Tel: +1 917 452 4400
www.accenture.com

Altran
251 boulevard Pereire
75017 Paris
France
Tel: +33 1 4409 6400
www.altran.net

Aon Consulting
200 East Randolph Street
Chicago, IL 60601
US
Tel: +1 312 381 4800
www.aon.com

Aquent
711 Boylston Street
Boston, MA 02116
US
Tel: +1 617 535 5000
www.aquent.com

Atos Origin
Tour les Miroirs, Bat C
18 avenue d'Alsace
92926 Paris La Défense 3 Cedex
France
Tel: +33 1 5591 2000
www.atosorigin.com

Bain & Company
Bain & Company Inc
131 Dartmouth Street
Boston, MA 02116
US
Tel: +1 617 572 2000
www.bain.com

BearingPoint
1676 International Drive
McLean, VA 22102
US
Tel: +1 703 747 3000
www.bearingpoint.com

BDO Seidman
330 Madison Ave
New York, NY 10017-5001
US
Tel: +1 212 885 8000
www.bdo.com

Booz Allen Hamilton
8283 Greensboro Drive
McLean, VA 22102
US
Tel: +1 703 902 500
www.bah.com

Boston Consulting Group
Exchange Place, 31st Floor
Boston, MA 02109
US
Tel: +1 617 973 1200
www.bcg.com

**BT Consulting & Systems
  Integration**
Guidion House
Ancells Business Park
Fleet
Hampshire GU51 2QP
UK
Tel: +44 1252 777 000
www.bt.com

CACI
CACI International Inc
1100 North Glebe Road
Arlington, VA 22201
US
Tel: +1 703 841 7800
www.caci.com

Capgemini
Place de l'Etoile
11 rue de Tilsitt
75017 Paris
France
Tel: +33 1 4754 5000
www.capgemini.com

CGI
1130 Sherbrooke Street West
5th Floor
Montreal, Quebec H3A 2M8
Canada
Tel: +1 514 841 3200
www.cgi.com

Ciber
5251 DTC Parkway, Suite 1400
Greenwood Village, CO 80111
US
Tel: +1 303 220 0100
www.ciber.com

Clark Consulting
102 South Wynstone Park Drive
North Barrington, IL 60010
US
Tel: +1 847 304 5800
www.clarkconsulting.com

**Computer Sciences Corporation
  CSC**
2100 East Grand Avenue
El Segundo, CA 90245
US
Tel: +1 310 615 0311
www.csc.com

Deloitte Touche Tomatsu
1633 Broadway
New York, NY 10019
US
Tel: +1 212 489 1600
www.deloitte.com

Dimension Data
The Campus
57 Sloane Street
Bryanston
Standon 2194
South Africa
Tel: +27 11 575 0000
www.didata.com

EDS
5400 Legacy Drive
Plano, Texas 75024
US
Tel: +1 800 566 9337
www.eds.com

Fujitsu Services
26 Finsbury Square
London EC2A 1SL
UK
Tel: +44 870 242 7799
www.uk.fujitsu.com

Gartner
56 Top Gallant Road
Stamford, CT 06904
US
Tel: + 1 203 964 0096
www.gartner.com

Gedas
Carnotstrasse 4
10587 Berlin
Germany
Tel: +49 30 3997 2999
www.gedas.com

Grant Thornton
175 West Jackson Boulevard
20th Floor
Chicago, IL 60601
US
Tel: +1 312 856 0200
www.grantthornton.com

Hay Group
100 Penn Square East
The Wanamaker Building
Philadelphia, PA 19107-3388
US
Tel: +1 215 861 2000
www.haygroup.com

Hewitt Associates
Hewitt Associates LLC
100 Half Day Road
Lincolnshire, IL 60069
US
Tel: +1 847 295 5000
was4.hewitt.com/hewitt/

Hewlett-Packard
3000 Hanover Street
Palo Alto, CA 94304-1185
US
Tel: +1 650 857 1501
www.hp.com

Horwath International
420 Lexington Avenue, Suite 526
New York, NY 10170-0526
US
Tel: +1 212 808 2000
www.horwath.com

IBM Business Consulting Services
New Orchard Road
Armonk, NY 10504
US
Tel: +1 914 499 1900
www-1.ibm.com

Infosys
Corporate Headquarters
Plot No 44 & 97A, Electronics City
Hosur Road
Bangalore 560 100
India
Tel: +91 80 2852 0261
www.infosys.com

Kurt Salmon Associates
650 Fifth Avenue, 30th Floor
New York, NY 10019
US
Tel: +1 212 319 9450
www.kurtsalmon.com

LogicaCMG
Stephenson House
75 Hampstead Road
London NW1 2PL
UK
Tel: +44 20 7637 9111
www.logicacmg.com

Management Consulting Group
Fleet Place House
2 Fleet Place, Holborn Viaduct
London EC4M 7RF
UK
Tel: +44 20 7710 5000
www.mcgplc.com

McKinsey & Co
55 East 52nd Street, 21st Floor
New York, NY 10022
US
Tel: +1 212 446 7000
www.mckinsey.com

Mellon
Mellon Financial Corporation
One Mellon Center
Pittsburgh, PA 15258-000
US
Tel: +1 412 234 5000
www.mellon.com

Mercer
1166 Avenue of the Americas
New York, NY 10036-2774
US
Tel: +1 212 345 5000
www.mercer.com

Milliman
1301 Fifth Avenue, Suite 3800
Seattle, WA 98101-2605
US
Tel: +1 206 624 7940
www.milliman.com

Monitor
Two Canal Park
Cambridge, MA 02141
US
Tel: +1 617 252 2000
www.monitor.com

Novell
404 Wyman, Suite 500
Waltham, MA 02451
US
Tel: +1 781 464 8000
www.novell.com

Oracle
500 Oracle Parkway
Redwood Shores, CA 94065
US
Tel: +1 650 506 7000
www.oracle.com

PA Consulting
PA Consulting Group
123 Buckingham Palace Road
London SW1W 9SR
UK
Tel: +44 20 7730 9000
www.paconsulting.com

Roland Berger
Arabellastrasse 33
81925 Munich
Germany
Tel: +49 89 9230 0000
www.rolandberger.com

The Salamander Organization
York Science Park
York YO10 5ZF
UK
Tel +44 870 161 1700
www.tsorg.com

SAP
Neurottstrasse 16
69190 Walldorf
Germany
Tel: +49 6227 747474
www.sap.com

Siebel
2207 Bridgepointe Parkway
San Mateo, CA 94404
US
Tel: +1 800 647 4300
www.siebel.com

Tata Consultancy Services
Tata Consultancy Services
Air India Building, 11th Floor
Nariman Point
Mumbai-400021
India
Tel: +91 22 5550 9422
www.tcs.com

Telcordia
One Telcordia Drive
Piscataway, NJ 08854-4157
US
Tel: +1 732 699 2000
www.telcordia.com

TietoEnator
Kronborgsgränd 1
16487 Kista
Sweden
Tel: +46 8 703 6264
www.tietoenator.com

Towers Perrin
335 Madison Avenue
New York, NY 10017-4605
US
Tel: +1 212 309 3400
www.towersperrin.com

T-Systems
Hahnstrasse 43 d
60528 Frankfurt-am-Main
Germany
Tel: +49 069 665310
www.t-systems.com

Unisys
Unisys Way
Blue Bell, PA 19424
US
Tel: +1 215 986 4011
www.unisys.com

Watson Wyatt
1717 H Street NW
Washington, DC 20006
US
Tel: +1 202 715 2000
www.watsonwyatt.com

2 Notes and references

3 The client market

Details of the public/private sector split in consulting fees can be found in *The UK Consulting Industry 2003/4*, available from the Management Consultancies Association (www.mca.org.uk). The report is updated annually. Kennedy Information publishes extensive research on the consulting industry globally (www.kennedyinfo.com).

A more detailed discussion of Armstrong and Brodie's findings can be found in *Dangerous Company: The Consulting Powerhouses and the Businesses They Save and Ruin*, by James O'Shea and Charles Madigan (Nicholas Brealey, London, 1997).

John Micklethwait and Adrian Wooldridge, *The Witch Doctors: What the Management Gurus are Saying, Why it Matters and How to Make Sense of It*, Heinemann, London, 1996.

David Collins, *Management Fads and Buzzwords: Critical-Practical Perspectives*, Routledge, London, 2000.

5 Projects

The study by PricewaterhouseCoopers that Max Wideman refers to is *Boosting Business Performance through Programme and Project Management*, by A. Nieto-Rodriguez and D. Evrard, published by PricewaterhouseCoopers in Belgium in 2004.

Those interested in Wideman's comments may also wish to refer to his book *The Project Time Frame: A Management Framework for Project, Program and Portfolio Integration* (Trafford Publishing, Canada, 2004).

7 The consulting firm

Chris Meyer and Stan Davis, *Blur: The Speed of Change in the Connected Economy* and *Future Wealth*, Capstone, 1998.

Chris Meyer and Stan Davis, *Future Wealth*, Harvard Business School Press, 2000.

10 Reputation

Readers interested in learning more about Marvin Bower should refer to the excellent biography by Barbara Elizabeth Haas Edersheim, *McKinsey's Marvin Bower: Vision, Leadership and the Creation of Management Consulting* (John Wiley, Hoboken, NJ, 2004.

Malcolm Gladwell, *The Tipping Point*, Abacus, London, 2002.

Further analysis of the tipping factors in financial scandals, from which this discussion is drawn, can be found in Fiona Czerniawska, *Consulting on the Brink: The Implications of Enron for the Consulting Industry* (Arkimeda, London, 2003).

11 Isolation

The first section of this chapter, on transformation outsourcing, is drawn from a more detailed report by Fiona Czerniawska. *Transformational Outsourcing: The Business Model of the Future?* was published by the MCA in 2004 and is summarised here with the kind permission of the MCA.

James Collins and Jerry Porras, *Built to Last: Successful Habits of Visionary Companies*, Random House, 1995.

Index